THE MACNEAN RESTAURANT COOKBOOK

The MacNean
Restaurant
Cookbook

NEVEN MAGUIRE

GILL & MACMILLAN

Gill & Macmillan
Hume Avenue, Park West, Dublin 12
with associated companies throughout the world
www.gillmacmillanbooks.ie

© Neven Maguire 2012

ISBN: 978 07171 5439 5

Compiled by Orla Broderick
Edited by Kristin Jensen
Food styling by Sharon Hearne-Smith
Photography by Joanne Murphy
Photos of MacNean Restaurant interior pp. xi, 24, 115, 282 © Lee Grace
Designed by www.grahamthew.com
Typeset by www.bnewdesigns.com
Indexed by Cliff Murphy
Printed and bound in Italy by L.E.G.O. SpA

543

PROPS SUPPLIED BY:

Slated: slated.ie. T: +353 86 825 9308

Avoca: H/O, Kilmacanogue, Bray, Co. Wicklow. T: 01 286 7466; E: info@avoca.ie; W: www.avoca.ie

Eden Home & Garden: 1–4 Temple Grove, Temple Road, Blackrock, Co. Dublin. T: 01 764 2004;
E: edenhomeandgarden@hotmail.com; W: www.edenhomeandgarden.ie

Meadows & Byrne: Dublin, Cork, Galway, Clare, Tipperary. T: 01 280 5444/021 434 4100;
E: info@meadowsandbyrne.com; W: www.meadowsandbyrne.com

Elizabelle: 23 Church Street, Listowel, Co. Kerry. T: 068 22593; W: www.elizabelle.com

House of Fraser: Dundrum Town Centre, Dublin 16. T: 01 299 1400; E: dundrum@hof.co.uk; W: houseoffraser.co.uk

The Blue Door: The Crescent, Monkstown, Co. Dublin. T: 01 230 1894; E: customerservice@thebluedoordirect.ie;
W: www.thebluedoordirect.ie

Arthur Price: House of Fraser, Dundrum Town Centre, Dublin 16

Contents

Neven Maguire and the History of MacNean Restaurant at Blacklion x

Acknowledgements xv

How to Run an Efficient Kitchen xvii

Menu Planning xxi

BREAKFAST

MacNean Special Porridge with Honey and Cream 2

Bircher Muesli with Granola 4

Poached Apricots with Star Anise and Yoghurt 5

Warm Prunes Marinated in Tea and Vanilla with Yoghurt 6

MacNean Special Breakfast 9

Scrambled Eggs with Burren Smoked Salmon 10

MacNean Eggs Benedict 13

Baked Eggs with Black Pudding Hash Browns 14

Morning Reviver Juice 15

Speckled Canary Juice 15

Breakfast Berry Zinger 15

Sunrise Juice 15

Banana and Pineapple Smoothie 16

Strawberry Booster Smoothie 16

Red Berry Smoothie 16

STARTERS

FISH

A Study of Shellfish 20

Tempura of Sole with Curried Mayonnaise and Chilli Jam 25

Seared Scallops with Confit of Pork Cheek and Cauliflower Textures 26

Crab Wontons with Enoki Mushrooms and Thai Broth 28

Confit Prawn Spring Rolls with Mango and Apple 31

Deconstructed Prawn Cocktail 32

POLTRY

Cinnamon Roasted Quail with Pea and Truffle Risotto 34

Salad of Wood Pigeon with Trio of Beetroot 37

Chicken Liver Parfait with Cherry Gel 38

Duck Confit with Crispy Fried Vegetables 39

Curried Chicken Spring Rolls with Pineapple Salsa 42

MEAT

Rabbit Confit with Wild Mushrooms in Kataifi Pastry 44

Saddle of Rabbit Stuffed with Black Pudding 47

Veal Sweetbreads with Carrot and Star Anise 48

Beef Satay with Pickled Cucumber 51

Smoked Belly of Pork with Creamed White Beans and Date Jam 52

Air-dried Beef Carpaccio with Roasted Beetroot and Mustard Cream 54

Pork and Wild Mushroom Wontons with Chinese Black Bean Sauce 56

VEGETABLES

Bruschetta of Wild Mushrooms and Asparagus 58

Crispy Goat's Cheese with Beetroot Panna Cotta 60

Ravioli of Swiss Chard and Ricotta with Smoked Garlic Foam 63

Ballyoak Cheese in Kataifi Pastry with Sauce Vierge 64

Salad of Grilled Vegetables and Aged Parmesan 65

SOUPS

Sweet Potato and Coconut Soup 66

Chestnut and Wild Mushroom Soup with Smoked Duck 69

Vera's Seafood Chowder 70

Vegetable Soup with Barley 73

Roast Pepper and Tomato Soup 74

Celeriac, Smoked Bacon and Apple Soup 76

Haricot Bean and White Truffle Oil Velouté 79

MAINS

FISH

Gratin of Cod with Prawns, Spinach and Pesto 82

Roast Turbot with Crab Cannelloni and Prawn Velouté 84

Hake with Cassoulet of Beans and Chorizo 87

Monkfish with Gnocchi, Wild Mushrooms, Sun-dried Tomato and Saffron Velouté 88

Smoked Salmon and Saffron Orzo 90

MacNean Fish Pie 91

Sea Trout with Aubergine Purée and Crispy Courgette Flowers Stuffed with Crab 92

Salmon Sausages with Creamed Leeks and Lemon Butter Sauce 94

POULTRY

Breast of Thornhill Duck with Sweet Potato Fondants 97

Trio of MacNean Chicken with Baby Carrots 98

Mum's Special Roast Chicken with Lemon, Garlic and Thyme 102

Roast Woodcock with Creamed Spinach and Offal Croûte 104

Sautéed Breast of Guinea Fowl and Stuffed Leg with Leeks and Girolle Mushrooms 106

Roast Goose with Cranberry and Apple Sausage Stuffing 109

Turkey and Leek Stroganoff with Wild and Basmati Rice 110

MEAT

Tasting of Irish Lamb (Herb-crusted Loin, Confit of Neck and Sweetbreads) 112

Braised Shoulder of Lamb with Mediterranean Couscous 116

Rump of Local Lamb with Pea Purée and Rosemary Jus 119

Assiette of Rare-breed Pork (Caramelised Belly, Smoked Bacon-wrapped Fillet and Pork and Leek Sausage) 120

Fillet of Dry-aged Beef with Braised Blade and Celeriac Purée 122

Peppered Steak with Gratin Potatoes and Whiskey Sauce 127

Roast Rib of Beef on the Bone with Yorkshire Puddings and Horseradish Cream 128

Stout-braised Shoulder of Pork with Potato and Apple Purée 130

Loin of Venison with Quinoa and Spinach 133

VEGETABLES

Celeriac and Baby Carrot Risotto with Sherry Vinegar Caramel and Crispy Potato Rosti 134

Open Lasagne with Roasted Vegetables 137

Avocado Spring Roll with Red Pepper Polenta 138

Pappardelle Pasta with Vegetables and Parmesan Foam 141

Warm Potato Pancakes with Leeks and Wild Mushrooms 142

Satay Vegetable Noodles 143

Aubergine and Potato Dhansak 144

Mediterranean Vegetable and Boilíe Pizza Tart 147

DESSERTS

The Orchard (Apple Panna Cotta with Apple Jelly, Glazed Apple Tart,
Apple Crumble and Apple Parfait) 150

Warm Chocolate and Pecan Brownie with Boozy Fudge Sauce 154

MacNean Cheesecake with Raspberries and White Chocolate 156

Toasted Coconut and Malibu Parfait with Pineapple Carpaccio and Coconut Sorbet 158

Lime Meringues with Fresh Fruit and Cream 160

Roasted Pineapple and Coconut Rice Pudding 161

Coconut Floating Islands with Coole Swan Crème Anglaise, Raspberries
and Spun Sugar Basket 162

Baked Alaska 165

Classic Tiramisu 166

Rhubarb and Strawberry Pudding 167

Passion Fruit and Orange Jelly with Vanilla Yoghurt and Granita 168

Summer Fruit Crumble 171

The Raspberry Plate (Baked Raspberry Shortcake, Buttermilk Mousse, Raspberry and
White Chocolate Parfait and Raspberry Sorbet) 172

Vanilla Crème Brûlée with Poached Irish Apple Compote 175

Sticky Toffee Pudding and Salted Whiskey Butterscotch Sauce 176

Trio of Chocolate (Warm Fondant, Delice and Opera Cake) 178

Chocolate Delice 182

Dessert Wine Matches 183

PETITS FOURS

Coconut and Malibu Marshmallows 186

MacNean Chocolate Orange Truffles 189

Madeleines 190

White Chocolate and Pistachio Fudge 193

Vanilla Macaroons with Chocolate and Peanut
    Butter Cream 194

Brandy Snaps with Chilli and Passion Fruit Cream 197

BREADS, CAKES AND BISCUITS

MacNean Wheaten Bread 200

Rosemary and Cranberry Soda Bread 203

Pizza Bread 204

Tomato and Parmesan Twister Bread Rolls 206

Irish Tea Bread 207

Sesame and Poppy Seed White Bread 209

Goat's Cheese and Red Onion Focaccia
    with Rosemary 210

Sun-dried Tomato Gluten-free Bread 213

Brioche 214

Prune and Armagnac Tart 215

Lemon and Sultana Scones 216

Oaty Chocolate Chip Cookies 217

Oatmeal Cookies 218

Shortbread Biscuits 220

Jammie Dodgers 221

The MacNean Celebration Cake 222

Sophie's Chocolate Biscuit Cake 225

BASIC RECIPES

Potato Sides 228

Vegetable Sides 232

Other Sides and Accompaniments 237

Vegetable Purées 242

Foams, Gels and Powders 245

Jams and Chutneys 248

Oils, Dressings and Mayonnaise 250

Stocks 252

Sauces, Syrups and Jus 255

Dessert Sauces 262

Ice Creams, Sorbets and Parfaits 265

Dessert Decorations 268

Food Suppliers 270

Specialist Kitchen Equipment 271

Index 274

Neven Maguire and the History of MacNean Restaurant at Blacklion
by Ross Golden-Bannon

When I was asked to write this introduction, I did not hesitate in agreeing for a moment – how could anyone resist the story of a tiny village on the border with Northern Ireland and how it reached national culinary prominence? From the first stories I heard from my family in Cavan to the talk around the food industry, it had been calling to me for some time. My first visit was a Sunday lunch where I found a standard of food that sang of seasonality and a business philosophy that deserved to succeed. This was folded into a style of cooking that drew from a wider world knowledge combined with skill and the luxury of rich local produce. They had me hooked.

Some restaurants have the luck to find themselves located in a city centre with a heavy footfall, and when this is combined with talent and good business acumen, they naturally thrive. The road to success for others is a more complicated one. The now-famed MacNean House and Restaurant in Blacklion, County Cavan, is just such a place. Set in the most westerly part of Cavan near the dramatic Cuilcagh Mountains and the fishing lakes of Lower and Upper Lough MacNean, for which the restaurant is named, it is the centre of Neven Maguire's world. But twenty years ago it was far from the minds of the culinary elites and it seemed unlikely that it would become a destination dining point for people across Ireland.

If you were to draw up a list of obstacles to success, you probably couldn't find any more dramatic, or indeed more painful, than those that faced Neven and his family. They suffered a bomb attack during the Troubles. They faced many years of struggle to make ends meet and in 1999 Neven's father, Joe Maguire, lost his life in a car accident returning from their café business in Sligo.

Nonetheless, Neven has thrived in the face of it with innumerable awards under his belt, from Best Chef in Ulster and Best Chef in Ireland to Best Restaurant, but he never fails to name check his parents in his success. This is no automated act of filial loyalty, but the heartfelt thanks of a son who recognises the influence of his father as a businessman and his mother as a professional chef.

1 MUM, NEVEN AND DAD

2 NEVEN

3 NEVEN WITH PAUL BOCUSE

4 WINNING BAILEYS YOUNG CHEF OF THE YEAR

5 WITH LÉA LINSTER

6 WITH GORDON RAMSAY

7 WHEN NEVEN WON WEDGEWOOD CHEF OF THE YEAR

8 NEVEN

On a sunny May day in 2012, I sat in the restaurant in Blacklion and talked to Neven and his mother, Vera Maguire (at the time in her seventieth year), about the story of the restaurant in Blacklion. As Neven's mother says, she has a 'lifetime of happy memories'. No doubt it is this spirit that Neven has inherited, as he remains almost permanently optimistic. His mother recalls Neven helping in the restaurant kitchen from an early age. She looks around the elegant room that Neven and his wife Amelda have created and describes what went before, painting a self-deprecating picture of the restaurant she ran. It was a boarding place for the Gardaí who were stationed across the road.

But this woman was no ordinary cook: all the sauces were made to order and when you look at the à la carte menu from 1989, you start to see the sort of work that was done. Vera says she 'had a hard neck', but returning diners spoke of fine food. In the middle of all this was Neven, eager to learn and to help.

The Maguires always ate in good restaurants. A table for eleven would be needed for the large family, as Vera and Joe Maguire believed children should try interesting, quality food. She also found ideas for her own menu from the restaurants they visited.

Nonetheless, it became increasingly difficult to do business and the restaurant finally closed from 1973 to 1989. Vera had always kept her hand in and was essentially doing outside catering during the gap, including the catering needs of the local golf club, accompanied by her trusty son, Neven.

When they reopened in May 1989 it turned out to be a sunny summer, which shone happily on their business too. The whole family helped in the restaurant, whether that meant chopping herbs, weeding the vegetable patch or the non-drinking brother advising on wine. As Neven's skills grew, his father would think nothing of hopping in the car and travelling just about anywhere for an ingredient the kitchen needed.

Neven trained in Fermanagh College in Enniskillen and worked his evenings in the restaurant. Eventually he ended up lecturing at his old alma mater too. While Blacklion was always home, he was keen to expand his knowledge and worked in Roscoff in Belfast with Paul and Jeanne Rankin, keen to soak up the knowledge a Michelin-starred restaurant could give him. He spent short stages in Moyclare Manor with Shay Curran, Arzak in San Sebastian and the Grand Hotel in Berlin. The first day he arrived at the Grand Hotel, the meat chef opened the fridge door and showed him the Irish lamb. The chef announced it was the best in the world, a statement that impressed the young Neven. After all, this hotel had 125 chefs covering five different restaurants, including The Golden Goose, their Michelin-starred restaurant, and they were using Irish ingredients.

Neven won the Eurotoque Bailey's Young Chef of the Year in 1994 and part of the prize was a stage with Léa Linster, the Michelin-starred Luxembourgian chef. She remains the only woman to be awarded the Bocuse d'Or and is a self-taught chef. She was a major influence on Neven and when he returned from the three-month stage with her, his food had changed radically. This was a turning point in his cooking style and he still considers her a major influence. He also still travels abroad for inspiration and knowledge to bring back home, though he is quick to point out that he never had any intention to stay away from Cavan and Blacklion.

Even today he still does stages every January or books himself into a course to add to his knowledge. This is not something many other chefs of his calibre would do. It marks him out not just as a man with an unwavering desire to excel, but a man with no place for ego in his life.

All this hard work and dedication could have come to nought without the power of television. His first appearances on RTÉ's *Open House* with Marty Whelan and Mary Kennedy grew into his popular shows today. His natural ability to perform has ensured the continued popularity of his shows and contributed to the popularity of his restaurant.

Neven's wife Amelda has been the able front-of-house person that all who visit will know for her calmness and warm welcome, but her work and influence go beyond this. With a background in accounting, she acts as a balance to Neven's more creative side. Food is always number one with Neven, but he feels that Amelda has worked to make the whole experience work for their customers.

The kitchen at MacNean is not one where people are allowed to get annoyed – they are expected to contribute their ideas to the menu. This is as much a reflection of what Neven's mother allowed him to explore as it is the wisdom of a good chef allowing new ideas to bloom. He describes his relationship with local producers and suppliers as one of 'great rapport', underplaying the prosperity he has brought to them and to the wider community. The very low staff turnover is also a testament to a long-term success story here.

Neven now sits at a very happy time in his life with newborn twins and the very able Amelda by his side. This book reflects a certain sense of taking stock. The recipes show how his food has evolved over the years – some are classics and some are modern. Previous books included some recipes from the restaurant but they were always aimed at the home cook. This is a celebration of what is cooked in the restaurant. It is a celebration of how his food and style have changed and grown.

Some recipes are aspirational, though elements can be taken from each and used as a single dish rather than attempting the whole thing. Sometimes people want a challenge and at other times they want the comfort of simpler food. For that reason, the book includes the daily recipes made for the staff, which contrast with the more complicated recipes from the menu – though no less delicious, of course.

The original building bought by Vera and Joe Maguire in 1968 has now grown to include the building next door and twenty accommodation rooms. Weekend sittings for the restaurants are at a premium. It has been a hard-fought journey and success is not something that comes easily or quickly. Neven knows that when you step outside what you are used to, you discover great things, but when you return, you also discover the excellence of what we have closest to us.

Enjoy the excellence of Neven's talent in these pages.

Ross Golden-Bannon
DUBLIN, MAY 2012

Acknowledgements

In the thirty years since the MacNean Restaurant opened its doors, there have been many people that played their part in getting us to where we are today. My dad, Joe, was a visionary and he always believed in Blacklion. With my Mum, Vera, at his side dreams could come true. Dad would be very proud of the restaurant today.

The third generation of Maguires has joined us recently and who knows what the future holds for Connor and Lucia? We are a family restaurant surrounded by a great team. Amelda, my lovely wife, has looked after front of house and loves meeting our customers. Currently she has her hands full at home! Over the years my brothers and sisters have all been involved in the restaurant. A big thank you to each and every one of them.

This book is about our food. It has evolved over the years and will continue to change, but at its core is the best of local produce, in season, combined with the influences I pick up on my travels. A huge thank you to my Head Chef Glen Wheeler, our Restaurant Manager Bláithín McCabe and all our wonderful staff – there are too many to mention. The restaurant would not be the success it is without each one of them; I really appreciate and admire the great job they all do. I also owe a great debt of gratitude to Peter Cumisky, whose advice has been invaluable for our restaurant wine list and also for recommending the wines in this book – I have learned so much from him.

This book simply could not have happened without my long-term collaborator, the incomparable Orla Broderick. She is so knowledgeable about food, so efficient, so helpful and always a joy to work with. She made an enormous contribution to this book.

Sharon Hearne-Smith is a talented food stylist and, apart from this book, she also works on my television shows. I am always thrilled with the results. Olivia Rafferty and Susan Murphy performed the crucial testing of the recipes. Zara McHugh, who works as my PA in MacNean, prepared all of the text as well as keeping on top of her myriad duties in the restaurant. Thank you, Zara.

Thanks also to Joanne Murphy for her inspiring photography and Graham Thew for his design. The Gill & Macmillan team were a pleasure to work with again. Thank you, Catherine Gough and Nicki Howard. And thank you to Michael Gill for his personal interest. They have given me the book of my dreams.

RTÉ has played a huge part in my career. It began when John Masterson believed in me and gave me my first break on *Open House* in 1998 – I can't thank him enough for that and for his friendship and support. Thank you to Purcell Masterson for advice and support over the years, and thanks particularly to Mary Tallent, who is the best publicist I could ask for. Thank you also to my many friends in the media who have been so supportive.

The Irish Farmers Journal has always been a great friend to me. Thank you to Mairead Lavery, David Leydon, and all the team – I enjoy my weekly column with you. And to everyone in Bord Bia for all their help and wonderful support in promoting Irish food.

A big thank you to all at Marla: Sheila Gallogly, Ann Marie Coonan, Lee Grace. They do a great job with my online and social media. To John Hickey, who is constantly working on new projects for me and is always there to give me great advice. Also to Eoin O'Flynn at Flogas for his continued support and friendship, and to John Martin who organises all my demos and makes sure things run smoothly.

David Hare has produced my television shows and has always been a pleasure to work with, along with cameraman Billy Keady and Ray de Brún on sound. Thank you also to Brian Walsh in RTÉ who has asked us back each year and has trusted us to deliver in prime time.

I love heading to Dublin on a Saturday morning to chat with the one and only Marian Finucane. Thank you to Marian and to Anne Farrell for the opportunity. It is great to be back on Friday mornings with my old *Open House*-mate Marty Whelan on Lyric FM. Thank you to Sinead Wylde and Al Ryan who keep Marty on track, and thank you, Marty, for doing me the honour of launching this book.

Finally, thank you to our customers. I hope you will keep on dining with us. We will do our level best to ensure that you enjoy the MacNean experience.

Neven

This book is dedicated to my wonderful mother, Vera, who started MacNean Restaurant. Thank you for all the love and inspiration you have given me over the years. I will always be grateful.

How to Run an Efficient Kitchen

In the restaurant we have to be very careful that there is little or no waste to ensure a healthy profit margin. After all, there's a huge amount of preparation time involved, and the chefs who do the work command full salaries – that is, their income isn't subsidised by tips. In other words, there's a labour cost that must be factored in.

If you enjoy entertaining, there's no doubt that costs can quickly spiral out of control. It's easy to get caught up in the excitement of planning a dinner party and overspend on ingredients, many of which won't even get used on the day. This is where running an efficient kitchen can help you cook the foods you want to eat and still be well within your means.

It's also important that you look at minimising waste. If you buy what you need and can use and you can store it effectively, then you're throwing less food away. It pays to do a little inventory review along with your meal/menu planning so you can make use of fresh foods that might otherwise go to waste. Just think of this aspect of economic cooking in this way – you paid for all of it, so you might as well use all of it.

I have found that by being a bit more conscious about how to maximise the use of your raw ingredients, it's relatively simple to keep your costs down. For instance, it's normally much cheaper to cook something yourself than buy it pre-made, and of course it's going to taste so much nicer. Try to be imaginative with your leftovers and use them as a basis for another meal. Also, you can save money by employing a range of tips that help you cook more efficiently.

Do you have your own herb garden? If not, you should. It's a great way to have fresh herbs at your doorstep without paying a high price for them at the supermarket. This year we've invested heavily and put in polytunnels so that we can grow the vegetables, salads and herbs we need. Obviously this is a large project, but I think everyone should consider growing some vegetables, no matter how limited your space is. Even if you don't have a patio, chillies and mini cucumbers can do extremely well in pots if you have a nice sunny spot indoors. The satisfaction of serving vegetables that you have grown yourself is hard to beat.

Learn about wild foods, when they are in season and how to recognise them. Everyone can probably get access to wild garlic in the spring and use it to make a variation on pesto. Pick elderflowers in the summer and make cordial or use them to flavour panna cotta. Blackberries are in abundance in the autumn and make the most wonderful crumbles or an accompaniment to crème brûlée. Probably the most popular winter wild food comes from the blackthorn. The small black-blue fruits, or sloes, are ready after the first hard frosts. I like to turn them into sloe gin, the perfect Christmas tipple or present.

How to Run an Efficient Kitchen: Ten Top Tips

I   Use leftover brioche to make breadcrumbs and freeze them for a later date so that you can use them for making goujons or potato croquettes.

2   Asparagus trimmings can form the base for a delicious soup.

3   Keep all the scraps when preparing sweet potato fondants (page 231) and use them for a purée or in soups and casseroles.

4   Leftover sugar syrup can be used in drinks or over a fresh fruit salad. Freeze in ice cube trays with tiny herb sprigs and edible flowers and use in cocktails or pre-dinner drinks.

5   The trimmings of a potato gratin (page 230) can all be put into a small baking dish and frozen. This will help make a delicious Sunday dinner at a later date with very little effort.

6   When you have gone to the trouble of making a complicated dish, consider freezing some of it so that it saves you a job the next time you're entertaining.

7   Most leftover sauces can be frozen in ice cube trays and easily defrosted as needed.

8   Consider using the cheaper cuts of meat when entertaining. They may take longer to prepare, but the flavour will be fantastic and you'll have the added bonus of having very little to do at the last minute.

9   If you go to the trouble of making purées and gels as garnishes, store them in the fridge or freeze them where possible. Just remember to always date and label them.

IO Use vegetable trimmings for stock, keeping any suitable bones in the freezer until you're ready to use them. Store stocks in small zip-lock bags in the freezer so that you have them on hand when you need them.

Menu Planning

There are so many factors that need to be taken into account when planning a menu that it can often seem like a difficult and daunting task, especially if you're not used to doing it regularly. The key to producing good food for your family and friends is to think about what excites you and work with that. Here you will find useful tips and information relating to all areas of menu planning.

Think about the people you're cooking for and what type of dishes they might enjoy. I often think it's nice to give your guests one ingredient that they might not have tried before. However, it's important to think about accessibility and make sure that you don't spend too much time running about trying to find particular ingredients.

Choose your dishes based on seasonality. If you're unsure, take a trip to your local farmers' market and ask the growers what's at its best. There is nothing as delicious as fresh, organic, seasonal fruits and vegetables. Sticking with fruits and vegetables of the season will not only guarantee the best flavour, but it also helps to keep costs down.

Always check the dietary requirements of your guests to make sure that you are catering for everyone. That said, I always like to make a little extra food just in case there's an allergy or food dislike that you're not aware of.

Think about what dishes can be done in advance or maybe even prepared and frozen beforehand. When entertaining at home, I would always aim to have at least one course made in advance, such as the dessert. Many dishes can also be prepared to a certain stage and then kept covered in the fridge until needed. I have included a Cook Ahead section below each recipe to help you demystify this area.

Try to get a good balance of texture, colour and types of cooking in your menu and aim not to overlap ingredients. It's also important not to make too many of the dishes too rich and heavy, as although delicious, your guests will start to struggle.

Work out a time plan for the evening and make a note about what times different things will need to go into the oven. This stops you from getting flustered once your guests arrive and allows you to enjoy and take part in the chat!

If you're nervous, maybe try out the dishes on close friends and family first. The less pressure you have on your shoulders, the better, and the more likely everyone is to enjoy the night. Once you have mastered a dish, then you can build on it and take it to the next level.

My favourite tip is, don't be a hero. If you need help, ask for it! Remember, the whole point of entertaining is to have a good time right along with your guests. I hope the recipes in this book inspire you to go into the kitchen and create something extraordinary.

BREAKFAST

MacNean Special Porridge with Honey and Cream

THIS IS ONE OF OUR SIGNATURE BREAKFAST DISHES. IT'S AMAZING HOW MANY PEOPLE GOING TO BED AT NIGHT TELL ME THAT THEY CAN'T WAIT TO TASTE THE PORRIDGE! ON COLD WINTER MORNINGS IT GETS YOU OFF TO A GOOD START AND TAKES NO MORE THAN 10 MINUTES TO COOK.

Serves 4

100g (4oz) porridge oats (organic if possible)

300ml (1/2 pint) milk (plus a little extra if necessary)

4 tbsp clear honey

4 tbsp Irish Mist

150ml (1/4 pint) cream

Place the porridge oats, milk and 150ml (1/4 pint) water in a heavy-based pan. Bring to the boil, then reduce the heat and simmer for 8–10 minutes, until the mixture has slightly thickened, stirring all the time. It's important that the porridge has a nice soft dropping consistency, so add a little more milk if you think it needs it.

To serve, spoon the porridge into warmed bowls. Drizzle each one with some honey and Irish Mist and serve with plenty of cream poured on top.

COOK AHEAD

One of the last things we do at night in the restaurant is steep the porridge oats in the milk and water in the fridge, as leaving them overnight makes them lovely and soft so that they cook much quicker. They can also be made the night before and reheated gently in a pan on the hob.

Bircher Muesli with Granola

THIS IS A GREAT RECIPE TO GET THE CHILDREN INVOLVED IN AND THE BEST PART IS THAT THEY WILL BE MUCH MORE LIKELY TO EAT IT FOR THEIR BREAKFAST! GET THEM TO ROLL UP THEIR SLEEVES AND USE A TEACUP TO MEASURE THE DIFFERENT INGREDIENTS.

Serves 4–6

For the bircher muesli:

225g (8oz) jumbo porridge oats

200ml (7fl oz) cream

150g (5oz) natural plain yoghurt

150ml (1/4 pint) freshly pressed apple juice

2 tbsp clear honey

1 tsp vanilla extract

1 Granny Smith apple

For the granola:

100g (4oz) mixed seeds (such as sunflower seeds, pumpkin seeds and/or sesame seeds)

40ml (1 3/4fl oz) maple syrup

25g (1oz) flaked almonds

To make the bircher muesli, mix the oats in a large non-metallic bowl with the cream, yoghurt, apple juice, honey and vanilla extract. Cover with clingfilm and set aside overnight in the fridge to soak.

To make the granola, preheat the grill to medium.

Place the mixed seeds in a bowl and drizzle in the maple syrup, stirring continuously until evenly combined. Tip the seed mixture onto a Swiss roll tin lined with parchment paper and spread out in an even layer. Place under the grill for 8–10 minutes, until light golden, stirring occasionally to break up any large lumps in the mixture. Add the flaked almonds, stirring to combine, and cook for another 5–10 minutes, until light golden, again stirring occasionally to prevent the edges from overcooking. Remove from the grill and leave to cool and harden. Transfer to an airtight container until needed.

In the morning, finish making the bircher muesli. Remove the core from the apple and then grate the apple into the softened oat mixture. It's important to keep the mixture quite wet.

To serve, divide the bircher muesli among martini glasses and sprinkle over the granola.

COOK AHEAD

This must be made 12 hours in advance, but it will keep for up to 2 days if kept covered with clingfilm in the fridge without adding the apple, which may brown.

Poached Apricots with Star Anise and Yoghurt

STAR ANISE IS A PRETTY STAR-SHAPED POD WITH A FLAVOUR THAT IS ALMOST OVERWHELMINGLY OF LIQUORICE, BUT WITH DEEPER SPICY UNDERTONES. MOST LARGE SUPERMARKETS SHOULD STOCK IT AND IT KEEPS QUITE WELL IN A COOL, DARK PLACE. IT ADDS AN EXOTIC FRAGRANT NOTE TO THE APRICOTS SO IT'S WELL WORTH SEEKING OUT.

Serves 4–6

50g (2oz) caster sugar

2 whole star anise

1 cinnamon stick

1/2 vanilla pod, split

300g (11oz) ready-to-eat dried apricots

150g (5oz) natural plain yoghurt

fresh mint leaves, to decorate

Place the sugar in a pan with 300ml (1/2 pint) water. Add the star anise, cinnamon stick and split vanilla pod. Bring to the boil, then tip in the apricots, reduce the heat and simmer gently for 15 minutes. Remove from the heat and leave to cool.

To serve, spoon the poached apricots into a small pan with the stock syrup and reheat gently. Ladle the warmed apricots into bowls and add a good dollop of the natural yoghurt. Decorate with the mint leaves.

COOK AHEAD

This will keep for up to 3 weeks in the fridge in a rigid plastic container, so it's worth making up a double batch if you're going to the trouble. To serve, simply reheat gently in a little of the stock syrup.

Warm Prunes Marinated in Tea and Vanilla with Yoghurt

I JUST LOVE THE COMBINATION OF PRUNES AND TEA AND WE ALWAYS HAVE IT ON THE MENU AS ONE OF OUR LIGHTER BREAKFAST OPTIONS. FEEL FREE TO EXPERIMENT WITH A MORE PERFUMED TEA, SUCH AS EARL GREY OR DARJEELING, BUT MY PERSONAL PREFERENCE IS DEFINITELY BARRY'S GOLD BLEND!

Serves 6

For the prunes:

100g (4oz) large pitted prunes

1 tea bag

1 tbsp caster sugar

1/2 vanilla pod, split in half and seeds scraped out

350g (12oz) Greek yoghurt

For the granola:

100g (4oz) mixed seeds (such as sunflower seeds, pumpkin seeds and/or sesame seeds)

40ml (1 3/4fl oz) maple syrup

25g (1oz) flaked almonds

To make the granola, preheat the grill to medium.

Place the mixed seeds in a bowl and drizzle in the maple syrup, stirring continuously until evenly combined. Tip the seed mixture onto a Swiss roll tin lined with parchment paper and spread out in an even layer. Place under the grill for 8–10 minutes, until light golden, stirring occasionally to break up any large lumps in the mixture. Add the flaked almonds, stirring to combine, and cook for another 5–10 minutes, until light golden, again stirring occasionally to prevent the edges from overcooking. Remove from the grill and leave to cool and harden. Transfer to an airtight container until needed.

Place the prunes, tea bag, sugar and vanilla pod in a small pan and pour in 175ml (6fl oz) water. Bring to a simmer and cook for 8–10 minutes, until the prunes are plump. Remove from the heat and leave to cool completely.

Remove the tea bag and vanilla pod from the prune mixture and discard. Pour the prune mixture into a liquidiser and blitz until smooth. Using a spatula, transfer to a bowl and cover with clingfilm. Chill in the fridge until needed.

In a separate bowl, mix the yoghurt and vanilla seeds together. Cover with clingfilm and chill until needed.

To serve, divide the prune purée among 6 x 120ml (4fl oz) martini glasses and spoon over the yoghurt to cover completely. Finally, scatter over a layer of the granola.

COOK AHEAD

The prune purée will keep for 2 weeks in the fridge and the granola keeps for 2 weeks in an airtight container. The layered martini glasses without the granola topping will sit happily in the fridge overnight covered with clingfilm.

MacNean Special Breakfast

THE SECRET TO A GOOD COOKED BREAKFAST IS THE QUALITY OF THE RAW INGREDIENTS AND IT IS BY FAR OUR MOST POPULAR MAIN COURSE BREAKFAST. IT'S IMPORTANT TO ME THAT IT LEAVES A MARKED IMPRESSION, AS IT'S GOING TO BE THE LAST THING CUSTOMERS HAVE TO EAT BEFORE THEY LEAVE. OBVIOUSLY YOU COULD GRILL EVERYTHING FOR A HEALTHIER OPTION. THE BOILED BOXTY IS MADE FOR US BY MY UNCLE GERRY BUT OF COURSE YOU CAN MAKE YOUR OWN OR USE IRISH POTATO FARLS INSTEAD.

Serves 4

8 small pork sausages

sunflower oil, for frying

2 ripe vine tomatoes, halved

butter, for grilling and frying

sea salt and freshly ground black pepper

4 slices black pudding

4 slices white pudding

8 back bacon rashers

4 slices boiled boxty

150g (5oz) button mushrooms, quartered or halved if large

4 eggs

fresh flat-leaf parsley sprigs, to garnish

Preheat the oven to 150°C (300°F/gas mark 2) and preheat the grill to medium.

Fry the sausages in a little sunflower oil in a frying pan over a medium heat, turning every now and then, for 8–10 minutes, until cooked through. Put onto a baking sheet and slide into the oven to keep hot.

Arrange the tomatoes cut side up on a grill rack, dot each one with a little butter and season to taste. Place the black and white pudding alongside and grill for 4–5 minutes, turning the puddings once, then keep warm with the sausages.

Meanwhile, wipe out the frying pan, add a teaspoon or two of oil and fry the rashers for 1–2 minutes on each side, until crisp and golden brown. Keep warm with the sausages, tomatoes and black and white pudding.

Heat another tablespoon of oil with the bacon fat left in the frying pan, add the boxty farls and fry for 1–2 minutes on each side, until crisp and golden. Put onto a second baking sheet and slide into the oven.

Melt a small knob of butter in a medium frying pan. Add the mushrooms and season to taste, then cook over a high heat for 2–3 minutes, or until tender, stirring occasionally. Set to one side.

Wipe the frying pan clean again, heat a thin layer of oil in it over a medium-high heat and break in the eggs. Season to taste and fry for a couple of minutes, spooning a little of the hot fat over the yolks until they are just set.

To serve, arrange the sausages on warmed plates with the tomatoes, black and white pudding, rashers and mushrooms. Arrange the fried boxty to one side and place a fried egg on top of each one. Garnish with the parsley sprigs to serve.

COOK AHEAD

Obviously a breakfast of this type is best made to order, but you can cook everything except the eggs and keep them in a preheated oven (100°C/200°F/gas mark 1/2) for up to 30 minutes but no longer, or it will begin to spoil.

Scrambled Eggs with Burren Smoked Salmon

THERE IS NOTHING NICER THAN THE COMBINATION OF FLAVOURS OF SMOKED SALMON AND SCRAMBLED EGGS. WE ARE LUCKY IN IRELAND TO HAVE SUCH GREAT SMOKED SALMON. MY FAVOURITE AT THE MOMENT IS FROM THE BURREN SMOKEHOUSE, AS I FIND IT VERY CONSISTENT IN FLAVOUR. THEY OFFER A GREAT MAIL ORDER SERVICE (SEE THE LIST OF SUPPLIERS ON PAGE 270 FOR DETAILS).

Serves 4

4 small clusters of cherry tomatoes on the vine

4 flat field mushrooms

1/4 tsp chopped fresh thyme

sea salt and freshly ground black pepper

2 tbsp rapeseed oil

6 eggs

3 tbsp milk or cream

1 tbsp snipped fresh chives, plus extra to garnish

40g (1 1/2oz) butter, softened

4 slices wholemeal bread

200g (7oz) smoked salmon slices

Preheat the oven to 220°C (425°F/gas mark 7) and preheat the grill.

Place the cherry tomatoes and mushrooms in a small roasting tin and sprinkle over the thyme. Season to taste and drizzle with the rapeseed oil. Roast for 15–20 minutes, until the mushrooms are tender and the cherry tomatoes are lightly charred and just beginning to burst.

Break the eggs into a bowl and add the milk or cream, chives and plenty of freshly ground black pepper. Blitz with a stick blender, as this helps make the resulting scrambled eggs even lighter and fluffier.

Heat a knob of the butter in a non-stick frying pan over a medium heat, until foaming. Add the egg mixture and whisk continuously for 2–3 minutes, until just set but still soft. Remove from the heat, as they will continue to cook. Check the seasoning and add a pinch of salt if you think it needs it.

Meanwhile, lightly toast the bread on a grill rack, then spread each piece of toast with the remaining butter and cut into triangles.

To serve, arrange two of the toasted bread triangles on each warmed plate. Top each one with the scrambled eggs and arrange the smoked salmon to the side. Add the roasted cherry tomatoes and field mushrooms, then garnish with the chives.

VARIATION
Smoked Kipper with Lemon Butter
Skin double smoked kipper fillets, removing any pin bones. Heat a large heavy-based frying pan and add a knob of butter and 1 tablespoon rapeseed oil. Gently fry the kippers for 1–2 minutes on each side, until cooked through. Add another knob of butter and a squeeze of lemon, then sprinkle over 1 teaspoon chopped fresh flat-leaf parsley and chives, swirling the pan to make an instant lemon butter sauce. Serve at once with the scrambled eggs and garnish with lemon wedges.

MacNean Eggs Benedict

THIS IS OUR VERSION OF EGGS BENEDICT: A POACHED EGG SERVED ON BRIOCHE WITH BACON AND A BUTTER SAUCE, WHICH IS MUCH LIGHTER THAN HOLLANDAISE. WE ALSO GIVE OUR CUSTOMERS THE OPTION OF HAVING IT WITH SMOKED SALMON OR WITH SPINACH AS A VEGETARIAN OPTION.

Serves 4

1 tbsp white wine vinegar

8 eggs

8 smoked streaky bacon rashers, rinds removed

40g (1 1/2oz) unsalted butter, softened

225g (8oz) baby spinach leaves

sea salt and freshly ground black pepper

1 brioche loaf, cut into 8 slices with ends discarded (page 214 or shop bought)

fresh chervil sprigs, to garnish

For the butter sauce:

100ml (3 1/2fl oz) cream

1 tsp prepared English mustard

2 tbsp softened butter

1 tsp cornflour, sifted

squeeze of lemon juice

1 tsp snipped fresh chives

sea salt and freshly ground black pepper

Heat a large pan with 2.25 litres (4 pints) water. Add the white wine vinegar and bring to the boil. Break each egg into the water where it is bubbling, then reduce the heat and simmer gently for 3 minutes, until the eggs are just cooked through but the yolks are still soft. Remove with a slotted spoon and plunge into a bowl of iced water.

Preheat the grill, then grill the bacon until crispy and golden brown.

Add half of the butter to a large pan over a medium heat and once it starts to foam, tip in the spinach. Sauté over a fairly high heat until just wilted. Season to taste and drain off any excess liquid on kitchen paper, then return to the pan and keep warm.

Meanwhile, stamp out 7.5cm (3in) rounds of brioche with a straight-sided cutter. Arrange the brioche rounds on a grill pan and cook for 2–3 minutes, until lightly toasted, turning once. Spread with the remaining butter.

To make the butter sauce, place the cream and mustard in a small pan and simmer for 1 minute. Whisk in the butter, cornflour and lemon juice, then continue to whisk for 2–3 minutes, until thickened. Stir in the chives and season to taste. Keep warm.

Bring a large pan of salted water to the boil. Add the poached eggs and cook for 1 minute to warm through.

To serve, place the brioche on warmed plates and spoon on small mounds of the spinach. Place slices of bacon on top of the spinach. Using a slotted spoon, remove the poached eggs from the pan and drain briefly on kitchen paper. Place an egg on the bacon and spoon over the butter sauce. Garnish with the chervil sprigs.

COOK AHEAD

The poached eggs will keep happily in the fridge in a large bowl of cold water for up to 24 hours. The butter sauce keeps for 4 days in the fridge in an airtight container. If using spinach, it can be cooked the day before and kept wrapped in kitchen paper in the fridge.

Baked Eggs with Black Pudding Hash Browns

AN IRISH TWIST ON THE CLASSIC OEUFS EN COCOTTE. TO MAKE THE EGGS MORE EXCITING, EXPERIMENT WITH ANOTHER FLAVOUR ADDITION – A LITTLE CHOPPED COOKED HAM OR PARMA HAM, DICED COOKED MUSHROOMS, A FEW HERBS OR SOME SLICED ARTICHOKE HEART CAN ALL GO INTO THE BASE BEFORE YOU CRACK IN THE EGG. FOR A REALLY EXTRAVAGANT ADDITION, ADD A DROP OR TWO OF WHITE TRUFFLE OIL OVER THE CREAM.

Serves 4

For the black pudding hash browns:

450g (1lb) Maris Piper potatoes, scrubbed clean

1 tsp snipped fresh chives

1 tsp chopped fresh flat-leaf parsley

sea salt and freshly ground black pepper

4 slices black pudding, about 5cm (2in) in diameter and outer casing removed

groundnut oil, for deep-frying

For the baked eggs:

butter, for greasing

4 tbsp Ballymaloe relish (from a jar)

4 large eggs

sea salt and freshly ground black pepper

4 tbsp cream

25g (1oz) Cheddar cheese, finely grated

hollandaise sauce (page 255), to serve

apple chutney (page 249), to serve

Preheat the oven to 190°C (375°F/gas mark 5).

Steam the potatoes for 10 minutes, then allow to cool slightly and peel off the skins. Coarsely grate the potatoes into a bowl and mix in the chives and parsley, then season generously – you should end up with 350g (12oz) in total.

Pat out 4 circles of the potato mixture, making sure they are larger than the black pudding slices. Place a slice of black pudding in the centre of each potato circle, then fold the potato edges in and around the filling and shape into an even-sized patty, each about 7.5cm (3in) in diameter and 2cm (3/4in) in height.

Heat the oil in a deep-fat fryer or deep-sided pan to 170°C (340°F). Carefully lower the black pudding hash browns into the oil and cook for 5 minutes, turning halfway through with a tongs to ensure that they cook evenly. Remove with a slotted spoon, then drain on kitchen paper and keep warm.

Meanwhile, prepare the baked eggs. Butter 4 ramekins and place 1 tablespoon of the relish in the bottom of each one. Crack in an egg and season with salt, then add 1 tablespoon cream to each ramekin and sprinkle over the Cheddar.

Arrange the ramekins in a roasting tin and pour in enough boiling water to come about halfway up each ramekin. Place in the oven and bake for 15 minutes, until the eggs are just set but the yolks are still runny. Set a ramekin on a warmed plate and add the black pudding hash browns. Pour the hollandaise on top of the eggs. Add a spoonful of the apple chutney to serve.

COOK AHEAD
The black pudding hash browns can be made up to 2 hours in advance and kept on a tray in the fridge covered with clingfilm. Any longer and the potato would be in danger of discolouring.

Morning Reviver Juice

THIS IS ROCKET FUEL FOR THE MORNING AND A GREAT WAY TO START THE DAY. FEEL FREE TO EXPERIMENT WITH DIFFERENT VEGETABLES DEPENDING ON WHAT'S AVAILABLE.

Makes about 800ml (1 pint 8fl oz)

4 eating apples

2 carrots

2 oranges, peeled

2 celery sticks

2.5cm (1in) piece of root ginger, peeled and chopped

Place the apples, carrots, oranges, celery and ginger in a juicer. Pour into glasses to serve.

> PREPARE AHEAD
> This juice can be made the night before and kept in a covered jug in the fridge. Give it a good stir before serving.

Breakfast Berry Zinger

WE ALWAYS HAVE A VARIETY OF JUICES AVAILABLE FOR OUR GUESTS, PREPARED BY OUR BREAKFAST CHEF, MARIE. THERE IS NO DOUBT THAT THIS JUICE IS A VERY HEALTHY WAY TO START YOUR DAY.

Makes about 700ml (1 pint 4fl oz)

150g (5oz) blueberries

100g (4oz) raspberries

100g (4oz) blackcurrants

300ml (1/2 pint) cranberry juice

Place the blueberries, raspberries and blackcurrants in a juicer. Transfer the juice to a blender and whizz with the cranberry juice. Pour into glasses to serve.

> PREPARE AHEAD
> This juice can be made the night before and kept in a covered jug in the fridge. Give it a good stir before serving.

Speckled Canary Juice

THIS TANGY JUICE HAS A FABULOUS COLOUR AND WOULD BE DELICIOUS SERVED AT ANY TIME OF THE DAY. IF YOU HAVE ANY LEFT OVER, IT MAKES AN EXCELLENT MIXER WITH YOUR FAVOURITE TIPPLE AND PLENTY OF ICE.

Makes about 500ml (16fl oz)

2 grapefruit, peeled

1 ripe pineapple, peeled, quartered and core removed

1 lime, peeled

6 fresh mint leaves

1 tbsp clear honey

Place the grapefruit, pineapple, lime and mint leaves in a juicer. Stir in the honey until dissolved, then pour into glasses to serve.

> PREPARE AHEAD
> This juice can be made the night before and kept in a covered jug in the fridge. Give it a good stir before serving.

Sunrise Juice

A REALLY REFRESHING WAY TO BEGIN THE DAY. TRY TO PICK A NICE RIPE MELON FOR EXTRA SWEETNESS.

Makes about 600ml (1 pint)

2 pink grapefruit, peeled

1 honeydew melon, cut into quarters, seeds removed and flesh roughly chopped (skin discarded)

1 lemon, peeled

Place the grapefruit, melon and lemon in a juicer. Pour into glasses to serve.

> PREPARE AHEAD
> This juice can be made the night before and kept in a covered jug in the fridge. Give it a good stir before serving.

Banana and Pineapple Smoothie

THIS BREAKFAST IN A GLASS IS THE PERFECT WAY TO START THE DAY. IF THE FRUIT IS NICE AND RIPE THERE'S NO NEED TO SWEETEN WITH SUGAR OR HONEY, BUT THAT, OF COURSE, IS PERSONAL PREFERENCE.

Makes about 900ml (1 1/2 pints)

2 bananas, peeled

1/2 fresh pineapple, cored, peeled and diced

275g (10oz) Greek yoghurt

300ml (1/2 pint) freshly pressed apple juice

handful of ice cubes

Place the bananas and pineapple in a liquidiser with the Greek yoghurt and apple juice. Blend until smooth and pour into tall glasses half filled with ice cubes. Serve at once.

PREPARE AHEAD
This smoothie can be made up to 2 hours in advance.

Strawberry Booster Smoothie

I USE FROZEN STRAWBERRIES HERE, AS THEY ARE JUST AS NUTRITIOUS AS FRESH BERRIES AND NORMALLY HALF THE PRICE. THE WHEAT GERM IS PACKED FULL OF NUTRIENTS AND IS ONE OF THE BEST SOURCES OF FOLIC ACID.

Makes about 900ml (1 1/2 pints)

225g (8oz) fresh or frozen strawberries

450g (1lb) natural plain yoghurt

225ml (8fl oz) semi-skimmed milk

2 tbsp honey (optional)

1 tbsp wheat germ

handful of ice cubes

Place the strawberries in a liquidiser with the yoghurt, milk, honey (if using) and wheat germ. Blend until smooth and pour into tall glasses half filled with ice cubes.

PREPARE AHEAD
This smoothie can be made up to 2 hours in advance.

Red Berry Smoothie

I NORMALLY USE FROZEN BERRIES STRAIGHT OUT OF THE FREEZER SO THAT YOU DON'T HAVE TO USE ANY ICE CUBES, BUT IT CAN BE HARD ON THE BLADES OF YOUR LIQUIDISER.

Makes about 1.2 litres (2 pints)

225g (8oz) fresh or frozen berries (such as a mixture of strawberries, raspberries, redcurrants and tayberries)

2 bananas, peeled

275g (10oz) natural yoghurt

600ml (1 pint) raspberry and cranberry juice

handful of ice cubes (optional)

Place the berries and bananas in a liquidiser with the yoghurt and juice. Process for 1 minute, until smooth. Alternatively, you can put everything into a large measuring jug and blend with a hand-held blender, moving it up and down, until smooth.

Half fill tall glasses with ice cubes, if using, and pour in the red berry smoothie to serve.

PREPARE AHEAD
This smoothie can be made up to 2 hours in advance.

STARTERS

Fish
A Study of Shellfish

THIS IS ONE OF OUR SIGNATURE DISHES ON THE MENU. IT HAS THE PERFECT BALANCE OF TEXTURE AND FLAVOUR FROM THE SELECTION OF SHELLFISH. IT'S A WONDERFUL SHOWCASE FOR THE FANTASTIC PRODUCE THAT IS HARVESTED FROM OUR OCEAN AND OUR CUSTOMERS LOVE IT.

Serves 6

For the crispy prawns in kataifi pastry:

150g (5oz) frozen kataifi pastry

25g (1oz) plain flour

sea salt and freshly ground black pepper

1 egg

50ml (2fl oz) milk

12 fresh Dublin Bay prawns, peeled and veins removed

groundnut oil, for deep-frying

chilli jam (page 248), to serve

curried mayonnaise (page 251), to serve

For the crab ravioli:

100g (4oz) organic salmon fillet, skinned, boned and cubed

1 egg yolk

1 tbsp cold cream

sea salt and freshly ground black pepper

1 tsp snipped fresh chives

1 tsp chopped fresh basil

100g (4oz) white crab meat

12 wonton wrappers

egg wash (made with 1 egg and 1 tbsp milk), to glaze

creamed leeks (page 234), to serve

prawn velouté (page 258), to garnish

To prepare the prawns, thaw the pastry while still in its plastic for a minimum of 2 hours before using. Once it's thawed it will be soft and pliable and ready to use, but remember when using it that you must always keep it well covered.

Place the flour in a shallow dish and season generously. Beat the egg with the milk and a pinch of salt in a separate shallow dish.

Toss the prawns in the seasoned flour until lightly coated, then dip briefly in the egg wash, then wrap well in kataifi pastry. To wrap the prawns, lay about 10g (1/4oz) of the kataifi pastry in a rectangle on a board. Sit a prawn across the width at the end closest to you and then roll it up away from you to completely enclose it. Place on non-stick parchment paper well spaced apart so that they don't get tangled up and cover with clingfilm. Chill until ready to use.

To make the ravioli, place the salmon in a food processor and blend briefly, then add the egg yolk and the cream and season to taste. Blend to a smooth consistency. Place in a bowl and stir in the chives and basil, then fold in the crab.

Lay out the wonton wrappers on a clean work surface. Brush one wrapper with a little of the egg wash. Place a generous spoonful of the crab mixture in the centre and place another wonton wrapper on top. Shape and seal well. Using a 6cm (2 1/4in) scone cutter, cut the ravioli to give a neat finish. Blanch in a pan of boiling salted water for 2 minutes, then remove with a slotted spoon and quickly refresh in a bowl of iced water. Arrange on a tray in a single layer and chill until needed.

Scrub the oyster shells then place one, wrapped in a clean tea towel, on a firm surface with the flattest shell uppermost and the hinge pointing towards you. Gripping the oyster firmly, insert an oyster knife into the gap in the hinge and twist to snap the shells apart. Slide the blade of the knife along the inside of the upper shell to sever the muscle that keeps the shells together. Lift the lid off the top shell and run the knife under the oyster to remove it from the shell. Repeat until all the oysters are taken out of their shells, but reserve the bottom half of the shells for presentation.

To prepare the scallops, pat them dry with kitchen paper. Detach the corals (roes) and save them for another dish. Heat a large frying pan until it's quite hot. Add a thin film

For the oysters:

6 Atlantic oysters

1 rindless smoked streaky bacon rasher

knob of butter

50g (2oz) spinach leaves, washed and tough stalks removed

3 tbsp flaked sea salt

lemon grass foam (page 246), to serve

For the scallops:

6 king scallops, roes removed

1 tbsp rapeseed oil

juice of 1/2 lemon

sea salt and freshly ground black pepper

sauce vierge (page 256), to serve

of rapeseed oil, then add the scallops and sear over a high heat for 1 minute on each side, until richly browned and crispy. Do this in batches if your frying pan isn't very large. Transfer them to a plate and add a squeeze of lemon juice, then season to taste.

To finish the prawns, heat the oil in a deep-fat fryer or a deep-sided pan to 160°C (325°F). Cook the coated prawns in batches of three for about 3 minutes, turning halfway through, until crisp and golden brown and the prawns are cooked through. Drain on kitchen paper.

To finish the crab ravioli, carefully place them in a pan of boiling salted water for 2 minutes to just warm through, then drain briefly on kitchen paper.

To finish the oysters, preheat the grill and grill the bacon for a couple of minutes, until crisp. Drain on kitchen paper. Melt the butter in a pan over a medium heat and add the spinach and a pinch of salt. Cook for a minute or so, stirring occasionally, until just wilted. Drain off any excess liquid and then spoon a small mound into each reserved oyster shell. Arrange on a warmed plate and keep warm. Add the raw oysters to the warm lemon grass foam and gently poach for 30 seconds. Carefully remove the oysters with a slotted spoon and place on top of the spinach in the oyster shells.

To serve, add the chilli jam and curried mayonnaise onto warmed plates and arrange the prawn in kataifi on top. Spoon the creamed leeks onto the plates and place the ravioli on top and garnish with the prawn velouté. Place each oyster shell on flaked sea salt and crumble over the smoked streaky bacon, then spoon over the lemon grass foam. Add a dollop of the sauce vierge and place a seared scallop on top.

COOK AHEAD
There is a lot of work to this dish, but it's worth it. Most of the elements can be prepared ahead and assembled at the last moment. The scallops can be opened and placed on damp kitchen roll in the fridge for up to 3–4 days or they can be frozen. The prawns can be wrapped in the kataifi pastry and chilled for up to 3–4 days until needed or they can be frozen. The crab ravioli can be made 2–3 days in advance and stored on a tray covered with clingfilm in the fridge or they can be frozen.

WINE
A crisp, dry, sparkling wine, especially Brut Champagne, would be very good with this recipe. Otherwise, try a white Burgundy from Côte de Beane or the Macon region. A dry Riesling from Alsace would also work well.

A STUDY OF SHELLFISH

Tempura of Sole with Curried Mayonnaise and Chilli Jam

THIS CRISPY SOLE IS COMPLETELY DELICIOUS WITH THE COMBINATION OF THE CURRIED MAYONNAISE AND CHILLI JAM. IT'S ONE RECIPE THAT ALWAYS MAKES A REAPPEARANCE ON THE MENU. ASK YOUR FISHMONGER TO PREPARE THE SOLE FOR YOU, AS IT'S A MESSY JOB THAT YOU'D NEED A VERY SHARP FILLETING KNIFE FOR.

Serves 6

groundnut oil, for deep-frying

2 egg whites

2 tbsp cream

150g (5oz) plain flour

2 tsp chilli powder

2 tsp curry powder

1 tsp sesame seeds

sea salt and freshly ground white pepper

600g (1lb 6oz) sole fillets, skinned, boned and well trimmed

curried mayonnaise (page 251), to serve

chilli jam (page 248), to serve

lightly dressed baby green salad leaves, to garnish

Heat the oil in a deep-fat fryer to 180°C (350°F). Whisk the egg whites and cream together in a shallow bowl and set aside. Place the flour, chilli powder, curry powder and sesame seeds in a separate bowl. Add 1/2 teaspoon salt and a large pinch of white pepper. Stir until well combined.

Cut the sole into small slices on the diagonal and dip into the egg mixture, making sure it is well coated, then gently shake off any excess. Dip the fish into the spiced flour until evenly coated. Deep-fry the fish for about 2 minutes, until golden and crispy. You may have to do this in batches, depending on the size of your deep-fat fryer. Remove from the oil and drain well on kitchen paper.

Arrange the crispy sole in the centre of warmed plates. Add a dollop of the curried mayonnaise and a squiggle of the chilli jam. Garnish with the salad leaves to serve.

COOK AHEAD
The sole fillets can be prepared and soaked in the egg mixture overnight.

WINE
Sancerre or Pouilly-Fumé from the Loire Valley, or try a crisp Muscadet or Chablis.

Seared Scallops with Confit of Pork Cheek and Cauliflower Textures

RICH AND TENDER PORK CHEEKS COMBINE PERFECTLY WITH SWEET, DELECTABLE SCALLOPS IN THIS EASILY PREPARED STARTER. ALTHOUGH THERE IS SOME PREPARATION INVOLVED, THE RESULTS ARE WELL WORTH THE EFFORT AND WILL HAVE YOUR GUESTS BEGGING FOR THE RECIPE! ORDER YOUR PORK CHEEKS FROM YOUR CRAFT BUTCHER AND GIVE A COUPLE OF DAYS' NOTICE.

Serves 6

For the scallops:

1 tsp rapeseed oil

18 large scallops, well trimmed

sea salt

cauliflower purée (page 243), to serve

dried cauliflower pieces (page 234), to serve

fresh pea shoots, to garnish

For the confit of pork cheek:

3 x 75–100g (3–4oz) pork cheeks, boned and trimmed

75g (3oz) coarse sea salt

6 fresh thyme sprigs

2 whole star anise

1 garlic clove, chopped

750ml (1 1/4 pints) duck fat

2 tbsp dark soy sauce

2 tbsp balsamic vinegar

2 tbsp maple syrup

creamed white beans (page 239), to serve

spinach purée (page 244), to serve

cauliflower foam (page 246), to serve

Place the pork cheeks on a plate and sprinkle over the salt, thyme, star anise and garlic. Cover with clingfilm and place in the fridge overnight to allow the flavours to infuse into the pork meat.

The next day, preheat the oven to 120°C (250°F/gas mark 1/2).

Rinse the excess spices off the marinated pork, removing all the salt, and dry thoroughly. To cook the pork, heat the duck fat in a casserole dish with a tight-fitting lid until melted, then carefully immerse the pork cheeks into the fat. Cover with foil and the lid, then place in the oven for about 4 hours, until the pork is meltingly tender and the flesh is just coming apart. Take out of the oven and leave to cool in the fat, then remove and dry with kitchen paper. Cut into 6 even-sized pieces and place on a plate covered with clingfilm until needed.

To finish cooking the pork cheeks, place the soy sauce, vinegar and maple syrup in a sauté pan. Bring to the boil and reduce to a honey consistency. Add the cold pork cheeks into the maple and balsamic syrup and warm through for 4–5 minutes, until caramelised and nicely sticky, turning regularly.

To cook the scallops, heat the rapeseed oil in a non-stick frying pan. Season the scallops with some salt, then sear the scallops for about 1 minute on each side, until golden brown and nicely caramelised. They should still be slightly undercooked in the middle. You may need to do this in batches depending on the size of your pan.

To serve, spoon a little of the cauliflower purée onto warmed plates, then using a spoon, swipe the purée. Add the scallops and top with a little more of the cauliflower purée, then garnish with the dried cauliflower pieces and pea shoots. Add the creamed white beans to each plate and place the pork cheek on top, then add a long swipe of the spinach purée alongside. Spoon the cauliflower foam alongside.

COOK AHEAD
The pork cheeks can be braised 24 hours in advance and caramelised just before serving. All the cauliflower elements can be made 24 hours in advance and kept in the fridge until needed. The scallops can be opened and placed on damp kitchen roll in the fridge for up to 3 or 4 days or they can be frozen.

WINE
Balance the rich hint of sweetness with a crisp, citrusy Albariño from Rias Baixas in north-west Spain. Another good choice is a ripe Antão Vaz from Portugal.

Crab Wontons with Enoki Mushrooms and Thai Broth

THIS DISH OFTEN APPEARS ON OUR TASTING MENU AND IS A FAVOURITE FOR SUNDAY LUNCH. I LEARNED TO MAKE THE BROTH WHILE TRAVELLING IN THAILAND, WHERE IT IS USED FOR BOTH FISH AND CHICKEN. TRY TO FIND FRESH OR FROZEN KAFFIR LIME LEAVES, AS I FIND THE DRIED ONES HAVE LOST A LOT OF THEIR FLAVOUR.

Serves 8

3 tbsp rapeseed oil

4 fresh or frozen kaffir lime leaves

1 lemon grass stalk, trimmed and thinly sliced

2.5cm (1in) piece of galangal, peeled and thinly sliced

400g can of coconut milk

300ml (1/2 pint) vegetable stock (page 252)

1 small red chilli, thinly sliced

1 tbsp sweet chilli sauce

2 tsp Thai fish sauce (nam pla)

2 tsp tomato purée

juice from 1/2 lime

sea salt and freshly ground black pepper

2 pak choi, cut into 2cm (3/4in) pieces on the diagonal

100g (4oz) enoki mushrooms

1 tsp soya lecithin

fresh micro coriander, to garnish

fresh red amaranth, to garnish

For the crab wontons:

100g (4oz) skinless salmon fillet, diced

2 egg yolks

100ml (3 1/2fl oz) cream, well chilled

200g (7oz) white crab meat

finely grated rind of 1/2 lemon

1 tbsp snipped fresh chives

1 tbsp chopped fresh basil

sea salt and freshly ground black pepper

24 wonton wrappers

egg wash (made with 1 egg and 1 tbsp milk), to glaze

To make the broth, heat 1 tablespoon of the oil in a pan over a medium heat and add the kaffir lime leaves, lemon grass and galangal. Stir well to combine and cook for 2 minutes. Stir in half the coconut milk along with the stock. Bring to the boil, then reduce the heat to a gentle simmer. Add the chilli, chilli sauce, fish sauce and tomato purée along with the remaining coconut milk and simmer for another 10 minutes, until slightly reduced and the flavours have had time to combine. Add the lime juice, then season to taste and pass through a sieve into a clean pan. The Thai broth is now ready to use.

To prepare the filling for the wontons, place the salmon in a food processor and blend for 2 minutes, until smooth. With the motor running, add the egg yolks followed by the cream until just combined. Transfer the salmon mixture to a bowl and fold in the crab meat, lemon rind and herbs. Season to taste, then cover with clingfilm and chill for at least 1 hour to firm up.

Lay the wonton wrappers out on a clean work surface. Brush all the edges with the egg wash. Place 1 teaspoon of the crab filling in the centre of the wrapper. Don't overfill or the filling will ooze out. Fold over to form a triangle, leaving the top flap edge 0.5cm (1/4in) away from the bottom edge. Fold the bottom edge over the top to stick down and seal to enclose the filling.

Poach the wontons in four batches in a large pan of salted boiling water for about 2 minutes. Check that they are cooked by cutting one in half. Remove from the water with a slotted spoon and keep warm while you cook the remainder. It's important that you cook these as close to serving as possible.

Heat a wok until smoking hot, then add the remaining 2 tablespoons of oil, swirling it up the sides. Tip in the pak choi and stir-fry for 1–2 minutes, until it is lightly wilted.

To serve, bring the Thai broth to a gentle simmer. Place the pak choi and the raw enoki mushrooms in the bottom of each warmed bowl and carefully arrange the cooked wontons on top. Hand blend the Thai broth with the soya lecithin until light and foamy, then spoon over the wontons. Garnish with the micro coriander and red amaranth. Any remaining broth can be served at the table.

COOK AHEAD The Thai broth can be made 24 hours in advance or frozen. The crab wontons can be cooked 24 hours in advance and stored in a bowl of iced water in the fridge. Steam for about 30 seconds to reheat when needed.

WINE A dry Riesling from the Clare Valley in Australia would be a great partner for crab dishes. Otherwise, try a dry Chenin Blanc from the Loire Valley, France.

Confit Prawn Spring Rolls with Mango and Apple

THIS IS AN INTERESTING WAY OF COOKING PRAWNS THAT WE RECENTLY STARTED TO DO IN THE RESTAURANT. THE CONFIT PROCESS MAKES THE PRAWNS REALLY TENDER SO THAT THEY MELT IN THE MOUTH. IT'S ACCOMPANIED BY MANGO AND APPLE, WHICH PROVIDE A GREAT FLAVOUR COMBINATION AND TEXTURE TO THE OVERALL DISH.

Serves 4

1 tbsp rapeseed oil

50g (2oz) white cabbage, shredded

2 spring onions, thinly sliced

1 small red onion, finely sliced

1 tbsp sweet chilli sauce

1 tbsp chilli jam (page 248)

1 tbsp chopped fresh coriander

finely grated rind of 1 lemon

sea salt and freshly ground black pepper

4 x 25cm (10in) square spring roll wrappers, cut into quarters

egg wash (made with 1 egg and 1 tbsp milk), to glaze

groundnut oil, for deep-frying

mango gel (page 247), to serve

basil purée (page 243), to serve

1 small ripe mango, peeled and cut into matchsticks (stone discarded)

1 small Granny Smith apple, cut into thin matchsticks (core discarded)

fresh micro leaves, to garnish

For the confit prawn:

300ml (1/2 pint) rapeseed oil

2 lemon grass stalks, trimmed and finely chopped

peeled rind of 1 lemon

450g (1lb) fresh Dublin Bay prawns, peeled and veins removed

Heat the rapeseed oil in a frying pan over a medium heat. Add the cabbage, spring onions and red onion and cook for 2–3 minutes, until the cabbage is just wilted, then tip into a bowl. Stir in the sweet chilli sauce, chilli jam, coriander and lemon rind. Season to taste and set aside until needed.

To confit the prawns, place the rapeseed oil, lemon grass and lemon rind in a pan. Gently warm the oil, but do not boil or it will be too hot and will overcook the prawns. Place the prawns into the warmed oil, making sure they are completely immersed, and gently simmer for 2–3 minutes, until the prawns are just cooked. Using a slotted spoon, remove the prawns onto kitchen paper and leave to cool. Break the prawns in half if large, then mix into the cooked cabbage mixture. This will keep in an airtight container for up to 2 days.

To fill the spring rolls, lay the spring roll wrapper squares on a clean work surface. Brush with egg wash on just one side and place a spoonful of the prawn and cabbage mixture in the centre of the wrapper. Fold one corner of the wrapper into the centre so that it covers the prawn mixture, then flip the ends in and roll tightly to form a sausage shape. Do not overfill or they will split. You'll end up with 16 in total.

When ready to serve, heat the groundnut oil in a deep-sided pan or in a deep-fat fryer to 180°C (350°F). Deep-fry the spring rolls for 2–3 minutes, until golden brown. Remove from the fryer and place on kitchen paper to catch any excess oil.

To serve, dot mango gel and basil purée from squeezy bottles onto warm plates. Arrange the mango and apple strips in a criss-cross design around the gel and purée. Trim the ends from each of the spring rolls, then arrange them standing upright together in the centre. Garnish with micro leaves.

COOK AHEAD
Prepare the prawn confit up to 24 hours in advance and keep well chilled. The spring rolls can be filled 2 hours before cooking and kept in the fridge. The mango and apple can also be prepared at the same time – just be sure to toss the apple in a little lemon juice to prevent it from going brown.

WINE
A spicy off-dry Alsace Gewürztraminer or a full-bodied Australian Chardonnay would work well here.

Deconstructed Prawn Cocktail

A TWIST ON AN OLD CLASSIC. WHEN MY MOTHER AND I WERE COOKING TOGETHER, IT WAS ALWAYS ONE OF THE MOST POPULAR DISHES. EVEN TODAY WE STILL GET REQUESTS FROM CUSTOMERS FOR IT, SO I'VE DEVELOPED A MODERN TAKE ON IT.

Serves 6

18 large raw tiger prawns, peeled and veins removed

1 garlic clove, crushed

1/4 red chilli, seeded and finely chopped

1 tbsp fresh lemon juice

1 tsp finely grated lemon rind

2 tbsp olive oil

100ml (3 1/2fl oz) mayonnaise (page 251)

2 tbsp tomato relish (shop bought)

1 ripe avocado, peeled, stone removed and roughly chopped

1 tsp chopped fresh coriander

1 tsp clear honey

1 tsp balsamic vinegar

sea salt and freshly ground black pepper

9 cherry vine tomatoes, halved

2 Little Gem lettuces, outer leaves discarded and stalk ends trimmed

basil purée (page 243), to garnish

pared lemon rind, to garnish

fresh micro coriander, to garnish

Pat the prawns dry with kitchen paper. Mix together the garlic, chilli, lemon juice and rind in a bowl and fold in the prepared prawns. Cover with clingfilm and chill for at least 15 minutes and up to 2 hours.

Heat 1 tablespoon of the olive oil in a frying pan. Add the prawns and stir-fry for 2 minutes, until cooked through and pink, then tip onto a plate and leave to cool. Cut in half down the length of the prawn.

Mix 4 tablespoons of the mayonnaise with half of the tomato relish and set aside to use as a garnish. Place the remainder in a liquidiser with the avocado, the rest of the tomato relish and the coriander and blend until smooth. Transfer to a squeezy bottle.

Mix together the honey, balsamic vinegar and the remaining 1 tablespoon of oil in a bowl and season to taste. Fold in the halved tomatoes.

To serve, arrange the prawns on plates and pipe the avocado mayonnaise alongside, then top with the Little Gem lettuce leaves. Add the tomato halves with the reserved tomato mayonnaise and the basil purée. Garnish with the lemon rind and micro coriander.

COOK AHEAD
The prawns can be cooked and chilled up to 8 hours in advance and covered with clingfilm.

WINE
A Verdejo wine from Rueda in Spain or from Australia would be a good match. A light-bodied red wine from Beaujolais would also be a good match.

Poultry
Cinnamon Roasted Quail with Pea and Truffle Risotto

THIS IS A NEW DISH ON OUR MENU THAT HAS DEVELOPED OVER TIME. THE CINNAMON GIVES A FANTASTIC AROMATIC SPICE TO THE DISH, WHICH IS A WONDERFUL CONTRAST TO THE CREAMY RISOTTO AND EARTHY LENTILS. QUAIL ARE AVAILABLE ALL YEAR ROUND AND ARE FAIRLY INEXPENSIVE.

Serves 4

4 x 175g (6oz) oven-ready quail

olive oil

1 tsp ground cinnamon

25g (1oz) butter, softened

2 tbsp rapeseed oil

150g (5oz) beech mushrooms, trimmed

1 tsp chopped fresh flat-leaf parsley

sea salt and freshly ground black pepper

4 quail's eggs

basil purée (page 243), to garnish

lemon olive oil powder (page 248), to garnish

balsamic lentils (page 240), to serve

raw enoki mushroom and micro salad bundles, tied together with chives

fresh micro salad, to garnish

For the pea and truffle risotto:

25g (1oz) peas, fresh or frozen

600ml (1 pint) chicken (page 253) or vegetable stock (page 252)

1 tbsp softened butter

1/2 small onion, diced

1 garlic clove, crushed

100g (4oz) Arborio rice (risotto)

25g (1oz) freshly grated Parmesan cheese

2 tsp white truffle oil

2 tsp chopped fresh mixed parsley and chives

sea salt and freshly ground black pepper

Place the quail in a shallow non-metallic dish. Rub olive oil all over them, then sprinkle over the cinnamon and rub it evenly into the flesh. Cover with clingfilm and chill overnight to allow the flavours to penetrate the flesh.

Preheat the oven to 200°C (400°F/gas mark 6).

To cook the risotto, blanch the peas until tender, then drain and set aside until needed. Heat the stock in a pan. Melt the butter in a separate sauté pan, then add the onion and garlic and sauté for 2 minutes. Add the Arborio rice. Stir well with a wooden spoon and slowly add a ladleful of the warm stock, stirring until absorbed. Continually add ladlefuls of the stock, stirring continuously until each ladleful is absorbed. Simmer gently for 20 minutes, stirring occasionally throughout. When the rice is nearly cooked, add the Parmesan, truffle oil and herbs along with the blanched peas. Season to taste. Keep warm but be careful not to overcook.

Meanwhile, to cook the prepared quail, heat an ovenproof non-stick pan over a medium heat. Add the butter and 1 tablespoon olive oil, then cook the quail for 2 minutes on each side, until golden brown. Place the pan in the oven and roast the quail for another 12 minutes. Turn once, making sure it's not too pink. Remove from the oven and leave to rest for at least 5 minutes, then carefully remove the legs and breast from the bone.

While the quail is roasting, heat 1 tablespoon of the rapeseed oil in a frying pan over a medium heat and fry the beech mushrooms for about 1 minute, until softened. Stir in the parsley and season to taste. Keep warm. Heat the remaining 1 tablespoon of rapeseed oil in a separate large frying pan and break in the quail's eggs. Cook for about 2 minutes, until the yolks are still soft. Drain on kitchen paper and then stamp out with a 4.5cm (1 3/4in) straight-sided cutter. Keep warm.

To serve, garnish each plate with the basil purée and lemon olive oil powder. Spoon on the risotto and sit the quail breasts on top. Add the balsamic lentils and put the legs on top, then add a fried egg to each plate. Spoon around the beech mushrooms and garnish with the mushroom and salad bundles and micro salad.

COOK AHEAD
The risotto can be half-cooked
up to 2 hours in advance and
then finished to order.

WINE
A good red wine choice would
be a Burgundy Pinot Noir, but a
full-bodied Australian
Chardonnay would
also be great.

Salad of Wood Pigeon with Trio of Beetroot

THE MAJORITY OF OUR WOOD PIGEON COMES FROM MY UNCLE FRANK, WHO HAS LAND IN WESTMEATH. IT HAS A WONDERFUL SWEET FLAVOUR AND IS NOT AT ALL GAMEY. THE SECRET IS TO SERVE IT PINK AND NOT BE TEMPTED TO OVERCOOK IT. THE COMBINATION AND TEXTURE OF THE BEETROOT WORK EXCEPTIONALLY WELL.

Serves 4

4 wood pigeon breasts, skinned

sea salt and freshly ground black pepper

2 tbsp rapeseed oil

4 quail eggs, at room temperature

12 slices beetroot carpaccio (page 236)

truffle mayonnaise (page 251), to serve

beetroot purée (page 245), to serve

lentil vinaigrette (page 251), to serve

50g (2oz) macadamia nuts, toasted and chopped

Frisée and baby Ruby chard dressed in olive oil, to garnish

For the beetroot crisps:

1 small raw beetroot (regular, white or golden)

sunflower oil, for deep-frying

sea salt

Preheat the oven to 180°C (350°F/gas mark 4).

Season the pigeon breasts on both sides. Heat an ovenproof frying pan over a medium heat and add the oil. Once the oil is sizzling, add the seasoned pigeon breasts and cook for 2 minutes on each side. Transfer to the oven and cook for another 4 minutes, until just cooked through but still pink in the middle. Remove from the oven and leave to rest for at least 5 minutes.

Meanwhile, place the quail eggs in a pan of boiling water and simmer for 2 minutes, until soft boiled. Drain, then cool under cold running water and take off the shells.

To prepare the beetroot crisps, it's best to put a pair of gloves on, otherwise you'll stain your hands. Trim the tops off the beetroots and then peel. Using a mandolin, carefully slice each beetroot as thinly as possible. Blanch the beetroot slices in a large pan of boiling salted water for 1 minute, until just tender but still with a little bite. Remove with a slotted spoon and drain well on kitchen paper. Heat a deep-fat fryer filled with sunflower oil to 170°C (340°F). Working in batches, deep-fry the beetroot for 30 seconds to 1 minute, until crisp and golden brown. Drain well on kitchen paper and season with salt.

To serve, arrange the beetroot carpaccio on plates. Slice the pigeon breasts in half and arrange on top. Cut the quail eggs in half and add to the plates, then add the truffle mayonnaise, beetroot purée and lentils. Scatter the macadamia nuts and beetroot crisps on top. Garnish with the Frisée and baby Ruby chard.

COOK AHEAD
All of the beetroot elements can be made up to 2 days in advance – just make sure you keep the crisps in an airtight container and the rest covered in the fridge.

WINE
Try a Tempranillo wine from Ribero del Duero or a South African Cabernet Sauvignon to match the earthy beetroot flavours.

Chicken Liver Parfait with Cherry Gel

I KNOW HOW EASY IT IS TO BUY PARFAIT THESE DAYS, BUT I MAKE MY OWN OCCASIONALLY. THIS RECIPE CAN BE PREPARED AHEAD AND WILL KEEP FOR 3-4 DAYS IN THE FRIDGE. I LOVE THE CONTRAST BETWEEN THE CHERRY GEL AND THE PARFAIT AND TEND TO SERVE IT IN THE RESTAURANT WITH SOME SLICES OF TOASTED BRIOCHE AND A SALAD. THIS CHICKEN LIVER PARFAIT CAN ALSO BE MADE IN 8 X 100ML (3 1/2FL OZ) INDIVIDUAL RAMEKINS. SIMPLY COOK AS DESCRIBED BELOW BUT REDUCE THE COOKING TIME TO 20-25 MINUTES, UNTIL JUST COOKED THROUGH BUT WITH A SLIGHT WOBBLE IN THE CENTRE.

Serves 8–12

400g (14oz) fresh chicken livers, well trimmed

300ml (1/2 pint) milk

100g (4oz) unsalted butter, softened

3 shallots, finely chopped

1 garlic clove, crushed

1 tsp chopped fresh thyme

1 tbsp ruby red port

5 eggs

1 tbsp cream

sea salt and freshly ground black pepper

cherry gel (page 247), to garnish

lightly toasted slices of brioche (page 214), to serve

lightly dressed salad leaves, to serve

Soak the chicken livers in the milk in a non-metallic bowl overnight. This will remove any traces of blood. The next day, drain off the milk and pat the livers dry with kitchen paper. Melt 25g (1oz) of the butter in a sauté pan over a low heat and gently sweat the shallots, garlic and thyme for 4–5 minutes, until softened but not coloured. Pour over the port and cook for 1 minute, until evaporated. Remove from the heat and leave to cool completely.

Meanwhile, preheat the oven to 180°C (350°F/gas mark 4).

Place the chicken livers in a food processor and blend for 2–3 minutes, until very smooth. Add the shallot mixture along with the eggs, cream, the remaining 75g (3oz) butter and plenty of seasoning. Blend again for about 30 seconds, until well combined.

Pass the chicken liver mixture through a fine sieve into a large jug and then pour into a 1.2 litre (2 pint) loaf tin that has been lined with clingfilm – the mixture should come two-thirds of the way up the sides (it rises up to the top during cooking). Cover with tin foil and place in a bain-marie (roasting tin half filled with boiling water) and cook for 1 hour, until set but still with a slight wobble in the middle. Remove the loaf tin from the bain-marie and take off the foil, then leave to cool completely. Wrap in clingfilm and place in the fridge until needed.

When ready to serve, invert the chicken liver parfait onto a flat plate or board and carefully peel away the clingfilm. Heat a large knife by dipping it in boiling water and wiping it dry, then cut the parfait into slices, discarding the end pieces.

To serve, arrange 2 slices of the parfait on each plate and drizzle around a little of the cherry gel to garnish. Add a slice of toasted brioche and some lightly dressed salad leaves.

COOK AHEAD
This parfait can be made up to 2 days in advance and kept chilled until needed.

WINE
A ripe and fruity Côtes du Rhône Villages would be a good match. For something really different, try this dish with a glass of sweet Sauternes.

Duck Confit with Crispy Fried Vegetables

ONE OF MY FAVOURITE RECIPES, DUCK IS ALWAYS SO POPULAR IN THE RESTAURANT THAT WHENEVER WE HAVE IT ON THE MENU, IT ALMOST ALWAYS SELLS OUT. IF YOU DON'T HAVE TIME TO COOK YOUR OWN YOU CAN BUY A VERY GOOD PRODUCT FROM SILVERHILL IN MONAGHAN, WHICH IS READILY AVAILABLE.

Serves 6

6 duck legs

6–7 fresh thyme sprigs

6 star anise

2 cinnamon sticks

1 garlic clove, peeled and sliced

4 tbsp coarse sea salt

1 litre (1 3/4 pints) duck fat

spinach purée (page 244), to serve

marmalade sauce (page 259), to serve

For the crispy vegetables:

sunflower oil, for deep-frying

1 large carrot, peeled

1 courgette

1 small beetroot, peeled

sea salt and freshly ground black pepper

To marinate the duck legs, place them in a single layer in a shallow non-metallic dish and scatter over the thyme, star anise, cinnamon, garlic and salt. Cover with clingfilm and place in the fridge overnight to allow the flavours to penetrate the duck.

Preheat the oven to 120°C (250F°/gas mark 1/2).

Rinse the marinade off the duck legs and pat them dry with kitchen paper. Return the duck legs to the dish. Heat the duck fat gently in a pan, then pour it over the duck legs to cover them completely. Place in the oven and cook for about 4 hours, until very tender and the meat is almost falling from the bone. Remove from the heat and leave to cool in the fat.

When ready to serve, preheat the grill to low. Remove the duck confit from the dish and brush off any excess fat. Arrange the duck legs on a grill rack skin side up, but don't put the rack too close to the grill or the skin will burn. Season with salt and cook for 10–15 minutes, until the skin is crisp and golden.

To prepare the crispy vegetables, heat a deep-fat fryer filled with sunflower oil to 170°C (340°F). Shave the carrot, courgette and beetroot into thin strips or ribbons using a potato peeler or mandolin. Make sure you do the beetroot last or you will discolour the other vegetables. Blanch the strips in a large pan of boiling salted water for 1 minute, until just tender but still with a little bite. Remove with a slotted spoon and drain well on kitchen paper. Working in batches, deep-fry the vegetable strips for 30 seconds to 1 minute, until crisp and golden brown. Drain well on kitchen paper and season to taste.

To serve, arrange the crispy duck confit on plates with the crispy vegetables. Add a swipe of spinach purée to each plate and drizzle over the marmalade sauce.

COOK AHEAD
The duck confit can be made 3 days in advance and stored in the fridge.

WINE
An earthy Pinot Noir from the Côtes de Nuits or a Merlot from St-Émilion in Bordeaux would be good with confit.

DUCK CONFIT WITH CRISPY FRIED VEGETABLES

Curried Chicken Spring Rolls with Pineapple Salsa

A REAL FAMILY FAVOURITE ON OUR LUNCH MENU. I MAKE THIS EVERY CHRISTMAS FOR THE FAMILY AND MY BROTHER KARLOUS HAS BEEN KNOWN TO EAT TWO OR THREE OF THEM. IF YOU WOULD PREFER TO COOK THESE IN THE OVEN, SIMPLY PREHEAT THE OVEN TO 180°C (350°F/GAS MARK 4). BRUSH THE TOPS AND SIDES OF THE SPRING ROLLS WITH EGG WASH AND ARRANGE ON A BAKING SHEET LINED WITH PARCHMENT PAPER. BAKE FOR 15-20 MINUTES, UNTIL CRISP AND GOLDEN BROWN.

Serves 4

2 x 150g (5oz) skinned chicken breast fillets

sea salt and freshly ground black pepper

1 tbsp mild curry powder

rapeseed oil, for cooking

knob of butter

1/4 head Savoy cabbage, tough stalk removed and leaves finely shredded (about 200g/7oz)

1/2 red onion, thinly sliced

1 spring onion, finely chopped

100g (4oz) shitake mushrooms, trimmed and sliced

3 tbsp sweet chilli sauce

3 tbsp chilli jam, plus extra to serve (page 248)

1 tbsp chopped fresh coriander

4 x 30cm (12in) spring roll wrappers, thawed if frozen

egg wash (made with 1 egg and 1 tbsp milk), to glaze

groundnut oil, for deep-frying

pineapple salsa (page 257), to serve

mango gel (page 247), to garnish

balsamic gel (page 247), to garnish

fresh micro coriander, to garnish

Preheat the oven to 180°C (350°F/gas mark 4).

Place the chicken in a baking dish and season, then sprinkle over the curry powder. Drizzle over a little rapeseed oil and add 1 tablespoon water into the tin – this stops the chicken from drying out. Bake for 15–20 minutes, until cooked through and tender. Leave to cool, then dice into 1cm (1/2in) cubes.

Heat the butter in a frying pan with a dash of rapeseed oil over a medium heat. Add the cabbage, red onion and spring onion. Toss until almost tender, then add the shitake mushrooms. Toss again for 2–3 minutes, until the mushrooms begin to wilt. Add the chilli sauce, chilli jam and coriander and toss until combined. Season to taste.

Lay out one spring roll wrapper on a clean work surface. It's important not to let the wrappers dry out, so keep them covered with a clean, damp tea towel until you need them. Imagine a diagonal line across the centre of the wrapper – brush the egg wash above that line and spoon the chicken mixture onto the centre along the line. Be careful not to overfill the spring rolls or they can burst during cooking. Fold the bottom corner up over the mixture, then turn the two outside corners in and roll up to meet the eggy corner to stick. Repeat to make the remaining 3 rolls.

Heat the groundnut oil in a deep-fat fryer or half fill a deep-sided pan to 180°C (350°F). Deep-fry 2 of the spring rolls for 4–5 minutes, until the spring rolls are golden brown, turning halfway through. Drain on kitchen paper and keep warm in a low oven or loosely covered with foil while you cook the remaining rolls.

To serve, slice each spring roll into three and arrange on warmed plates with the pineapple salsa and chilli jam. Garnish each plate with the mango gel, balsamic gel and micro coriander.

COOK AHEAD

These spring rolls can be made 2–3 hours in advance. The mixture may be made up to 2 days before you want to cook it, but you cannot leave the spring rolls wrapped overnight, as the juices can seep through the wrapper.

WINE

A white wine with a hint of sweetness would be great with this recipe. Try a Gewürztraminer or an off-dry German Riesling.

Meat
Rabbit Confit with Wild Mushrooms in Kataifi Pastry

THIS RECIPE IS PART OF A MUCH MORE COMPLEX DISH THAT WE SERVE IN THE RESTAURANT (PAGE 47), BUT IT'S ALSO DELICIOUS SERVED AS A STARTER ON ITS OWN. YOU'LL NEED QUITE A BIT OF DUCK FAT FOR THIS RECIPE, WHICH IS AVAILABLE FROM YOUR BUTCHER OR LARGE SUPERMARKETS. IF YOU DON'T HAVE ENOUGH, COMBINE IT WITH PEANUT OIL OR CHICKEN FAT, OR JUST USE EITHER INSTEAD. IN THE RESTAURANT WE KEEP THE FAT FROM ANY DUCK CARCASSES AND FREEZE IT IN PLASTIC BAGS. I TAKE IT OUT AS NEEDED, SIMMER IT IN WATER TO RENDER IT AND STRAIN IT THROUGH A FINE SIEVE BEFORE USING.

Serves 2 (makes 4)

For the rabbit confit in kataifi pastry:

1 tbsp rapeseed oil

2 rabbit legs, trimmed (150g (5oz) in total)

1 onion, roughly chopped

2 garlic cloves, cut in half, skin on

1.2 litres (2 pints) duck fat

2 fresh thyme sprigs

2 fresh rosemary sprigs

100g (4oz) frozen kataifi pastry

25g (1oz) plain flour

sea salt and freshly ground black pepper

1 egg

groundnut oil, for deep-frying

mango salsa (page 257), to serve

chilli jam (page 248), to serve

aioli (page 251), to serve

lightly dressed baby salad leaves, to garnish

Preheat the oven to 120°C (250°F/gas mark 1/2).

To make the confit, heat the rapeseed oil in a large non-stick frying pan over a medium heat, then add the rabbit legs and brown all over, turning regularly with tongs. Add the onion and garlic and cook for another 5 minutes, until golden brown. Place the rabbit, onion and garlic in an ovenproof casserole dish with the duck fat and herbs. Cover with foil and then with a lid. Cook for 2–3 hours, until the rabbit legs are meltingly tender. Leave the rabbit legs to rest in the duck fat until cool.

To prepare the mushroom duxelles, heat the rapeseed oil in a large frying pan over a medium heat. Add the mushrooms, shallot and garlic and sauté for 2–3 minutes, until just tender. Add the Madeira, cream and herbs. Reduce for 2 minutes, then season to taste. Remove from the heat and leave to cool.

Remove the cooked rabbit confit from the duck fat and pat dry with kitchen paper. Remove the meat from the bones and roughly chop. Place in a bowl and then stir in the cooked mushroom duxelles. Mix well to combine and season to taste. This mixture will keep in the fridge for 2 days or it can be frozen. Divide the rabbit mixture into 4 portions and press it firmly together in the shape of a small sausage, then chill for 20 minutes to firm up.

Allow the kataifi pastry to thaw, still in its plastic wrapping, for a minimum of 2 hours before using. Once thawed, it will be soft and pliable and ready to use, but remember that you must keep it covered with a clean, damp tea towel when not in use.

Place the flour in a shallow dish and season to taste. In a separate shallow dish, beat the egg with a pinch of salt. Toss the rabbit confit shapes in the seasoned flour until lightly coated, then dip briefly in the beaten egg mixture. Divide the kataifi pastry into 4 and spread out on a clean work surface into 4 rectangular shapes.

For the mushroom duxelles:

1 tbsp rapeseed oil

75g (3oz) mixed wild mushrooms, diced

1 shallot, finely diced

1 small garlic clove, crushed

1 tsp Madeira

1 tsp cream

1 tsp chopped fresh mixed herbs (such as chives, basil and flat-leaf parsley)

sea salt and freshly ground black pepper

Sit a rabbit confit shape at the end closest to you, across the width of the pastry, and roll it up away from you to completely enclose. Place the wrapped rabbit confit, well spaced apart, on a baking sheet lined with parchment paper. Cover with clingfilm and chill until ready to use.

Just before serving, heat the oil in a deep-fat fryer or a deep-sided pan to 160°C (325°F). Cook the rabbit confit in kataifi pastry for 2–3 minutes, turning halfway through, until crisp and golden brown and the rabbit is warmed through. Drain on kitchen paper.

To serve, cut each rabbit confit in kataifi pastry in half and use as required. If serving as a starter, arrange on warmed plates with the mango salsa, chilli jam and aioli. Garnish with the lightly dressed baby salad leaves.

COOK AHEAD
The rabbit confit in kataifi pastry will sit happily overnight in the fridge or can be frozen for up to 3 weeks.

WINE
A red wine choice is a ripe Chianti Classico, but an Alsace Gewürztraminer is also great with rabbit.

Saddle of Rabbit Stuffed with Black Pudding

MANY OF OUR CUSTOMERS HAVE FOND MEMORIES OF EATING RABBIT IN THEIR CHILDHOOD AND THIS DISH IS AN EXCELLENT EXAMPLE OF HOW TO GET THE BEST USE OUT OF THIS UNDERRATED GAME. ORDER THE RABBIT FROM YOUR LOCAL CRAFT BUTCHER AND ASK HIM FOR THE CAUL FAT AS WELL.

Serves 4

100g (4oz) skinless chicken breast fillet, diced

100g (4oz) black pudding, outer casing removed

50ml (2fl oz) cream

1 egg yolk

1/2 tsp chopped fresh flat-leaf parsley

1/2 tsp chopped fresh basil

1 saddle of rabbit, boned and fillets removed (2 loins and 2 bellies)

2 sheets caul fat, each about 15cm (6in) square (from a pig)

sea salt and freshly ground black pepper

1 tbsp rapeseed oil

basil purée (page 243), to garnish

mango gel (page 247), to garnish

balsamic gel (page 247), to garnish

truffle mayonnaise (page 251), to garnish

balsamic lentils (page 240), to serve

garlic foam (page 245), to garnish

mango salsa (page 257), to serve

4 rabbit confit with wild mushrooms in kataifi pastry (pages 44–45)

fresh micro salad, to garnish

To make the stuffing for the rabbit, place the chicken breast in a food processor with the black pudding. Blend for about 30 seconds, then add the cream, egg yolk and herbs and blend to a soft, smooth consistency. Transfer to a bowl.

Place one rabbit belly on a sheet of the caul fat and top with the rabbit loin, then season. Spread about 2 tablespoons of the chicken mousse mixture in the middle of the rabbit loin. Roll the edge of the rabbit belly nearest to you around the mousse. Wrap well in the caul fat – this will naturally stick together. Repeat the process for the other belly and loin. Cover with clingfilm and chill for at least 1 hour to firm up.

Preheat the oven to 180°C (350°F/gas mark 4).

Heat an ovenproof frying pan with the rapeseed oil over a medium heat. Add the rabbit parcels and cook for 6–7 minutes, until golden brown on all sides, turning regularly with a tongs. Transfer to the oven and cook for another 12–15 minutes, until firm to the touch. Remove from the oven and leave to rest for at least 5 minutes, then carve in half.

To serve, garnish each warmed plate with the basil purée, mango gel, balsamic gel and truffle mayonnaise. Add spoonfuls of the balsamic lentils and sit the rabbit saddle on top, then spoon over the garlic foam. Add spoonfuls of the mango salsa and place the rabbit confit in kataifi on top. Garnish with the micro salad.

COOK AHEAD
Most of this dish needs to be made in advance. The rabbit can be stuffed and chilled up to 2 days ahead. The legs can be confited at least 2 days in advance; however, they are best wrapped in the kataifi pastry no more than 2 hours in advance. Keep them covered with clingfilm in the fridge to prevent them from drying out.

WINE
A ripe, juicy New World Pinot Noir from South Africa or New Zealand would match this recipe well. An alternative would be an Italian Barbera with lots of cherry fruit flavours.

Veal Sweetbreads with Carrot and Star Anise

VEAL SWEETBREADS ARE ONE OF MY FAVOURITE MEATS, WHICH I'LL ALWAYS ORDER IF I SPOT ON A MENU. I LOVE THE SOFTNESS AND RICHNESS OF THE INSIDE AND THE CRISPY CARAMELISED OUTSIDE. HERE I'VE SCENTED THEM WITH FRAGRANT STAR ANISE.

Serves 4

2 x 300g (11oz) veal sweetbreads, well trimmed and cleaned

1 onion, sliced

1 carrot, sliced

6 star anise

5 black peppercorns

4 fresh thyme sprigs

1 bay leaf

200ml (7fl oz) milk

sea salt

1 tbsp rapeseed oil

knob of butter

carrot and ginger purée (page 244), to serve

bread croûtes (page 240), to serve

carrot and ginger foam (page 246), to serve

fresh micro coriander, to garnish

For the caramelised baby carrots:

4 baby carrots, trimmed, peeled and cut into 2.5cm (1in) lengths

1 tsp softened butter

1/4 tsp clear honey

sea salt and freshly ground black pepper

For the carrot scrolls:

4 baby carrots, trimmed and peeled

Clean the sweetbreads under cold running water, then put in a non-metallic bowl of salted water. Place in the fridge overnight to soak.

The next day, remove the sweetbreads from the fridge and rinse very well under cold running water. Place in a pan with the onion, carrot, two of the star anise, the peppercorns, thyme and bay leaf. Pour in the milk and add 200ml (7fl oz) water. Place on a low heat and bring to the boil, then add the veal sweetbreads and simmer for 4–5 minutes. Remove from the heat and set aside until cool.

Strain away the liquid from the sweetbreads and discard with the vegetables. Using a small sharp knife, clean away the outer membrane and then cut each sweetbread in half. Season with salt.

Heat the oil in a large frying pan over a low heat. Add the butter and once it stops sizzling, add the sweetbreads, presentation side down. Cook for 7–8 minutes, until golden brown and caramelised. Remove and quickly drain on kitchen paper – you may have to do this in batches depending on the size of your pan.

To prepare the caramelised baby carrots, cook the baby carrots in a pan of boiling salted water for about 2 minutes, until tender. Drain, then return to the pan and toss in the butter and the honey until evenly coated. Season to taste.

To prepare the carrot scrolls, pare the baby carrots into ribbons on a Japanese mandolin so that each one gives you 4 strips. Blanch for 20 seconds in a pan of boiling salted water. Drain and once cool enough to handle, roll each ribbon into a scroll shape. Set aside until needed.

To serve, place the cooked sweetbreads in the centre of the warmed plates. Add some of the carrot and ginger purée, caramelised baby carrots, bread croûtes and carrot scrolls. Spoon over the carrot and ginger foam and garnish with the remaining star anise and the micro coriander.

COOK AHEAD
The sweetbreads can be prepared 24 hours in advance and kept covered with clingfilm in the fridge, then pan-fried to serve.

WINE
An Australian oaked Chardonnay is a good white wine choice. If you prefer red, try a good-quality Beaujolais Cru.

Beef Satay with Pickled Cucumber

ANOTHER ONE OF MY FAMILY FAVOURITES. I HAVE MY ELDEST BROTHER KENNETH TO THANK FOR THIS RECIPE, WHICH HE ALWAYS MAKES FOR A FAMILY GATHERING. IT WORKS EQUALLY WELL WITH CHICKEN OR PORK AND IS GREAT COOKED ON THE BARBECUE.

Serves 6

3 garlic cloves, crushed

4 tbsp pineapple juice

4 tbsp light soy sauce

4 tsp caster sugar

1 tsp Chinese five spice

550g (1lb 4oz) rump or sirloin steak, cut lengthways into thin strips (each about 2.5cm (1in) long)

pickled cucumber (page 236), to serve

fresh micro coriander, to garnish

For the satay sauce:

1/2 carrot, grated

2 tsp white wine vinegar

2 tsp rapeseed oil

1 small onion, finely diced

1/2 red pepper, cored and cut into strips

1/2 green pepper, cored and cut into strips

2 garlic cloves, crushed

1/2 tsp freshly grated root ginger

200g can of coconut milk

100g (4oz) crunchy peanut butter

50ml (2fl oz) sweet chilli sauce

50ml (2fl oz) dark soy sauce

2 tsp tomato purée

25g (1oz) cashew nuts, toasted and chopped (optional)

sea salt and freshly ground black pepper

Place the garlic, pineapple juice, soy sauce, sugar and five spice in a shallow non-metallic dish and mix until well combined. Tip in the steak and using your hands, rub in the marinade. Cover with clingfilm and chill for at least 3–4 hours, though overnight is best.

To make the satay sauce, place the carrot in a small bowl with the white wine vinegar. Set aside to soak for 1 hour.

Heat the oil in a heavy-based pan over a medium heat. Add the onion, peppers, garlic and ginger. Sweat for 5 minutes, stirring regularly. Add the coconut milk, peanut butter, chilli sauce, soy sauce, tomato purée and 3 tablespoons water to the pepper mixture. Stir well, then bring to the boil and simmer for 10–15 minutes, stirring occasionally, until slightly reduced and thickened.

Remove the satay sauce from the heat, then stir in the soaked carrot mixture along with the cashew nuts, if using. Season to taste and transfer to a bowl. Cover with clingfilm and chill until needed.

To cook the beef satay, preheat a charcoal grill or griddle pan. Thread the marinated steak onto 18 x 15cm (6in) soaked bamboo skewers. Cook for 6–8 minutes, turning occasionally, until slightly charred and cooked through. Brush the rest of the marinade over the skewers to help keep them moist while they are cooking.

Arrange the beef satay on warmed plates with small dishes of the pickled cucumber and satay sauce to the side of each one. Garnish with the micro coriander to serve.

COOK AHEAD
The marinated steak can be left in the fridge for up to 3 days.

WINE
A juicy, fruity Italian red will match these flavours – try a Chianti Classico or a Valpolicella.

Smoked Belly of Pork with Creamed White Beans and Date Jam

WE GET THIS SMOKED PORK BELLY FROM OUR EXCELLENT LOCAL CRAFT BUTCHER, KEVIN MCGOVERN, BASED IN BELLEEK IN CO. FERMANAGH. IT'S COAL SMOKED AND HAS A VERY SIMILAR TASTE TO KASSLER, THE GERMAN DISH, WHICH IS TRADITIONALLY SERVED WITH SAUERKRAUT. USE ANY LEFTOVER TRIMMINGS FOR PASTA CARBONARA. THE BRAISING JUICE CAN BE USED FOR A CELERIAC SOUP OR CAN BE FROZEN.

Serves 4

1 large carrot, diced

1 large onion, diced

1 leek, trimmed and diced

4 garlic cloves, sliced

2 fresh thyme sprigs

2 star anise

900g (2lb) smoked pork belly, boned but with skin on and scored

sea salt and freshly ground black pepper

600ml (1 pint) freshly pressed apple juice

450g (1lb) creamed white beans (page 239)

date jam (page 249), to serve

sweet potato purée (page 244), to serve

2 pieces of crisp Parma ham

fresh micro salad, to garnish

Preheat the oven to 150°C (300°F/gas mark 2).

Arrange the vegetables in a raised bed in the middle of a large, deep roasting tin. Tuck in the garlic, thyme and star anise and lay the pork belly on top. Season generously. Pour in the apple juice and add enough water to come halfway up the sides of the tin, then cover tightly with foil.

Roast the smoked pork belly for 4–5 hours – you'll know the pork is cooked when the flesh is just coming away. You may need to top up the water a little during this time, as you must be careful that it doesn't dry out.

Remove the pork carefully from the braising juices (reserve to use as a stock for soup). Place the cooked pork on a baking sheet lined with clingfilm, then place another baking sheet on top with cans on top to weigh it down. This will give the pork a firm, even shape. Allow to cool in the fridge overnight.

When ready to serve, preheat the oven to 200°C (400°F/gas mark 6). Slice the pork into eight 5cm x 3.5cm (2in x 11/2in) rectangles and arrange on a large baking sheet. Place in the oven for 5 minutes or crisp under a hot grill. You can also pan-fry the rectangles in a little rapeseed oil for 2–3 minutes on each side, until crisp around the edges and golden brown.

To serve, spoon the creamed white beans into the centre of each warmed plate and place 2 pieces of crispy pork belly on top. Dot around some of the date jam, followed by smears of the sweet potato purée. Break the Parma ham into small pieces and use to garnish the date jam, then scatter around with the micro salad.

COOK AHEAD
The smoked pork belly needs to be cooked at least 24 hours in advance, but up to 3 days is fine. It can also be frozen.

WINE
Try a smoky Pinotage from South Africa or a Syrah wine from the south of France with this dish.

Air-dried Beef Carpaccio with Roasted Beetroot and Mustard Cream

THIS IS A GREAT DISH FOR A DINNER PARTY OR SPECIAL OCCASION AND IS BOUND TO IMPRESS. WE SOURCE THE BEEF FROM JAMES MCGEOGH IN OUGHTERAD, CO. GALWAY. HE IS ONE OF THE BEST CRAFT ARTISAN BUTCHERS IN THE COUNTRY AND DOES A FANTASTIC MAIL ORDER SERVICE.

Serves 6

18 slices air-dried beef

50g (2oz) walnut pieces

675g (1 1/2lb) small beetroot (each one weighing about 75g/3oz)

2 fresh thyme sprigs

4 tbsp balsamic vinegar

2 tbsp rapeseed oil, plus extra for dressing

sea salt and freshly ground black pepper

25g (1oz) fresh small watercress sprigs

juice of 1/2 lemon

50g (2oz) Parmesan shavings

For the mustard cream:

100g (4oz) crème fraîche

2 tbsp freshly grated horseradish

1 tbsp wholegrain mustard

sea salt and freshly ground black pepper

Preheat the oven to 220°C (450°F/gas mark 7).

Remove the air-dried beef from the fridge 30 minutes before you intend to use it to allow it to come back to room temperature.

Place the walnut pieces in a small baking tin and roast for 3–4 minutes, until toasted. Set aside.

Scrub the beetroot, then trim off the tops and pat dry with kitchen paper. Place in a roasting tin with the thyme and drizzle over the balsamic vinegar and rapeseed oil. Season, then cover with tin foil and roast for 1 hour, until the beets can be pierced easily with a knife. Leave to cool, then cut into quarters and toss back into the cooking juices once cut.

Meanwhile, make the mustard cream. Place the crème fraîche, horseradish and wholegrain mustard into a bowl with 1 teaspoon water and mix well to combine, then season to taste.

To serve, arrange 3 slices of the air-dried beef in a slightly overlapping layer on each plate. Place the roasted beetroot to the side and drizzle some of the beetroot cooking juices on top, then dribble the mustard cream over some of the beef. Dress the watercress with rapeseed oil and lemon juice and scatter alongside the beef. Finish with the Parmesan shavings and toasted walnut pieces.

COOK AHEAD
The dressing and beetroot can be made 24 hours in advance and kept covered in the fridge until needed.

WINE
The earthy flavours of a Burgundy Pinot Noir would be a good match, as would a Rioja Reserve.

Pork and Wild Mushroom Wontons with Chinese Black Bean Sauce

THIS IS ONE OF THE MOST POPULAR STARTERS IN THE RESTAURANT, WHERE I SOMETIMES USE A CHICKEN MOUSSE WITH CRAB AS AN ALTERNATIVE FILLING. PACKETS OF WONTON WRAPPERS CAN BE FOUND IN SPECIALIST ASIAN STORES OR ON THE INTERNET. NORMALLY THEY COME IN PACKETS OF ABOUT 40, SO YOU'LL BE ABLE TO FREEZE THE REMAINDER.

Serves 6

2 tbsp rapeseed oil

175g (6oz) mixed mushrooms, finely chopped (such as shiitake, chestnut and chanterelle)

2 shallots, finely diced

1 garlic clove, crushed

25g (1oz) butter, softened

1 tbsp Madeira or port

120ml (4fl oz) cream, well chilled

2 tbsp chopped fresh mixed herbs (such as chives, basil, flat-flat parsley and thyme)

sea salt and freshly ground black pepper

225g (8oz) lean pork shoulder or leg, diced

2 egg yolks

24 wonton wrappers, thawed if frozen

egg wash (made with 1 egg and 1 tbsp milk), to seal

Chinese black bean sauce (page 256), to serve

smoked bacon foam (page 246), to serve

fresh micro coriander, to garnish

For the crispy noodles:

groundnut oil, for deep-frying

100g (4oz) flat rice noodles

For the sesame pak choi:

3 baby pak choi, trimmed and leaves separated

1 tbsp toasted sesame seeds

1 tbsp toasted sesame oil

sea salt and freshly ground black pepper

Heat the oil in a large frying pan over a medium heat. Add the mushrooms, shallots and garlic and stir to combine, then add the butter and sauté for 2–3 minutes. Stir in the Madeira or port, 1 tablespoon of the cream and 1 tablespoon of the herbs. Reduce for 2 minutes, then season to taste and leave to cool.

Place the pork in a food processor with the egg yolks, half of the mushroom mixture and the remaining cream. Add two pinches of salt and blend to make a smooth mousse. Place the mousse in a bowl, then stir in the rest of the mushrooms and herbs. Mix well to combine and season.

Bring a large pan of salted water to the boil and keep it boiling while you assemble the wontons. Lay the wonton wrappers out on a clean work surface. Brush all the edges with the egg wash. Place 1 teaspoon of the pork filling in the centre of the wrapper. Don't overfill or the filling will ooze out. Fold over to form a triangle, leaving the top flap edge 0.5cm (1/2in) away from the bottom edge. Fold the bottom edge over the top to stick down and seal to enclose the filling.

The wontons are now ready to poach. Put them into the boiling water as soon as possible after filling them and poach for about 3 minutes, until cooked through and floating to the top. Remove with a slotted spoon and drain well before placing on a plate.

When ready to steam, arrange the wontons in a single layer in a steamer and cook for about 5 minutes, until heated through.

To make the crispy noodles, heat the groundnut oil in a deep-fat fryer or deep-sided pan to 190°C (375°F). Drop in small batches of the noodles and cook for 20–30 seconds, until puffed up and crispy. Drain well on kitchen paper.

To prepare the pak choi, blanch the pak choi leaves in boiling water for 30 seconds, then drain well and gently pat dry with kitchen paper. Heat a large frying pan or wok over a medium heat and add the sesame seeds, then toss for a few minutes, until golden. Add the sesame oil and pak choi and stir-fry for no more than 30 seconds, until just wilted. Season to taste.

To serve, arrange the sesame pak choi and steamed wontons on warmed plates. Spoon over the black bean sauce followed by the smoked bacon foam. Garnish with the micro coriander and finish with the crispy noodles.

WINE
A spicy Alsace Gewürztraminer or a Loire Valley red would be a good partner here.

COOK AHEAD
The wontons may be prepared in advance up to the point when they are first poached, then placed in a bowl of iced water to cool completely. Lay them out in a single layer on a tray lined with damp kitchen roll and cover with cling-film, then chill for up to 24 hours before steaming.
The crispy noodles can be made up to 4 hours in advance and kept in an airtight container until needed. The pak choi can also be blanched up to 4 hours in advance and kept covered in the fridge until needed.

Vegetables
Bruschetta of Wild Mushrooms and Asparagus

THIS IS A SIMPLE AND TASTY STARTER, WHICH IS STILL VERY POPULAR IN THE RESTAURANT. THE SWEETNESS OF THE BRIOCHE REALLY COMPLEMENTS THE VEGETABLES. EXPERIMENT WITH ANY SELECTION OF WILD MUSHROOMS THAT ARE AVAILABLE.

Serves 4

1 tbsp rapeseed oil

1/2 small red onion, thinly sliced

1 garlic clove, finely chopped

200g (7oz) mixed wild mushrooms, diced (such as chanterelle, shiitake and oyster)

sea salt and freshly ground black pepper

1/2 tsp chopped fresh basil

1/2 tsp chopped fresh flat-leaf parsley

1/2 tsp snipped fresh chives

24 asparagus spears

8 slices of brioche (page 214)

2 tsp softened butter

100g (4oz) beech mushrooms, stalks trimmed

1 tbsp toasted pine nuts

beetroot purée (page 245), to garnish

basil purée (page 243), to garnish

balsamic gel (page 247), to garnish

snipped fresh chives, to garnish

fresh red amaranth, to garnish

Preheat the grill to medium and heat a large heavy-based frying pan over a medium heat. Add 1/2 tablespoon of the rapeseed oil and sauté the onion and garlic for 2 minutes. Tip in the diced wild mushrooms and cook for 10 minutes, until very soft and tender and all the liquid has evaporated. Season to taste, then stir in the herbs and keep warm.

Trim and peel the asparagus to give attractive tips, then blanch in boiling salted water for 2–3 minutes, depending on their size. Drain and cool down quickly by plunging them into a bowl of iced water to prevent them from cooking any further. Drain again and place on a plate lined with kitchen paper until needed.

Meanwhile, cut the brioche into discs using a 7cm (2 3/4in) straight-sided cutter or cut into 6cm (2 1/2in) squares. Arrange on the grill rack and cook for a few minutes, until crispy and golden on both sides.

Heat another frying pan over a high heat. Add the remaining 1/2 tablespoon of the rapeseed oil and the butter. Once the butter stops sizzling, tip in the beech mushrooms and season to taste. Sauté for 3–4 minutes, until just cooked through and tender. Toss in the blanched asparagus tips for the last minute to just heat through.

To serve, spread the mushroom mixture on the toasted brioche and arrange 2 slices on each warmed plate. Spoon the beech mushrooms and asparagus on top and scatter over the toasted pine nuts. Garnish the plates with the beetroot purée, basil purée and balsamic gel, then scatter over the chives and red amaranth.

WINE
Try a ripe New World Sauvignon Blanc from New Zealand or Australia.

Crispy Goat's Cheese with Beetroot Panna Cotta

IF YOU PREFER TO BAKE THE GOAT'S CHEESE, SIMPLY COOK IT IN AN OVEN PREHEATED TO 180°C (350°F/GAS MARK 4) FOR ANOTHER 5-10 MINUTES, UNTIL WARMED THROUGH AND SOFT. AS YOU CAN SEE IN THE PHOTO, WE USE A RECTANGULAR SILICONE MOULD TO MAKE THE PANNA COTTAS IN, WHICH ARE AVAILABLE FROM GOOD CATERING SHOPS OR ONLINE. OURS ARE 5CM (2IN) LONG ON THE TOP OF THE MOULD AND 2.5CM (1IN) WIDE.

Serves 4

25g (1oz) fresh white breadcrumbs

1 tbsp finely chopped fresh flat-leaf parsley

1 tsp toasted pine nuts, finely chopped

1 tsp sesame seeds

sea salt and freshly ground black pepper

1 egg

25g (1oz) plain flour

150g (5oz) log of Corleggy or Ryefield goat's cheese, cut into 4 slices

groundnut oil, for deep-frying

12 slices beetroot carpaccio (page 236)

basil purée (page 243), to serve

fresh affilia cress, to garnish

fresh pea shoots, to garnish

fresh mixed micro salad, to garnish

For the beetroot panna cotta:

225g (8oz) raw beetroot

1 tbsp agar agar powder

300ml (1/2 pint) cream

100g (4oz) soft goat's cheese (no rind)

sea salt and freshly ground black pepper

To make the beetroot panna cotta, place the beetroot in a pan, cover with water and bring to the boil over a medium heat. Reduce the heat, cover with a lid and simmer for 30–40 minutes, until completely tender when pierced with a knife. Drain and leave to cool, then peel and roughly chop the flesh. Place in a food processor and blend to a purée – you'll need 50g (2oz) for the panna cotta; place the rest in a small squeezy bottle to use as a garnish.

Dissolve the agar agar in 4 tablespoons of cold water in a small pan, whisking continuously. Bring it to the boil, then reduce the heat and simmer for 1 minute, until dissolved. Remove from the heat and leave to cool a little.

Place the cream in a heavy-based pan and bring to the boil, then remove from the heat. Whisk the cooled agar agar mixture into the cream. Stir in 50g (2oz) of the beetroot purée, then beat in the goat's cheese until evenly combined. Season to taste and place in 4 x 120ml (4fl oz) dariole moulds that are base-lined with parchment paper. Leave in the fridge for 2–3 hours to set, or you can make them the day before and leave overnight.

To prepare the crispy goat's cheese, mix the breadcrumbs with the parsley, chopped nuts and sesame seeds in a shallow dish. Season to taste. In a separate dish, beat the egg and season lightly. Season the flour and place in another shallow dish. Lightly coat the goat's cheese in the seasoned flour, then dip each slice into the beaten egg, gently shaking off any excess. Place in the breadcrumb mixture so that it is completely coated. Place on a flat tray lined with parchment paper in the fridge for at least 30 minutes (or overnight covered with clingfilm is fine) to firm up.

Preheat the oven to 180°C (350°F/gas mark 4).

Heat the oil in a deep-sided pan or deep-fat fryer to 180°C (350°F) and cook the breaded goat's cheese for 1–2 minutes, until golden brown. Carefully remove from the oil and transfer to a plate lined with kitchen paper to drain off any excess oil. Arrange on a baking sheet and place in the oven for another 3–4 minutes, until heated through but still holding their shape.

To serve, dip the panna cotta moulds in just-boiled water for 5–10 seconds, then carefully invert the panna cotta onto the plates. Add 3 slices of the beetroot carpaccio to each plate. Put a dot of the beetroot purée on the plate to prevent the crispy goat's cheese from slipping, then place on top. Garnish with the rest of the beetroot purée and the basil purée. Scatter over the affilia cress, pea shoots and mixed micro salad.

COOK AHEAD
The panna cotta can be made up to 2 days in advance and/or put in the freezer overnight or even an hour covered with clingfilm. This makes them easier to unmould. Simply place on a tray at room temperature for an hour before you want to serve, then unmould as described above. You can also have the goat's cheese crumbed up to 2 days in advance.

WINE
Sancerre, Loire Valley Sauvignon Blanc or an earthy Burgundy Pinot Noir.

Ravioli of Swiss Chard and Ricotta with Smoked Garlic Foam

THIS DISH IS A CLEVER WAY OF LOOKING LIKE YOU HAVE GONE TO THE TROUBLE OF MAKING YOUR OWN PASTA. INSTEAD, THE SECRET IS TO USE WONTON WRAPPERS, WHICH CAN BE FOUND IN ASIAN SUPERMARKETS OR ON THE INTERNET. WE HAVE STARTED TO GROW OUR OWN CHARD FOR THE RESTAURANT. YOU CAN ALSO USE GOLDEN OR RUBY CHARD OR EVEN BABY SPINACH WORKS VERY WELL.

Serves 4

1 tbsp rapeseed oil

1 small red onion, finely diced

2 garlic cloves, finely chopped

4 Swiss or Ruby chard leaves, tough stalks removed (if unavailable, use 100g (4oz) baby spinach leaves)

200g (7oz) ricotta cheese

1 tbsp shredded fresh basil

sea salt and freshly ground black pepper

40 wonton wrappers, thawed if frozen

1–2 tbsp plain flour, for dusting

egg wash (made with 1 egg and 1 tbsp milk), for sealing

smoked garlic foam (page 245), to serve

fresh micro Ruby chard, to garnish

fresh wild rocket, to garnish

4 tbsp toasted pine nuts, to garnish

25g (1oz) Parmesan cheese, pared into shavings, to garnish

Heat the rapeseed oil in a pan over a medium heat and sauté the onion and garlic for about 5 minutes, until softened but not browned. Remove with a slotted spoon and set aside in a bowl. Add the chard and cook for 2–3 minutes, stirring regularly, until just wilted. Remove from the heat, drain and leave to cool completely.

Squeeze out any excess moisture from the chard mixture and then finely chop. Place in the bowl with the reserved onion and stir in the ricotta cheese and basil. Season to taste and mix well to combine.

Place 20 wonton wrappers on a lightly floured work surface and spoon 1 heaped teaspoon of the chard mixture into the centre of each one. Brush a little egg wash around the edges, then carefully cover with the remaining wonton wrappers, pressing gently to shape into ravioli. You can use a 6cm (2 1/2in) fluted cutter to shape each ravioli if you like and discard the leftover scraps of wonton pastry.

To cook the ravioli, bring a large pan of salted water to the boil, then add the ravioli and cook for about 2 minutes, until just cooked through and floating at the top of the pan. Drain well on kitchen paper.

To serve, arrange 5 ravioli on each warmed plate. Spoon over the smoked garlic foam and garnish with the micro chard and wild rocket, then sprinkle the toasted pine nuts and Parmesan shavings on top.

COOK AHEAD
The filling for the ravioli can be made up to 24 hours in advance and kept covered in the fridge until needed, but it's best to fill the ravioli just before serving.

WINE
A white Bordeaux Sauvignon/Semillon blend, like Graves, or a good-quality Italian Soave.

Ballyoak Cheese in Kataifi Pastry with Sauce Vierge

THIS IS A FABULOUS LOCAL CHEESE MADE ABOUT 30 MINUTES FROM THE RESTAURANT. THE SOFT MELTING CHEESE ENCASED IN THE CRISPY PASTRY IS A GREAT COMBINATION. THE KATAIFI PASTRY IS FOUND IN MOST ASIAN SUPERMARKETS IN THE FROZEN SECTION. THIS RECIPE ALSO WORKS WELL WITH A GOOD-QUALITY IRISH BRIE CHEESE.

Serves 4

200g (7oz) frozen kataifi pastry

2 tbsp plain flour

sea salt and freshly ground black pepper

1 egg

50ml (2fl oz) milk

450g (1lb) smoked Ballyoak cheese

groundnut oil, for deep-frying

chilli jam (page 248), to serve

sauce vierge (page 256), to serve

lightly dressed mixed lettuce leaves, to serve

Thaw the pastry while still in its plastic for a minimum of 2 hours before using. Once it's thawed it will be soft and pliable and ready to use, but remember that you must keep it covered with a clean, damp tea towel when not in use.

Place the flour in a shallow dish and season generously. Beat the egg with the milk and a pinch of salt in a separate shallow dish.

Cut the cheese into 12 even-sized pieces, each one roughly the size of your thumb, then toss in the seasoned flour until lightly coated. Dip briefly in the egg wash. To wrap the cheese, lay about 10g (1/4oz) of the kataifi pastry in a rectangle on a board. Sit a cheese wedge across the width at the end closest to you, then roll it up away from you to completely enclose it. Place on a baking sheet lined with parchment paper well spaced apart so that they don't get tangled up and cover with clingfilm. Chill until ready to use.

Just before serving, heat the oil in a deep-fat fryer or a deep-sided pan to 160°C (325°F). Cook the coated cheese wedges in batches for about 3 minutes, turning halfway through, until crisp and golden brown and the cheese is warmed through. Drain on kitchen paper.

To serve, place 3 pieces of crispy cheese on each plate. Spoon a little chilli jam to the side with a little of the sauce vierge alongside. On the third part of the plate, arrange a small pile of dressed lettuce leaves.

COOK AHEAD
The cheese can be wrapped in the pastry up to 24 hours in advance and kept in the fridge.

WINE
A south of France Viognier or Italian Pinot Grigio.

Salad of Grilled Vegetables and Aged Parmesan

THE SECRET TO THIS DISH IS THE SELECTION AND QUALITY OF THE VEGETABLES. FEEL FREE TO EXPERIMENT BY ADDING A LITTLE FRESH CHILLI OR DIFFERENT HERBS. THIS WOULD ALSO BE DELICIOUS SERVED WITH GRILLED GOAT'S CHEESE.

Serves 4

12 asparagus spears

2 small courgettes, each cut on the diagonal into 6 pieces

2 vine tomatoes, halved

1 red onion, cut into 4 slices (ends discarded)

1 yellow pepper, halved, seeded and cut into quarters

1 small aubergine, cut into slices

1 garlic clove, crushed

1 tsp chopped fresh thyme

5 tbsp extra virgin olive oil

sea salt and freshly ground black pepper

1 tbsp chopped fresh basil

4 tsp balsamic and port syrup (page 260)

25g (1oz) wild rocket

100g (4oz) aged Parmesan cheese, pared into shavings

4 tbsp basil pesto (page 256)

Preheat the oven to 180°C (350°F/gas mark 4).

Heat a large griddle pan until smoking hot. Place the asparagus, courgettes, tomato halves, red onion, pepper, aubergine, garlic and thyme in a large bowl. Add 3 tablespoons of the oil, then season to taste. Toss until well combined, then add to the griddle pan. Cook the vegetables in batches for about 2 minutes on each side, until lightly charred.

Transfer to a roasting tin and drizzle over the remaining 2 tablespoons of oil. Place in the oven and roast for 8–10 minutes, until all the vegetables are completely tender but not overcooked.

To serve, arrange the grilled vegetables on warmed plates and scatter over the basil, then drizzle over the balsamic and port syrup. Garnish with the wild rocket, then scatter over the Parmesan shavings. Drizzle over the basil pesto to serve.

WINE
An-off dry German Riesling or Australian Semillon.

Soups
Sweet Potato and Coconut Soup

COCONUT MILK IS ONE OF MY FAVOURITE INGREDIENTS AND IT MAKES A FANTASTIC CREAMY BASE FOR ALL THE OTHER
ROBUST FLAVOURS IN THIS ASIAN-STYLE SOUP. CHOOSE FIRM SWEET POTATOES WITH ORANGE FLESH FOR THEIR VIBRANT
COLOUR.

Serves 4–6

450g (1lb) sweet potatoes, cut into cubes

2 tbsp sunflower oil

1 onion, finely chopped

1 leek, trimmed and finely chopped

1 lemon grass stalk, trimmed and halved

1 red chilli, halved, seeded and thinly sliced

1 tsp freshly grated root ginger

1.25 litres (2 1/4 pints) vegetable stock (page 252) or chicken stock (page 253)

4 tsp tomato purée

400g can coconut milk

sea salt and freshly ground black pepper

chilli oil (page 250), to garnish

fresh micro coriander, to garnish

Preheat the oven to 200°C (400°F/gas mark 6).

Place the sweet potatoes in a baking tin, drizzle over 1 tablespoon of the sunflower oil and roast for 20–30 minutes, until tender. Set aside.

Heat the remaining 1 tablespoon of oil in a pan over a medium heat. Add the onion, leek, lemon grass, half the chilli and the ginger and sweat for 4 minutes, stirring occasionally. Add the roasted sweet potato with the stock and tomato purée, then bring to the boil. Reduce the heat and simmer for 10 minutes, until the liquid has slightly reduced and all the vegetables are completely tender.

Pour the coconut milk into the pan, reserving about 3 tablespoons from the top of the can as a garnish, and cook for another 5 minutes, stirring constantly. Season to taste. Remove the lemon grass and then blend with a hand blender until smooth.

To serve, ladle the soup into warmed bowls and swirl in the reserved coconut milk. Add a drizzle of the chilli oil, then sprinkle over the reserved chilli slices and micro coriander.

COOK AHEAD
This soup can be made up to 2–3 days in advance and kept covered in the fridge. It can also be frozen for up to 1 month but may need to be blitzed with a hand blender when reheating, as it may split.

WINE
An Alsace Gewürztraminer or German Riesling.

Chestnut and Wild Mushroom Soup with Smoked Duck

STOCK UP ON CANS OF VACUUM-PACKED CHESTNUTS, WHICH ARE NORMALLY READILY AVAILABLE IN GOOD DELIS, SHOPS AND LARGE SUPERMARKETS AT CHRISTMASTIME. IF YOU WANT TO KEEP THE SOUP VEGETARIAN, GARNISH IT WITH SOME SAUTÉED MUSHROOMS INSTEAD OF THE SMOKED DUCK.

Serves 8–10

50g (2oz) dried mixed wild mushrooms

1 tbsp rapeseed oil

450g (1lb) peeled chestnuts, chopped (canned or vacuum packed)

100g (4oz) smoked duck, thinly sliced

1 large onion, finely chopped

sea salt and freshly ground black pepper

1 tsp chopped fresh thyme

1.2 litres (2 pints) chicken stock (page 253) or vegetable stock (page 252)

200ml (7fl oz) cream

mushroom purée (page 244), to garnish

snipped fresh chives, to garnish

fresh micro herbs, to garnish

Place the dried wild mushrooms in a heatproof bowl and pour in 400ml (14fl oz) of boiling water to cover. Set aside for 20 minutes, until they have plumped up. Drain the mushrooms and gently squeeze them dry, reserving the soaking liquid.

Heat a large pan over a medium heat and add the rapeseed oil. Add the chestnuts, half of the smoked duck, the onion and drained wild mushrooms and sweat gently for 10 minutes, until golden brown, stirring occasionally. Season to taste.

Add the thyme to the pan with the reserved soaking liquid and stock, stirring to combine. Bring to the boil, then reduce the heat and simmer for another 20 minutes. Stir in the cream and allow to heat through for 1 minute, then whizz with a hand blender until as smooth as possible. Season to taste, then blitz again with a hand blender until light and foamy, tilting the pan to get the maximum effect.

To serve, ladle the soup into warmed bowls. Garnish each one with the mushroom purée, reserved smoked duck, chives and micro herbs.

COOK AHEAD
This soup can be made up to 2–3 days in advance and kept covered in the fridge. It can also be frozen for up to 1 month but may need to be blitzed with a hand blender when reheating, as it may split.

WINE
An earthy Burgundy Pinot Noir or an oaked Australian Chardonnay.

Vera's Seafood Chowder

THIS IS A VERY FILLING SOUP THAT IS ACTUALLY A RECIPE OF MY MUM'S THAT WE HAVE BEEN MAKING ON AND OFF IN THE RESTAURANT FOR YEARS. USE THE VERY BEST-QUALITY FISH AND SHELLFISH FOR THE BEST FLAVOUR.

Serves 6

1 tbsp rapeseed oil

1 tbsp butter, softened

2 large potatoes, cut into 1cm (1/2in) dice

1 small onion, cut into 1cm (1/2in) dice

1 carrot, cut into 1cm (1/2in) dice

1/2 small leek, cut into 1cm (1/2in) dice

1 tbsp plain flour

sea salt and freshly ground black pepper

150ml (1/4 pint) dry white wine

300ml (1/2 pint) fish stock (page 254)

100g (4oz) skinless salmon fillet, cut into cubes

100g (4oz) smoked coley fillet, cut into cubes

100g (4oz) cooked mussel meat

100g (4oz) cooked peeled prawns

150ml (1/4 pint) cream

1 tsp chopped fresh flat-leaf parsley

1 tsp chopped fresh dill

1 tbsp parsley oil (page 250), to garnish

fresh micro salad, to garnish

Heat the oil in a large pan over a medium heat and then add the butter. Once it stops sizzling, tip in the potatoes, onion, carrot and leek and cook for 5 minutes, until softened but not coloured. Add the flour and cook on a low heat for 2 minutes, stirring continuously. Season to taste.

Gradually pour the wine into the pan and allow it to bubble down, stirring continuously. Add the stock and bring to the boil. Reduce the heat and simmer for 5 minutes. Stir in the salmon and coley and simmer for 5 minutes, then add the mussel meat, prawns and cream and simmer for another 2–3 minutes, until warmed through. Stir in the herbs and season to taste.

To serve, ladle the soup into warmed bowls and garnish each one with the parsley oil and micro salad.

COOK AHEAD
This soup can be made up to 24 hours in advance and kept covered in the fridge. Just be careful when reheating not to allow it to come to the boil or the fish will lose its texture.

WINE
Splash out on a rosé Champagne, rosé Cava or a ripe Chardonnay from Macon in Burgundy.

Vegetable Soup with Barley

TO ME, THIS SOUP IS THE CLOSEST THING YOU'LL GET TO A HUG IN A BOWL! IT'S MY MOTHER'S RECIPE AND SOMETHING SHE ALWAYS MADE FOR ME AS A CHILD. I NOW SOMETIMES MAKE IT FOR AMELDA WHEN SHE'S FEELING POORLY.

Serves 4–6

50g (2oz) pearl barley

1 tbsp rapeseed oil

2 celery sticks, diced

1 onion, diced

1 carrot, diced

1 small leek, trimmed and diced

1 tsp chopped fresh thyme

50g (2oz) rindless streaky bacon, diced (optional)

1.2 litres (2 pints) chicken stock (page 253) or vegetable stock (page 252)

1–2 tsp cornflour, sifted (optional)

1 tbsp chopped fresh flat-leaf parsley

sea salt and freshly ground black pepper

crusty bread, to serve (optional)

Place the pearl barley in a sieve and rinse well under cold running water.

Heat the rapeseed oil in a pan over a medium heat and stir in the celery, onion, carrot, leek and thyme. Add the bacon, if using, and sauté for 5 minutes, until the vegetables are softened and the bacon is sizzling.

Pour the stock into the vegetable mixture, add in the rinsed barley and bring to the boil, then reduce the heat and simmer for about 20 minutes, until the vegetables and barley are completely tender but still holding their shape.

If you want to thicken the soup, mix the cornflour with a little of the liquid from the soup and then stir it back into the pan. Give the soup a good stir and simmer for another minute or two to cook out the cornflour. Stir in the parsley and season to taste.

To serve, ladle the soup into warmed bowls and have a separate basket of crusty bread.

COOK AHEAD
This soup keeps well in the fridge for up to 2 days covered with clingfilm.

WINE
A Bordeaux white Sauvignon Blanc/Semillon blend or an Italian Pinot Grigio.

Roast Pepper and Tomato Soup

THIS IS A GREAT SOUP TO MAKE WHEN YOU HAVE A GLUT OF TOMATOES OR ONES THAT ARE SLIGHTLY PAST THEIR BEST. LIKE MANY OF THE SOUPS THAT WE NOW SERVE IN THE RESTAURANT, IT USES NO FLOUR TO THICKEN IT, SO IT'S SUITABLE FOR COELIACS. IT'S EXCELLENT HOT OR COLD AND I OFTEN PUT IT ON THE VEGETARIAN MENU.

Serves 4–6

1kg (2 1/4lb) vine-ripened tomatoes, halved

2 red peppers, quartered and seeds removed

2 tbsp rapeseed oil

1 tsp balsamic vinegar

1/2 tsp chopped fresh thyme

1 large onion, finely chopped

2 garlic cloves, crushed

900ml (1 1/2 pints) vegetable stock (page 252) or chicken stock (page 253)

sea salt and freshly ground black pepper

basil pesto (page 256), to garnish

deep-fried basil sprigs, to garnish

MacNean wheaten bread (page 200), to serve

Preheat the oven to 190°C (375°F/gas mark 5).

Arrange the tomato and pepper halves in a baking tin, cut side up. Drizzle over 1 tablespoon of the rapeseed oil and sprinkle the vinegar and thyme on top. Place in the oven and roast for 20–25 minutes, until softened and lightly charred.

Heat the remaining 1 tablespoon of oil in a pan over a medium heat. Add the onion and garlic and sweat for 10 minutes, until lightly golden, stirring occasionally. Add the roasted tomatoes and peppers and the stock and bring to the boil. Reduce the heat and simmer for 10–15 minutes, until slightly reduced, then blitz with a hand blender until smooth. Season lightly and pass through a sieve for a really smooth finish.

When ready to serve, return the smooth soup to a clean pan and reheat gently, stirring occasionally. Do not allow it to boil for too long or it will lose some of its wonderful vibrant colour.

To serve, ladle the soup into warmed bowls. Garnish each one with the basil pesto and a deep-fried basil sprig. Arrange on plates with the wheaten bread to serve.

COOK AHEAD
This soup can be made up to 3 days in advance and kept covered with clingfilm in the fridge. It can also be frozen for up to 1 month.

WINE
A juicy ripe Beaujolais Village or a New Zealand Sauvignon Blanc.

Celeriac, Smoked Bacon and Apple Soup

THIS IS A SOUP THAT I LOVE TO SERVE IN THE RESTAURANT IN THE AUTUMN, WHEN LOCAL APPLES ARE AT THEIR BEST. THE CELERIAC WORKS VERY WELL WITH THE APPLE AND IS A VEGETABLE THAT I WISH PEOPLE WOULD USE MORE, AS IT HAS A FANTASTIC FLAVOUR AND IS REALLY VERY VERSATILE. IT MAKES A LARGE QUANTITY BUT IT FREEZES VERY WELL.

Serves 10–12

25g (1oz) butter

1 tbsp rapeseed oil

100g (4oz) rindless smoked streaky bacon

2 small onions, sliced

1 celeriac, peeled and diced

1 eating apple, peeled, cored and chopped

1 tsp chopped fresh thyme

1.2 litres (2 pints) vegetable stock (page 252) or chicken stock (page 253)

600ml (1 pint) freshly pressed apple juice (unsweetened)

600ml (1 pint) cream

sea salt and freshly ground black pepper

apple and vanilla gel (page 247), to garnish

celeriac purée (page 244), to garnish

steamed diced celeriac, to garnish

green apple matchsticks, to garnish

fresh pea shoots, to garnish

Heat a large heavy-based pan. Add the butter and rapeseed oil and once the butter has melted and is foaming, tip in the bacon, onions, celeriac, apple and thyme. Leave to sweat for about 10 minutes, until they are just beginning to colour, stirring occasionally to ensure they cook evenly.

Pour the stock and apple juice over the vegetable mixture, then bring to the boil and simmer for 30 minutes, until all the vegetables are completely tender and the liquid has slightly reduced. Stir in the cream and season to taste, then allow to cook for another minute or two. Use a hand blender to blend the soup until smooth or do it in batches in a food processor.

To serve, reheat the soup gently and season to taste, then ladle into warmed bowls. Garnish with apple and vanilla gel, celeriac purée, steamed celeriac, apple matchsticks and pea shoots.

COOK AHEAD
This soup can be made 2 days in advance and kept in the fridge covered with clingfilm. It can also be frozen for up to 1 month.

WINE
An Australian Riesling or Semillon.

Haricot Bean and White Truffle Oil Velouté

OF COURSE YOU COULD USE ANY WHITE BEANS FOR THIS SOUP, BUT HARICOT BEANS ARE A FAVOURITE OF MINE IN THE RESTAURANT. THEY'RE A SMALL, OVAL, PLUMP AND CREAMY-WHITE BEAN WITH A MILD FLAVOUR AND SMOOTH, BUTTERY TEXTURE. WITH LITTLE FLAVOUR OF THEIR OWN, THEY ABSORB OTHER AROMAS AND FLAVOURS VERY WELL, WHICH MAKES THEM PERFECT TO USE IN A SOUP LIKE THIS.

Serves 6–8

225g (8oz) dried haricot beans

1 tbsp rapeseed oil

1 small onion, finely chopped

1 tsp chopped fresh thyme

sea salt and freshly ground black pepper

1.2 litres (2 pints) vegetable stock (page 252) or chicken stock (page 253)

200ml (7fl oz) cream

2–3 tbsp white truffle oil

toasted pine nuts, to garnish

fresh micro herbs, to garnish

Soak the haricot beans overnight in a large bowl of cold water. Drain and place in a very large pan and cover with 1.2 litres (2 pints) of water. Bring to the boil and boil rapidly for 10 minutes, then cover and simmer for 30 minutes, until just tender. Drain and set aside until needed.

Heat a large pan over a medium heat and add the oil. Add the cooked haricot beans with the onion and thyme and sweat gently for 10 minutes, stirring occasionally. Season to taste.

Add the stock, stirring to combine. Bring to the boil, then reduce the heat and simmer for another 20 minutes. Remove 3 tablespoons of the cooked white beans and set aside to use as a garnish. Stir in the cream and allow to heat through for 1 minute, then whizz with a hand blender until as smooth as possible but with a foamy top. Season to taste.

To serve, ladle the soup into warmed wide-rimmed bowls. Drizzle over the truffle oil and garnish each one with the reserved haricot beans, toasted pine nuts and micro herbs.

COOK AHEAD
This soup keeps very well for 2–3 days in the fridge covered with clingfilm. It can also be frozen for up to 1 month.

WINE
A ripe Chardonnay from the south of France or the New World.

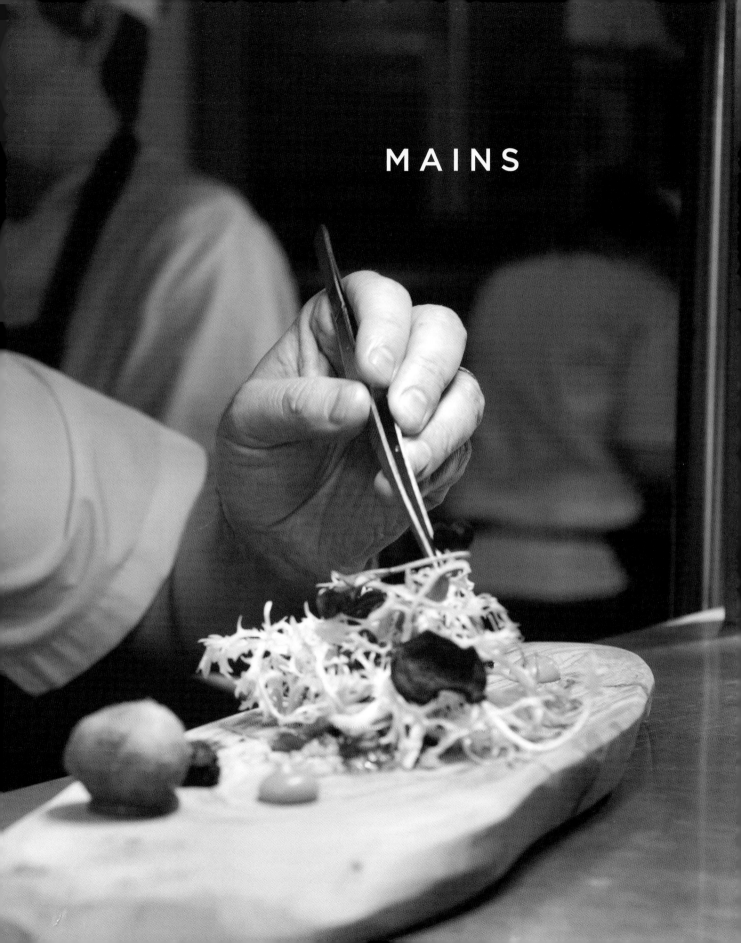

MAINS

Fish
Gratin of Cod with Prawns, Spinach and Pesto

THIS HAS TO BE ONE OF THE MOST POPULAR FISH DISHES IN THE RESTAURANT AND IS SERVED AS A SMALL STARTER AND A MAIN COURSE. IT HAS BEEN ON THE MENU FOR AS LONG AS I CAN REMEMBER AND REALLY IS HARD TO BEAT. YOU CAN REPLACE THE COD WITH HAKE, HADDOCK OR ANY FIRM-FLESHED WHITE FISH.

Serves 4

4 x 175g (6oz) cod fillets, pin boned and scaled

sea salt and freshly ground black pepper

16 raw Dublin Bay prawns, peeled and veins removed

6 tbsp chopped fresh basil

125g (4 1/2oz) mozzarella cheese, sliced

4 tsp chilli jam (page 248)

4 tbsp basil pesto (page 256)

smoked salmon and saffron orzo (page 90), to serve

fresh micro basil, to garnish

For the spinach:

50g (2oz) butter

225g (8oz) spinach, tough stalks removed

pinch of caster sugar

sea salt and freshly ground black pepper

Preheat the oven to 200°C (400°F/gas mark 6).

To sauté the spinach, heat a pan over a medium heat and add the butter. Once it has stopped foaming, quickly sauté the spinach with the sugar until soft and wilted. Season to taste and drain well on kitchen paper to remove the excess moisture.

Place the cod on a baking sheet lined with non-stick parchment paper and season the cod. Arrange the spinach on top, then carefully put 4 prawns on top of each fillet. Sprinkle over the basil and arrange the mozzarella on top. Drizzle over the chilli jam with 2 tablespoons of the basil pesto. Cook for 15–20 minutes, until golden brown.

Place a pile of the smoked salmon and saffron orzo in the centre of each plate and using a fish slice, carefully arrange a gratin of cod on top. Drizzle around the rest of the basil pesto and garnish with micro basil.

COOK AHEAD
This gratin can be prepared 2–3 hours in advance and kept covered with clingfilm in the fridge.

WINE
A ripe Macon-Villages, a Burgundy Chardonnay or a Pinot Blanc from Alsace. Or why not splash out on a rosé Champagne or Cava?

Roast Turbot with Crab Cannelloni and Prawn Velouté

THIS IS ONE OF THE MOST HIGHLY PRIZED FISH THAT CAN BE CAUGHT IN OUR WATERS. IT CAN BE EXPENSIVE, WHICH IS WHY I'VE SERVED IT HERE WITH SOME DELICIOUS CRAB CANNELLONI SO THAT THE FISH STRETCHES A BIT FURTHER. SAMPHIRE IS A SEA VEGETABLE THAT GROWS ABUNDANTLY ON SHORELINES, IN MARSHY SHALLOWS AND ON SALTY MUDFLATS. IT HAS A CRISP TEXTURE AND TASTES OF THE SEA. IF YOU DON'T SEE ANY ON THE WET FISH COUNTER, ASK YOUR FISHMONGER TO GET SOME FOR YOU AND THEY NORMALLY WILL OBLIGE.

Serves 6

1kg (2 1/2lb) turbot fillet

1 tbsp rapeseed oil

sea salt and freshly ground black pepper

25g (1oz) butter

2 fresh thyme sprigs

juice of 1/2 lemon

12 asparagus tips

25g (1oz) samphire, well picked over

carrot purée (page 244), to serve

wilted spinach (page 233), to serve

prawn velouté (page 258), to serve

fresh micro coriander, to garnish

For the crab cannelloni:

100g (4oz) organic salmon fillet, skinned, boned and cubed

pinch of cayenne pepper

1 egg yolk

1 tbsp cold cream

sea salt and freshly ground black pepper

1 tsp snipped fresh chives

1 tsp chopped fresh basil

1 tsp chopped fresh coriander

100g (4oz) white crab meat

3 fresh pasta sheets (page 241 or shop bought)

Trim the turbot fillet and carefully remove the skin and bones. Cut into 6 even-sized pieces and arrange on a tray. Cover with clingfilm, then place in the fridge until needed.

To make the cannelloni, place the salmon and cayenne pepper in a food processor and blend briefly, then add the egg yolk, cream and seasoning, and blend to a smooth consistency. Place in a bowl and stir in the herbs, then fold in the crab and season with pepper. Place the mousse into a piping bag fitted with a 1.5cm (3/4in) plain nozzle.

Place the lasagne sheets lengthways away from you onto individual sheets of clingfilm. Pipe the mousse onto each pasta sheet on the edge that is closest to you, in a long sausage shape. Use the clingfilm to lift the pasta around the mousse to create a cylinder shape. Roll the clingfilm tightly at both ends to create a sausage shape and place in the fridge for at least 1 hour to firm up.

When ready to cook, place the cannelloni in a steamer set over simmering water and steam for 15–20 minutes, until cooked and firm to the touch, then cut in half through the clingfilm. Discard the clingfilm and trim down the ends.

Heat the rapeseed oil in a large frying pan over a medium heat. Season the turbot fillets on both sides and carefully place in the heated frying pan. Add the butter and cook for 2–3 minutes, depending on the thickness of the fish fillets. Turn over and add the thyme sprigs to the pan, then continue to cook the fish until golden brown and just cooked through. Add a squeeze of lemon and then remove the turbot from the heat.

Meanwhile, place the asparagus in a steamer and scatter the samphire on top. Cook over a medium heat for 2–3 minutes, until just tender but still with a little bite.

To serve, place the carrot purée on warmed plates with the spinach and arrange the turbot on top, then spoon over the prawn velouté. Place the crab cannelloni to one side and arrange the asparagus and samphire in a guard of honour over the top. Garnish with the micro coriander.

COOK AHEAD The crab cannelloni can be made up to 24 hours in advance. They can also be precooked 1 day ahead and gently reheated in the steamer until just warmed through.

WINE Turbot cries out for the best-quality Burgundy Chardonnay. Time to open the prized bottle of Meursault or Montrachet.

Hake with Cassoulet of Beans and Chorizo

HAKE HAS A LOVELY SOFT TEXTURE AND SLIGHT SWEETNESS WHEN IT'S VERY FRESH. IT'S HIGHLY REGARDED BY CHEFS, AS IT OFFERS GREAT VALUE FOR MONEY. ASK YOUR FISHMONGER FOR THE HAKE FILLETS FROM THE CENTRE CUT SO THAT THEY ARE NICE AND CHUNKY. THE COMBINATION OF THE CHORIZO AND BEANS GIVES THIS DISH A REAL SPANISH FLAVOUR.

Serves 4

60g (2 1/4oz) mixed dried beans (such as haricot, cannellini, borlotti and black-eyed beans)

2 tbsp rapeseed oil

100g (4oz) raw chorizo

150ml (1/4 pint) vegetable stock (page 252)

1 tbsp softened butter

sea salt and freshly ground black pepper

2 tsp chopped fresh flat-leaf parsley

1 tsp snipped fresh chives

4 x 150g (5oz) skinless hake fillets, pin bones removed

red pepper gel (page 247), to garnish

basil purée (page 243), to garnish

red pepper foam (page 246), to garnish

fresh micro basil, to garnish

Preheat the oven to 200°C (400°F/gas mark 6).

Place the beans in a large pan with plenty of water and a good pinch of salt. Bring to a simmer and cook for 20–30 minutes, until tender. Drain and refresh under cold running water.

Heat 1 tablespoon of the rapeseed oil in a heavy-based pan over a medium heat. Add the chorizo and sauté for 2–3 minutes, until sizzling. Remove the chorizo and drain on kitchen paper.

Place the stock, the butter, the reserved cooked chorizo and the beans in a pan and bring to the boil, then reduce the heat and simmer for a few minutes, until warmed through. Season to taste and stir in the parsley and chives. Keep warm.

Arrange the hake on a piece of parchment paper in a steamer. Drizzle with the remaining 1 tablespoon oil and steam for 8–10 minutes, until just cooked and tender. The cooking time obviously depends on the thickness of the fish fillets.

To serve, spoon the bean and chorizo cassoulet onto the centre of each warmed plate and arrange the hake on top, skin side up. Garnish with the red pepper gel and basil purée, then spoon over the pepper foam and scatter with the micro basil.

COOK AHEAD
The bean and chorizo cassoulet can be made up to 2 days in advance and kept covered with clingfilm in the fridge. Simply warm through when needed.

WINE
Try an Albariño from Galicia, Spain, or a white Rioja, also from Spain.

Monkfish with Gnocchi, Wild Mushrooms, Sun-dried Tomato and Saffron Velouté

MONKFISH IS A FIRM-TEXTURED FISH AND IS VERY POPULAR WITH OUR CUSTOMERS. THE VELOUTÉ GOES WELL WITH ANY FISH, AS ITS FLAVOUR ISN'T TOO OVERPOWERING. THE GNOCCHI ALSO WORKS WELL ON ITS OWN WITH A PARMESAN FOAM (PAGE 246) AS A STARTER OR LIGHT SUPPER.

Serves 4

2 tbsp rapeseed oil

4 x 175g (6oz) monkfish tails, trimmed

16 baby carrots

4 baby leeks, trimmed and cut into 1cm (1/2in) lengths

1 tbsp softened butter

100g (4oz) wild mushrooms, trimmed and quartered or halved, depending on their size (such as Piedmont, girolles and cepes)

sea salt and freshly ground black pepper

wilted spinach (page 233), to serve

16 potato gnocchi (page 231)

sun-dried tomato and saffron velouté (page 258), to serve

fresh micro coriander and basil, to garnish

Preheat the oven to 200°C (400°F/gas mark 6).

Heat 1 tablespoon of the rapeseed oil in a large ovenproof frying pan over a medium heat and sear the monkfish pieces all over for 3–4 minutes, until crisp and golden. Transfer to the oven and roast for another 10–12 minutes, until firm to the touch and just cooked through. Keep warm.

Using a vegetable peeler, peel and trim the baby carrots into cones. Blanch in a pan of boiling salted water for 4 minutes, then drain and quickly refresh under cold running water. Blanch the baby leeks in a separate pan of boiling salted water, then drain and quickly refresh under cold running water.

Meanwhile, heat 2 frying pans over a medium heat. Add the remaining 1 tablespoon of the oil to one of them with 1 teaspoon of the butter and then tip in the mushrooms. Sauté for 2–3 minutes, until just cooked through and tender. Season to taste and keep warm.

Add the rest of the butter to the other frying pan and sauté the carrot cones and baby leeks for a minute or so, until just warmed through

To serve, spoon the spinach onto each warmed plate. Slice each piece of monkfish in half and arrange on top. Scatter around the gnocchi, wild mushrooms, carrot cones and baby leeks. Spoon over the sun-dried tomato and saffron velouté and garnish with the micro coriander and basil.

WINE
A rich, full-bodied Chardonnay from South Africa or Oregon or try a dry rosé from Spain or France.

Smoked Salmon and Saffron Orzo

THIS IS FANTASTIC SERVED AS A SIMPLE SUPPER ON ITS OWN, OR TRY IT WITH MY GRATIN OF COD (PAGE 82) OR THE SALMON SAUSAGES (PAGE 94). ALTERNATIVELY, OMIT THE SMOKED SALMON AND USE A HANDFUL OF DICED SUN-DRIED TOMATOES INSTEAD FOR A LOVELY VEGETARIAN OPTION. ORZO PASTA IS A RICE-SHAPED PASTA ALSO KNOWN AS RISONI. IT IS TRADITIONALLY USED IN SOUPS AND PILAFS, BUT I THINK IT WORKS WONDERFULLY SERVED AS A SIDE DISH.

Serves 4

2 large pinches of saffron threads

350g (12oz) orzo pasta

225ml (8fl oz) cream

finely grated rind of 1 lemon

sea salt and freshly ground black pepper

1 tbsp chopped fresh basil

1 tbsp snipped fresh chives

225g (8oz) smoked salmon slices, diced

oven-dried cherry tomatoes (page 237) or semi sun-dried tomatoes, to garnish (optional)

Bring a large pan of salted water to the boil with the saffron. Tip in the orzo pasta, stir once and then cook for 12–15 minutes, until just al dente, or according to the package instructions. Drain the pasta well under cold running water.

Place the cream in a pan with the lemon rind. Bring to the boil, then reduce the heat and simmer for 2 minutes. Add the cooked orzo and simmer for another 5 minutes, stirring occasionally. Season to taste and stir in the herbs and salmon. Allow to warm through.

To serve, use as required if you're having it as a side order or divide among warmed wide-rimmed bowls and garnish with the oven-dried cherry tomatoes or semi sun-dried tomatoes, if liked.

COOK AHEAD
This can be made up to 2 days in advance, covered with clingfilm and kept in the fridge.

WINE
Pinot Blanc from Alsace or treat yourself with Brut Champagne or Cava.

MacNean Fish Pie

FISH PIE IS A REAL STAPLE OF IRISH FAMILY COOKING AND EVERYONE HAS THEIR OWN WAY OF MAKING IT. THIS IS MY VERSION, WHICH EVERYONE ALWAYS SEEMS TO ENJOY. WE OFTEN MAKE A VERSION OF IT FOR A STAFF SUPPER USING THE TRIMMINGS THAT ARE LEF TOVER FROM PORTIONING THE FISH FOR SERVICE.

Serves 6–8

350g (12oz) haddock, skin on and pin bones removed

350g (12oz) smoked cod, skin on and pin bones removed

350g (12oz) salmon fillets, skin on and pin bones removed

sea salt and freshly ground white pepper

900ml (1 1/2 pints) milk

1 large bay leaf

800g (1lb 12oz) potatoes

50g (2oz) butter

100g (4oz) mature Cheddar cheese, grated

1 tbsp basil pesto (page 256)

225g (8oz) leeks, thinly sliced

1 small onion, thinly sliced

150ml (1/4 pint) dry white wine

50g (2oz) plain flour

1 tbsp chopped fresh flat-leaf parsley

150g (5oz) cooked peeled prawns

2 tbsp crème fraîche

2 heaped tbsp toasted breadcrumbs

steamed broccoli florets, to serve

Preheat the oven to 160°C (325°F/gas mark 3).

Remove any stray pin bones from the haddock, cod and salmon and season generously, then place in a roasting tin with the milk and bay leaf. Poach in the oven for 10–15 minutes, until the fish flakes easily when tested with a knife.

Remove the fish from the tin and take off any remaining skin. Flake the flesh, checking for bones that might have been overlooked. Strain the leftover milk into a measuring jug until you have 600ml (1 pint). Discard the bay leaf.

Increase the oven temperature to 180°C (350°F/gas mark 4).

Cut the potatoes into even-sized pieces and place in a large pan of salted water. Bring to the boil and cook for about 20 minutes, until tender. Drain and return to the pan to dry out a little. Mash well and beat in half of the butter along with the Cheddar cheese and basil pesto. Season to taste.

Melt the remaining butter in a small pan and gently cook the leeks and onion for about 5 minutes. Pour in the white wine and reduce by half. Add in the flour and cook for 1 minute, stirring constantly. Gradually pour in the reserved poaching milk and stir until you have a smooth sauce. Season and reduce the heat. Add the parsley and simmer for 3 minutes, stirring occasionally.

Fold the prawns into the parsley sauce with the flaked fish and crème fraîche and cook for 2 minutes. Be careful not to boil the mixture because the fish will break up and the sauce will go mushy.

Spoon the fish mixture into a shallow ovenproof dish. Top it with the cheesy mash and sprinkle over the breadcrumbs. Bake for about 20 minutes, until the top is golden brown and bubbling.

To serve, divide among warmed plates and add some broccoli to each one.

COOK AHEAD
Although this fish pie can be made in advance, it is best made fresh or the fish and prawns are in danger of overcooking.

WINE
A rich, ripe, buttery Chardonnay from the New World would work really well with this recipe.

Sea Trout with Aubergine Purée and Crispy Courgette Flowers Stuffed with Crab

SIMILAR TO SALMON IN COLOUR, SEA TROUT LIVES OFF CRUSTACEANS AND IN MY OPINION HAS THE BEST FLAVOUR OF ALL TROUT. IT IS BEST SERVED SLIGHTLY PINK AND STILL QUITE MOIST.

Serves 4

4 courgette flowers, still attached to tiny courgettes

2 fresh pasta sheets (page 241 or shop bought)

16 asparagus tips, well trimmed

4 x 175g (6oz) sea trout fillets, pin boned and trimmed (with skin still on)

sea salt and freshly ground black pepper

1 tbsp rapeseed oil

1 tbsp softened butter

groundnut oil, for deep-frying

wilted spinach (page 233), to serve

aubergine purée (page 242), to serve

spinach purée (page 244), to garnish

prawn velouté (page 258), to garnish

For the crab filling:

50g (2oz) white crab meat

25g (1oz) ricotta cheese

1 tbsp chopped semi sun-dried tomatoes

1 tsp chopped fresh basil

sea salt and freshly ground black pepper

For the batter:

100g (4oz) plain flour, plus 25g (1oz) for dusting

250ml (9fl oz) chilled sparkling water

To prepare the filling for the stuffed courgette flowers, mix together the crab meat, ricotta, sun-dried tomatoes and basil in a bowl, then season to taste and cover with clingfilm. Spoon into a piping bag fitted with a 2.5cm (1in) plain nozzle and place in the fridge for a couple of hours to firm up.

Trim the courgette flowers from the courgettes, then cut each courgette into 4 slices and reserve. Open the courgette flowers and using the piping bag, fill them with the ricotta crab mixture. Twist the end of each flower to keep the stuffing in place.

To make the batter, sieve the flour into a bowl. Pour the sparkling water into a shallow dish, gradually whisking in the sieved flour and making sure there are no lumps. The batter should look like pouring cream. Set aside until needed.

Cut each pasta sheet into 6 strips lengthways. Blanch in a pan of boiling salted water for a minute or so, until just tender and al dente. Drain with a slotted spoon and refresh under cold running water. Drain and then roll into scroll shapes.

Blanch the courgette slices for 30 seconds, then drain with a slotted spoon and quickly refresh under cold running water. Blanch the asparagus tips for a minute or two, then drain and refresh under cold running water.

To prepare the sea trout, using a very sharp knife, score the skin in thin parallel lines and season the flesh side lightly. Heat a non-stick frying pan over a medium heat and add the oil and 1 teaspoon of the butter. Once the butter stops sizzling, place the trout skin side down and cook gently for 4–5 minutes to get the skin crispy, then carefully turn over and cook for a further 2–3 minutes to brown lightly.

To cook the flowers, preheat a deep-fat fryer or deep-sided pan filled with groundnut oil to 180°C (350°F). Carefully dip the flowers into the flour to lightly dust them, then quickly dip them in the batter, swirling to coat. Place them in the hot oil, being careful that they don't stick to the basket, and deep-fry for about 2 minutes, until crisp and golden. Remove from the oil and drain on kitchen paper. Keep warm.

Meanwhile, heat a frying pan with the rest of the butter. Add the pasta, courgette and asparagus and sauté for 1–2 minutes, until just warmed through. Keep warm.

To serve, place some wilted spinach in the middle of each warm plate and place the sea trout on top, crispy skin side up. Next, spoon or swipe the aubergine purée beside the fish and carefully arrange the stuffed courgette flower on the side of the plate. Garnish with spinach purée and spoon the prawn velouté on top.

COOK AHEAD
The crab filling for the courgette flowers can be made 24 hours in advance,
but don't fill them more than 2 hours before you plan to cook them.

WINE
An off-dry Riesling from Alsace or Germany or try a New Zealand Pinot Gris.

Salmon Sausages with Creamed Leeks and Lemon Butter Sauce

ANOTHER POPULAR RESTAURANT DISH THAT IS JUST THAT LITTLE BIT DIFFERENT AND BOUND TO IMPRESS YOUR GUESTS. THE SALMON SAUSAGE MIXTURE OR THE ACTUAL COOKED SAUSAGES CAN BE MADE UP TO 24 HOURS IN ADVANCE, LEAVING VERY LITTLE TO DO LAST MINUTE.

Serves 4

450g (1lb) organic salmon fillet, skinned, boned and diced (well chilled)

sea salt and freshly ground black pepper

1 egg yolk

pinch of cayenne pepper

100ml (3 1/2fl oz) cream, well chilled

3 raw Dublin Bay prawns, shelled, veins removed and finely chopped

2 tsp snipped fresh chives, plus extra to garnish

1 tbsp rapeseed oil

knob of butter

creamed leeks (page 234), to serve

lemon butter sauce (page 13), to serve

To make the salmon sausages, blitz the salmon to a purée in a food processor. Season to taste, then add the egg yolk and cayenne pepper. Blend again until smooth. With the motor running, slowly add the cream through the feeder tube. Stop the machine as soon as the cream has been incorporated. Scrape into a bowl, then stir in the prawns and chives.

Place a piece of clingfilm on the work surface that is about 20cm x 25cm (8in x 10in) in size. Spoon an eighth of the salmon mixture in the centre across the width of the clingfilm, then fold the long ends of the clingfilm over tightly and form into a sausage shape about 2.5cm (1in) thick and 8.5cm (3 1/2in) long, twisting the ends to seal. Repeat with the remaining mixture to make 8 sausages in total and refrigerate for at least 10 minutes to rest (up to 24 hours is fine).

Bring a large pan of water to a simmer and gently poach the salmon sausages, still in the clingfilm, for 5 minutes, turning halfway through as they rise to the surface, until slightly firm to the touch. Carefully remove the sausages (to avoid them breaking) and place them in a large bowl of iced water to cool down immediately, then place in the fridge until needed.

When ready to serve, heat a large non-stick frying pan over a medium heat. Carefully remove the clingfilm from the salmon sausages. Add the rapeseed oil and butter to the heated frying pan and gently fry the sausages for 4–5 minutes, turning occasionally, until warmed through and golden brown. Remove and drain on kitchen paper. Keep warm.

To serve, spoon the creamed leeks into the centre of warmed plates and carefully arrange 2 salmon sausages on top of each one. Drizzle with the lemon butter sauce and garnish with the chives.

COOK AHEAD
These sausages can be made up to 24 hours in advance and kept covered with clingfilm in the fridge.

WINE
A white wine choice would be a Pinot Gris from Alsace. A light red wine like Beaujolais or Burgundy Pinot Noir would also be a good match.

HEAD CHEF GLEN WHEELER

Poultry
Breast of Thornhill Duck with Sweet Potato Fondants

KEN MOFFIT IS ONE OF OUR OLDEST SUPPLIERS AND OPERATES LESS THAN 5 MINUTES FROM THE RESTAURANT. HE REARS A SPECIFIC BREED CALLED PEKING DUCK, WHICH ARE SMALLER THAN USUAL AND ARE SPECIALLY BRED FOR FLAVOUR.

Serves 4

4 x 275g (10oz) duck breasts, well trimmed

1 tbsp cracked black pepper

sea salt

1 tbsp clear honey

creamed cabbage (page 233), to serve

8 sweet potato fondants (page 231)

spinach purée (page 244), to serve

sweet potato purée (page 244), to serve

honey and clove sauce (page 259), to serve

garlic confit (page 236), to garnish

Preheat the oven to 200°C (400°F/gas mark 6) and preheat the grill to medium.

Score the fat on the duck in a criss-cross pattern. Season the duck on both sides with the cracked black pepper and salt. Heat a large ovenproof frying pan over a medium to high heat and add the duck breasts, skin side down (this helps render the duck fat, giving it a crispy skin,) and cook for about 2 minutes, until the skin is crisp.

Turn the duck breasts over and cook for another minute, then transfer the frying pan to the oven and cook for 8 minutes for a pink finish or 10 minutes if you prefer your duck a little more well done. For the last few minutes of the cooking time, brush the skin of the duck breasts with the honey, which will give a wonderful flavour and caramelise the skin. Leave to rest in a warm place for 5 minutes, without covering.

To serve, carve the duck breasts into thin slices and arrange on warmed plates on a bed of creamed cabbage with 2 of the sweet potato fondants to one side. Add the spinach and sweet potato purées, then drizzle over the honey and clove sauce. Finally, garnish with the garlic confit.

WINE
Either a Burgundy white Chardonnay or red Pinot Noir would be a good match for this recipe. Alternatively, a Rioja Reserve goes very well with oven-cooked duck.

Trio of MacNean Chicken with Baby Carrots

THIS IS A FANTASTIC SHOWCASE FOR OUR LOCAL FERMANAGH FREE-RANGE CHICKEN, WHICH HAS A WONDERFUL TEXTURE AND FLAVOUR. I JUST LOVE DISHES LIKE THIS IN THE KITCHEN, AS IT USES ALMOST EVERY PART OF THE CHICKEN, LEAVING BEHIND JUST THE CARCASS, WHICH I THEN USE IN STOCK.

Serves 4

For the stuffed chicken thigh:

1 tbsp softened butter

15g (1/2oz) wild mushrooms, diced (such as cepes, shiitake or oyster)

1 tsp chopped fresh mixed herbs (such as chives, flat-leaf parsley and basil)

1 rindless smoked bacon rasher

1 small chicken breast, diced (75g (3oz) in total)

1 egg yolk

50ml (2fl oz) cream, well chilled

sea salt and freshly ground black pepper

1 chicken thigh, boned but with skin still on

1 tbsp rapeseed oil, plus a little extra

For the braised drumsticks:

1 tbsp rapeseed oil

4 chicken drumsticks

1 onion, diced

1 carrot, diced

1 celery stalk, diced

1 garlic clove, chopped

100ml (3 1/2fl oz) red wine

1 tbsp chopped fresh thyme

500ml (16fl oz) chicken stock (page 253)

sea salt and freshly ground black pepper

To prepare the stuffed chicken thigh, heat a frying pan over a medium heat. Add half the butter and once it stops sizzling, tip in the mushrooms. Cook gently for a few minutes, until soft. Stir in the herbs and transfer to a bowl to cool. Preheat the grill and cook the bacon until crispy, then drain on kitchen paper before chopping very finely.

To make the mousse, place the chicken breast in a food processor and blend for 1 minute. Add the egg yolk, followed by the cream. Blend for 1–2 minutes. Season to taste, then stir in the bacon and cooled mushroom mixture.

Place the chicken thigh between 2 sheets of clingfilm. Use a rolling pin to flatten it out until it's twice its original size and quite thin. Remove the top layer of clingfilm and place the mousse stuffing on the thigh, then spread the mixture lengthways down the centre along the thigh. Roll the meat over the stuffing so that it forms a sausage shape. When rolled, wrap each thigh tightly in oiled tin foil to keep its shape. Twist the ends of the tin foil so that it looks like a Christmas cracker. Chill in the fridge for at least 2 hours to firm up.

To prepare the braised drumsticks, heat a large sauté pan with a lid over a medium heat. Add the rapeseed oil and fry the chicken drumsticks skin side down for at least 10 minutes, until nicely browned. Turn over and brown the other side, then remove from the pan.

Add the vegetables and garlic to the pan you've cooked the chicken in and sauté for 5 minutes, until browned, scraping up any sediment from the bottom of the pan with a wooden spoon. Add the red wine and thyme and simmer for 5 minutes, until slightly reduced.

Return the browned chicken drumsticks to the pan along with the stock. Cover with a piece of foil and the lid and simmer for 50 minutes, until the drumsticks feel tender when pierced with a fork and the meat is almost ready to fall off the bone. When the chicken drumsticks are cooked, strain the sauce into a clean pan and discard the vegetables. Reduce the sauce down for 15–20 minutes, until you have achieved a rich, glossy sauce. Return the chicken drumsticks and gently heat for 5 minutes, spooning the sauce over to glaze. Season to taste.

For the sautéed breasts:

2 large chicken breasts, halved, with skin on

sea salt and freshly ground black pepper

25g (1oz) butter

2 tbsp rapeseed oil

smoked bacon foam (page 000), to garnish

For the baby carrots:

4 baby carrots, scrubbed

1 tsp softened butter

potato purée (page 228), to serve

wilted spinach (page 233), to serve

carrot purée (page 244), to serve

Meanwhile, preheat the oven to 180°C (350°F/gas mark 4) to cook the chicken breasts and finish cooking the prepared chicken thigh.

Poach the rested stuffed thigh, still in the foil, in a pan of simmering water for 10–15 minutes, until just cooked, then remove from the pan and carefully peel off the tin foil. Heat the rest of the butter and the rapeseed oil in a large heavy-based frying pan over a medium heat and gently brown the chicken for 3–4 minutes, turning regularly. Remove from the pan, then leave to rest for about 5 minutes before trimming off both ends and cutting into 4 even-sized slices. Keep warm.

To sauté the chicken breasts, season them all over. Heat a large, non-stick, ovenproof frying pan over a medium heat. Add the butter and oil and once the butter stops sizzling, add the chicken pieces skin side down. Cook for 3 minutes on both sides, then transfer to the oven to finish cooking for 10–12 minutes, until just cooked through but still very moist. Remove from the oven and leave to rest for at least 5 minutes. Keep warm.

Meanwhile, cut each of the baby carrots into 3 pieces. Blanch in a pan of boiling water for 2–3 minutes, until tender. Drain and refresh under cold running water. Heat a frying pan with the butter over a medium heat. Add the baby carrot pieces and sauté for 1–2 minutes, until warmed through.

To serve, place the potato purée on warmed plates with the braised drumsticks and spoon over the sauce. Add the wilted spinach and carrot purée, then top with the chicken breast and slices of stuffed chicken thigh, respectively. Spoon the smoked bacon foam over the chicken breast to garnish. Add the baby carrot pieces.

COOK AHEAD

A lot of this dish can be prepared 24 hours in advance. The drumsticks can be braised and the thighs can be stuffed and poached. Keep both on a tray in the fridge, covered with clingfilm. The breast is best cooked to order.

WINE

A Sauvignon Blanc/Semillon blend from either Bordeaux or Australia would be great with these flavours. A good quality dry rosé would also work well.

TRIO OF MACNEAN CHICKEN WITH BABY CARROTS

Mum's Special Roast Chicken with Lemon, Garlic and Thyme

THIS RECIPE HAS BEEN COOKED IN OUR HOUSE FOR AS LONG AS I CAN REMEMBER, BUT NOW I'VE ADDED MY OWN TWIST AFTER BEING INSPIRED BY HESTON BLUMENTHAL. HE RECOMMENDS BRINING THE CHICKEN THE DAY BEFORE TO GUARANTEE A JUICY AND SUCCULENT BIRD EVERY TIME.

Serves 4

250g (9oz) fine sea salt

1.5kg (3lb) whole chicken

1 bunch fresh thyme sprigs

1 lemon

75g (3oz) butter, softened

2 garlic cloves, crushed

sea salt and freshly ground black pepper

8 small carrots, peeled

4 red onions, peeled and halved

2 celery sticks, chopped in half

1 leek, chopped in half

1 garlic bulb, broken into cloves (but not peeled)

3 tbsp rapeseed oil

1 tbsp plain flour

120ml (4fl oz) white wine

600ml (1 pint) chicken stock (page 253) or vegetable stock (page 252)

100g (4oz) baby carrots, scrubbed and halved lengthways

50g (2oz) fresh or frozen peas

1 tsp chopped fresh mint

roast potatoes (page 229), to serve

Dissolve the salt in a large pan with 3.9 litres (7 pints) water. Leave to cool, then place the chicken in a large container with the thyme, reserving 1 decent sprig to use later. Pour over enough of the brine to ensure the chicken is completely covered. Place in the fridge overnight, then remove the chicken from the liquid. Rinse under cold running water and pat dry with kitchen paper.

Preheat the oven to 230°C (450°F/gas mark 8).

Finely grate the rind from the lemon and place the rind in a bowl, reserving the lemon. Strip the thyme leaves from the stalks of the reserved thyme sprig (save the stalks) and add to the lemon rind. Mix most of the butter (reserving 1 teaspoon) with the crushed garlic, then season to taste.

Loosen the skin from the chicken breasts, starting at the cavity end and working your hand underneath to release. Spread the butter evenly under the skin and lay the skin back down on top. Slash the chicken legs several times with a sharp knife (this is to help ensure crispy skin once cooked).

Place the carrots, onions, celery, leek and garlic cloves in a roasting tin, tossing to coat in 1 tablespoon of the rapeseed oil. Sit the chicken on top of the vegetables and drizzle all over with the remaining oil, then season well, rubbing it all over and right into the slashes.

Cut the reserved lemon in half and put it inside the chicken's cavity with the reserved thyme stalks. Place the chicken in the oven and immediately reduce the heat to 200°C (400°F/gas mark 6). Roast the chicken for 1 hour 20 minutes, until the chicken is tender and cooked through, basting the chicken halfway through cooking.

When the chicken is cooked, remove from the oven and transfer the chicken to a board. Put the carrots and red onions on a warmed plate. Cover each with tin foil and leave to rest for 15 minutes while you make the gravy. Using a large spoon, carefully remove most of the fat from the tin, then place the tin directly on the heat. Stir in the flour, then holding the tin steady, mash up the remaining vegetables as much as possible with a potato masher to release their juices.

Pour the wine into the tin and allow it to bubble down, stirring continuously to blend the flour in. Pour in the stock and bring to the boil, then reduce the heat and simmer for about 10 minutes, stirring occasionally, until slightly reduced and thickened. Take a large jug and set a sieve into it, then pour in the gravy mixture and use a ladle to push all of the liquid and some of the vegetables through with the back of the spoon. Stir in the juices from the resting chicken and season to taste. Transfer to a warmed gravy boat.

Meanwhile, blanch the baby carrots and peas in a pan of boiling salted water for 3–4 minutes, until tender. Drain and refresh under cold running water. Heat the remaining 1 teaspoon of butter in a frying pan over a medium heat. Add the carrots and peas and toss until warmed through. Season to taste and add the mint, tossing to coat evenly. Keep warm.

To serve, carve the chicken into slices and arrange on warmed plates with the reserved carrots and red onion halves, the roast potatoes and buttered baby carrots and peas. Pour over the gravy to serve.

COOK AHEAD
The chicken needs to be brined 24 hours in advance. It can then be kept for another 24 hours on a plate covered with clingfilm in the fridge.

WINE
A ripe, buttery oaked Chardonnay from Australia or California will balance the citrus flavour. Roast chicken also never says no to a good Burgundy Pinot Noir.

Roast Woodcock with Creamed Spinach and Offal Croûte

WE ARE VERY LUCKY IN CAVAN TO GET A LOT OF GAME. FRANCIS MAGUIRE IS A LOCAL GUN CLUB MEMBER WHO LIVES ONLY 15 MINUTES FROM THE RESTAURANT. WOODCOCK IS ONE OF THE STARS OF THE SEASON AND WE HAVE ONE FRENCH CUSTOMER WHO COMES EVERY YEAR TO ENJOY THIS DISH.

Serves 4

4 whole woodcock

25g (1oz) butter

1 shallot, diced

1 garlic clove, crushed

1 tsp chopped fresh thyme, plus 4 sprigs

1 tbsp Cognac

1 tbsp Madeira

100ml (3 1/2fl oz) cream

1/2 tsp chopped fresh flat-leaf parsley

sea salt and freshly ground black pepper

4 streaky bacon rashers

2 tbsp rapeseed oil

creamed spinach (page 233), to serve

celeriac purée (page 244), to serve

caramelised baby onions (page 235), to serve

4 crispy potato rosti (page 228), to serve

garlic foam (page 245), to garnish

spinach purée (page 244), to garnish

4 bread croûtes (page 240), to serve

For the port jus:

200ml (7fl oz) beef stock (page 253)

2 tsp ruby red port

1 tsp chopped fresh thyme

2 tsp softened butter

50g (2oz) beech mushrooms, stalks trimmed

Preheat the oven to 200°C (400°F/gas mark 6).

Gut the woodcock and wash well under cold running water, reserving the liver, heart, kidneys and the intestines, which also can be kept as it is a very clean bird. Trim them down and finely chop the flesh or get your butcher to do this for you.

Melt the butter in a pan over a medium heat. Add the chopped offal, shallot, garlic and chopped thyme and sauté for 2 minutes. Sprinkle over the Cognac and Madeira and flambé, then add the cream and parsley and season to taste. Reduce the heat and simmer for 5 minutes, until reduced and slightly thickened. Keep warm.

Place a thyme sprig into the cavity of each woodcock, then wrap in a streaky bacon rasher. Heat a large ovenproof frying pan over a high heat and add the oil. Quickly sear the woodcocks for about 5 minutes, until golden, turning regularly with a tongs. Transfer to the oven and roast for another 5–8 minutes, until tender but still pink.

Meanwhile, to make the port jus, place the beef stock in a heavy-based pan and add the port and thyme. Mix well to combine and bring to the boil, then reduce the heat and simmer for 6–8 minutes, until you have achieved a sauce consistency. Heat the butter in a frying pan over a medium heat and sauté the beech mushrooms for 1–2 minutes, until just tender. Drain on kitchen paper and add to the jus at the last minute and allow to just warm through.

To serve, spoon the creamed spinach, celeriac purée and caramelised baby onions onto warmed plates and add the potato rosti. Remove the legs and breast from the woodcock, discarding the bacon, then arrange on the plates. Garnish with the garlic foam and spinach purée. Drizzle around the port jus with beech mushrooms. Put a bread croûte on the side of each plate and top with the offal mixture.

COOK AHEAD
The game mixture will keep in the fridge for 2 days covered with clingfilm.

WINE
This recipe calls for a strong, full-bodied red. Try a Salice Salentino or similar red from southern Italy. Another option would be a Côtes du Rhône Villages from France.

Sautéed Breast of Guinea Fowl and Stuffed Leg with Leeks and Girolle Mushrooms

THIS IS A GREAT WAY OF USING THE ENTIRE GUINEA FOWL, WHICH HAS A LOVELY FLAVOUR AND ISN'T TOO STRONG. IT'S AN EXCELLENT ALTERNATIVE TO CHICKEN AND VERY POPULAR FOR SUNDAY LUNCH. DON'T BE AFRAID TO ASK YOUR LOCAL CRAFT BUTCHER TO CUT IT INTO THE PORTIONS YOU NEED. I'M SURE THEY'LL BE HAPPY TO OBLIGE.

Serves 4

150g (5oz) girolle mushrooms, trimmed

3 tbsp rapeseed oil

50g (2oz) butter

25g (1oz) leeks, diced

1/4 tsp chopped fresh thyme

1 chicken breast fillet, skinned and diced

1 egg yolk

50ml (2fl oz) cream

1 tbsp chopped fresh mixed herbs (such as chives, basil and flat-leaf parsley)

sea salt and freshly ground black pepper

2 guinea fowl legs

4 guinea fowl breasts (skin on)

1 baby carrot

8 baby leeks

1 tsp clear honey

wilted Cos lettuce (page 232), to serve

spinach purée (page 244), to serve

mushroom foam (page 245), to garnish

red wine jus (page 261), to garnish

Pick out 16 small girolle mushrooms and trim down, then set aside. Dice the remaining 50g (2oz) mushrooms to add to the chicken mousse. Heat 1 tablespoon of the oil in a frying pan over a medium heat and add a knob of the butter. Once the butter stops sizzling, tip in the diced mushrooms, leeks and thyme. Sauté for 4–5 minutes, until the mushrooms are tender and softened. Remove from the heat and leave to cool completely.

To make the chicken mousse, place the chicken breast in a food processor with a pinch of salt and blend for 1 minute, then add the egg yolk and cream and blend for 3–5 minutes, until smooth. Spoon the chicken mousse into a bowl and stir in the leek and mushroom mixture until well mixed. Add the herbs and season to taste. Transfer to a bowl and cover with clingfilm, then chill for at least 1 hour to firm up.

To prepare the guinea fowl legs, place them on a clean work surface and using a sharp knife, carefully remove the bones. Put each boned leg between 2 sheets of clingfilm, leaving plenty of room between them. Use a rolling pin or meat mallet to flatten them out until each one is twice its original size and quite thin.

Remove the top layer of clingfilm from the flattened legs and place half of the chilled mousse stuffing on each leg, spooning the mixture lengthways down the centre. Roll the meat over the stuffing so that it forms a sausage shape. When rolled, wrap each leg tightly in oiled tin foil to keep its shape. Twist the ends of the tin foil so that it looks like a Christmas cracker. Chill in the fridge for at least 2 hours to firm up.

When ready to cook, bring a large, deep pan of water to a gentle simmer. Carefully lower in the stuffed legs, still wrapped in the tin foil, and cook for approximately 15–20 minutes, until they're firm to the touch. Remove from the water and set aside until needed.

Meanwhile, to cook the guinea fowl breasts, preheat the oven to 200°C (400°F/gas mark 6). Heat an ovenproof frying pan over a medium heat, then add 1 tablespoon of the oil and a knob of butter. Season the guinea fowl breasts and place in the heated frying pan, skin side down. Cook for 2–3 minutes on both sides, until golden brown. Transfer to the oven and cook for another 10–12 minutes, until just cooked through but still moist. Keep warm.

Peel off the tin foil from the cooked stuffed legs. Heat an ovenproof frying pan over a medium heat with the remaining tablespoon of oil and a knob of butter. Add the stuffed guinea fowl legs and gently brown for 4–5 minutes, until warmed through, turning regularly. Transfer to the oven and roast for another 8–10 minutes. Remove from the pan, then leave to rest for about 5 minutes before trimming off both ends. Cut each stuffed guinea fowl leg in half and keep warm.

Meanwhile, using a solferino spoon (6mm melon baller), make tiny carrot balls and blanch in a pan of boiling salted water for 2 minutes. Drain with a slotted spoon and quickly refresh under cold running water. Trim the baby leeks and cut each one into 3 x 2.5cm (1in) lengths. Blanch for 20–30 seconds, then drain and quickly refresh under cold running water.

Heat the remaining knob of butter in a frying pan over a medium heat and sauté the reserved girolle mushrooms for a few minutes, until almost tender. Add the blanched carrot balls and leeks and allow to just warm through. Drizzle over the honey and toss to glaze, then season to taste. Keep warm.

To serve, spoon the wilted Cos lettuce onto warmed plates and add a guinea fowl breast and a piece of stuffed leg to each one. Add the spinach purée and scatter over the girolles, carrot and leeks. Spoon over the mushroom foam and red wine jus.

COOK AHEAD
The stuffed legs can be prepared and poached 24 hours in advance. Arrange on a tray and cover with clingfilm until needed. Finish cooking to order.

WINE
French wines always seem perfect with game. With this recipe, try a St-Émilion or a cru Beaujolais Fleurie.

SAUTÉED BREAST OF GUINEA FOWL AND STUFFED LEG WITH LEEKS AND GIROLLE MUSHROOMS

Roast Goose with Cranberry and Apple Sausage Stuffing

THIS IS WHAT WE'D ALWAYS HAVE AT A FAMILY CHRISTMAS, SERVED WITH ALL THE TRIMMINGS. FREE-RANGE GEESE ARE NOW IN PLENTIFUL SUPPLY DURING THE FESTIVE PERIOD. MAKE SURE YOU SAVE THE DRAINED-OFF FAT AND USE IT TO MAKE CRISPY ROAST POTATOES.

Serves 8

6kg (12lb) oven-ready goose, at room temperature

1 tsp salt

2 tbsp redcurrant jelly

1 tbsp balsamic vinegar

1 tbsp ruby red port or red wine

finely grated rind of 1 orange

braised red cabbage (page 234), to serve

small bunch of fresh thyme, to garnish

honey and clove sauce (page 259), to serve

For the stuffing:

2 tbsp rapeseed oil

2 eating apples, peeled, cored and cut into thin slices

350g (12oz) sausage meat

100g (4oz) dried cranberries

100g (4oz) walnut halves, chopped

75g (3oz) fresh white breadcrumbs

1 tbsp chopped fresh thyme

sea salt and freshly ground black pepper

To make the stuffing, heat the oil in a large frying pan over a medium heat. Add the apples and sauté for 3–4 minutes, until softened and golden. Transfer to a bowl and leave to cool. Once cool, add the sausage meat, cranberries, walnuts, breadcrumbs and thyme, stirring gently until evenly mixed. Season to taste.

Preheat the oven to 200°C (400°F/gas mark 6).

Place the goose on a rack set over a roasting tin. Pour over a full kettle of boiling water, then drain off the water from the roasting tin. To stuff the goose, start at the neck end, where you'll find a flap of loose skin – gently loosen this away from the breast and you'll be able to make a triangular pocket. Pack two-thirds of the stuffing inside as far as you can go and make a neat round shape on the outside, then tuck the neck flap under the goose and secure it with a small skewer. Rub all over with the salt. Press the remaining stuffing into the base of a 225g (8oz) loaf tin and set aside.

Weigh the goose and calculate the cooking time, allowing 15 minutes per 450g (1lb) plus 15 minutes – a 6kg (12lb) goose should take about 3 1/2 hours. Place in the oven to roast, draining off excess fat every 30 minutes or so. After 1 hour, reduce the oven temperature to 180°C (350°F/gas mark 4). Continue to cook, still draining the fat off every half an hour.

Remove the goose from the oven 30 minutes before the end of the cooking time. Warm the redcurrant jelly, balsamic vinegar, port or wine and orange rind in a small pan. Bring to a simmer, stirring until the jelly dissolves, then cook for 4–5 minutes, until syrupy. Brush all over the goose. Return the goose to the oven with the reserved tin of extra stuffing and cook for the final 30 minutes, until completely tender. Transfer the goose to a serving platter and cover with foil, then leave to rest for 10 minutes. Spoon the cranberry and apple stuffing into a warmed bowl and keep warm.

To serve, garnish the roast goose with the thyme and bring to the table. Turn the tin of extra stuffing onto a warmed plate. Carve the goose into slices and arrange on warmed plates, discarding any excess fat. Add some of the stuffing to each plate with the braised red cabbage. Hand around a gravy boat of the honey and clove sauce and allow guests to help themselves.

COOK AHEAD
The stuffing can be made up to 2 days in advance and kept covered with clingfilm in the fridge.

WINE
With this recipe, you need a wine with plenty of acidity. An Alsace Riesling would work well, as would a Loire Valley red from Chinon or Bourgueil.

Turkey and Leek Stroganoff with Wild and Basmati Rice

FOR THOSE EVENINGS WHEN MY STAFF JUST WANT INSTANT COMFORT FOOD, YOU CAN'T GO FAR WRONG WITH THIS VARIATION ON AN OLD FAVOURITE. OBVIOUSLY THE TURKEY COULD BE SUBSTITUTED WITH CHICKEN OR BEEF DEPENDING ON WHAT TAKES YOUR FANCY.

Serves 4

225g (8oz) wild and basmati rice

1 tbsp sunflower oil

knob of butter

175g (6oz) chestnut mushrooms, sliced

1 garlic clove, crushed

450g (1lb) turkey breast steaks, cut into strips

2 small leeks, trimmed and sliced on the diagonal

1/4 tsp paprika, plus a little extra to garnish

sea salt and freshly ground black pepper

1 tbsp white wine vinegar

150ml (1/4 pint) chicken stock (page 253)

4 tbsp dry white wine

2 tsp tomato purée

1 tsp Dijon mustard

4 tbsp soured cream

1 tbsp chopped fresh basil

Bring a large pan of water to the boil. Add the rice and return to the boil, then give it a good stir and turn down to a low heat. Cook for the length of time given on the packet instructions – they all vary.

Heat a large frying pan over a medium heat. Add the oil and butter and once the butter stops foaming, add the mushrooms and garlic. Sauté for 2–3 minutes, until just tender. Scatter in the turkey and leeks, then sprinkle in the paprika and cook for another minute or two, stirring, until just sealed. Season to taste.

Add the white wine vinegar and allow it to bubble right down, then add the stock, wine, tomato purée and mustard and simmer for a few minutes, stirring occasionally, until reduced by half. Stir the soured cream into the pan, bring to a simmer, then reduce the heat and simmer gently for a couple of minutes. Cook until the sauce has thickened and slightly reduced and the turkey is tender but still moist. Stir in the basil.

To serve, divide the cooked rice among warmed plates and spoon the turkey and leek stroganoff alongside. Finish with a light dusting of paprika to serve.

COOK AHEAD:
This could be made up to 24 hours in advance and kept covered in the fridge. Reheat gently in a frying pan to serve.

WINE
A ripe Chardonnay from the south of France or a Côtes du Rhône red would be a good match.

Meat
Tasting of Irish Lamb
(Herb-crusted Loin, Confit of Neck and Sweetbreads)

WE ARE VERY LUCKY TO GET ALL OUR LAMB DIRECT FROM RING OF KERRY LAMB. LAMB NECK IS ONE OF THE MOST UNDERRATED CUTS OF LAMB, AS PEOPLE ONLY THINK OF USING IT IN A STEW, BUT IT TURNS INTO SOMETHING QUITE MAGICAL DURING THE CONFIT PROCESS. YOU CAN ALSO CONFIT THE SHOULDER OR SHANK WITH EXCELLENT RESULTS.

Serves 4

For the confit neck of lamb:

1 lamb neck, trimmed (about 225g (8oz) in total)

3 garlic cloves, sliced

2 fresh thyme sprigs

2 fresh rosemary sprigs

600ml (1 pint) duck fat

1 tbsp rapeseed oil

knob of butter

For the herb-crusted loin:

150ml (1/4 pint) rapeseed oil

2 garlic cloves, crushed

1 tbsp chopped fresh rosemary

1 tbsp Dijon mustard

2 x 500g (1lb 2oz) lamb loins, well trimmed

50g (2oz) white breadcrumbs

2 tbsp chopped fresh mixed herbs (such as mint, basil and flat-leaf parsley)

egg wash (made with 1 egg and 1 tbsp milk), for brushing

Preheat the oven to 130°C (275°F/gas mark 1).

To make the confit, place the lamb neck in a small casserole dish with the garlic, herbs and duck fat. Cover with foil and cook in the oven for 3 hours, until completely tender but still holding its shape. Leave to sit in the duck fat to rest. When cooled, remove the lamb and pat dry with the kitchen paper, then roll tightly with tin foil to create a round cylinder shape about 2.5cm (1in) in diameter and 12.5cm (5in) long. Place in the fridge overnight to firm up.

To marinate the lamb loins, mix the oil in a shallow non-metallic dish with the garlic, rosemary and mustard. Add the lamb, turning to coat, then cover with clingfilm and chill overnight to allow the flavours to combine.

To prepare the herb crust, place the breadcrumbs in a food processor with the mixed herbs and blend for 5 minutes, until green and fragrant. Remove the lamb loin from the marinade and wipe off any excess with kitchen paper, then brush over the egg wash and press on a thick layer of the breadcrumbs. Put on a plate and chill until needed.

Rinse the sweetbreads very well under cold running water, then place in a pan with the milk. Add the onion, carrot, peppercorns, thyme and bay leaf. Place on a low heat and bring to a gentle simmer, then remove from the heat and set aside to cool down completely.

Strain the liquid from the sweetbreads and discard. Using a small, sharp knife, clean away the outer membrane and any sinew. Cut the sweetbreads into quarters and season with salt, then coat in the seasoned flour, shaking off any excess. Dip in the egg wash, then roll in the breadcrumbs until well coated. Put on a plate and cover with clingfilm and chill until needed.

To roast the herb-crusted loins, preheat the oven to 200°C (400°F/gas mark 6). Allow the lamb to come back to room temperature, then arrange on a roasting tin with a wire rack. Roast for 8–10 minutes, until the crusts are golden and the lamb is medium rare. Leave to rest for 15 minutes, then carve each one in half.

For the sweetbreads:

50g (2oz) lamb sweetbreads, soaked in cold salted water overnight in the fridge

100ml (3 1/2fl oz) milk

1/2 onion, sliced

1/2 carrot, sliced

3 black peppercorns

2 fresh thyme sprigs

1 bay leaf

sea salt

25g (1oz) seasoned plain flour

egg wash (made with 1 egg and 1 tbsp milk), for dipping

100g (4oz) fresh white breadcrumbs

groundnut oil, for deep-frying

For the baby carrots:

8 baby carrots, trimmed and peeled

1 tsp softened butter

1/2 tsp chopped fresh flat-leaf parsley

sea salt and freshly ground black pepper

2 onion tart tatin, halved (page 235), to serve

pea and mint purée (page 242), to serve

garlic confit (page 236), to garnish

rosemary jus (page 260), to garnish

garlic foam (page 245), to garnish

While the lamb is in the oven, trim the ends off the lamb neck confit and then cut into 4 x 2.5cm (1in) thick pieces and remove the tin foil. Heat a large frying pan over a medium heat and add the oil and butter. Once the butter is sizzling, add the lamb pieces and cook for 2–3 minutes on each side, until crisp and golden brown.

Blanch the baby carrots for 3–4 minutes in a pan of boiling salted water. Drain and quickly refresh under cold running water. Heat the butter in a frying pan over a medium heat and add the carrots to just warm through. Tip in the parsley and toss until evenly coated. Season to taste.

To cook the sweetbreads, heat the oil until it reaches 190°C (350°F) in a deep-fat fryer or deep-sided pan. Deep-fry for about 2 minutes, until golden brown, then drain on kitchen paper and keep warm.

To serve, arrange a piece of lamb loin, confit and sweetbread on each warmed plate with half an onion tart tatin. Add the pea purée to each plate and garnish with the garlic confit, rosemary jus and garlic foam.

COOK AHEAD

A lot of preparation can be done in advance. The confit of neck and sweetbreads can be made up to 2 days in advance and the loins can be marinated overnight. Just make sure that everything is well covered and chilled and never mix cooked and raw meats together on the same tray.

WINE

Rioja Reserve goes well with almost all lamb dishes. Alternatively, try a Nebbiolo wine from Piedmont, Italy, such as Barolo or Barbaresco.

TASTING OF IRISH LAMB

Braised Shoulder of Lamb with Mediterranean Couscous

A VERSION OF THIS DISH OFTEN MAKES AN APPEARANCE ON OUR SUNDAY LUNCH MENU OR I HAVE IT AS AN ELEMENT ON A TASTING PLATE OF IRISH LAMB. I JUST LOVE TO SHOWCASE THE VERSATILITY OF LAMB. MAKE SURE YOU ASK YOUR LOCAL BUTCHER TO TRIM, BONE AND ROLL THE SHOULDER FOR YOU SO THAT YOU END UP WITH A NICE SHAPE FOR PRESENTATION.

Serves 4

3 tbsp rapeseed oil

675g (1 1/2lb) boned lamb shoulder, rolled and tied at intervals with string

2 carrots, diced

2 celery sticks, diced

1 leek, diced

1 onion, diced

3 garlic cloves, finely chopped

1.2 litres (2 pints) beef stock (page 253)

600ml (1 pint) red wine

2 fresh thyme sprigs

2 fresh rosemary sprigs

1 tbsp tomato purée

sea salt and freshly ground black pepper

2 tbsp Madeira

1 tbsp balsamic vinegar

1 tsp light brown sugar

knob of butter

Mediterranean couscous (page 238), to serve

oven-dried cherry tomatoes (page 237), to garnish

caramelised baby onions (page 235), to garnish

red pepper gel (page 247), to garnish

fresh micro coriander, to garnish

Preheat the oven to 160°C (325°F/gas mark 3).

Heat 1 tablespoon of the oil in a large frying pan over a medium heat. Add the lamb shoulder and brown all over for 6–8 minutes, turning regularly with tongs. Add the carrots, celery, leek, onion and garlic and cook for another 10 minutes, until the vegetables are golden brown.

Place the lamb and vegetables in a large, deep roasting tin. Cover with the stock, red wine, herbs and tomato purée. Season to taste, then cover with foil and cook in the oven for 3 hours, until the lamb is really tender. Leave to cool completely and rest in the juices.

Once it has cooled, remove the lamb from the pan. Strain the juices into a clean bowl and discard the vegetables. Cover the juices and keep in the fridge until needed. Cut off the string, then tightly roll the lamb in a double layer of tin foil to create a firm sausage shape. When cold, place in the fridge overnight to firm up.

Place the reserved braising juices in a pan and add in the Madeira, vinegar and sugar. Bring to the boil and cook for 25–30 minutes, until reduced by half to a sauce consistency. Season to taste and keep warm.

When ready to serve, remove the tin foil from the lamb cylinder and trim off the ends, then carve into 4 x 5cm (2in) slices. Heat a large frying pan over a medium heat and add the remaining 2 tablespoons of the oil and the knob of butter. Once the butter stops sizzling, add the lamb pieces and cook for 2–3 minutes on each side, until crisp and golden brown and nicely warmed through.

To serve, spoon the Mediterranean couscous onto each warmed plate using a 9cm (3 3/4in) cooking ring. Place the crispy braised lamb on top and spoon over the braising jus. Garnish each plate with the oven-dried cherry tomatoes, caramelised baby onions, red pepper gel and micro coriander.

COOK AHEAD
This whole dish can be prepared up to 2 days in advance. The shoulder is best cooked at least the day before so that it can be rolled really tight to give the joint a good shape.

WINE
Try a Côtes du Rhône from Rasteau or Gigondas, or a Cabernet Sauvignon-based wine from Bordeaux.

Rump of Local Lamb with Pea Purée and Rosemary Jus

WE OFTEN PUT THIS ON OUR SUNDAY LUNCH MENU WHEN LAMB IS IN SEASON, AS IT IS A DELICIOUS CUT OF MEAT THAT OFFERS GOOD VALUE. WE HAVE JUST STARTED GROWING BROAD BEANS, WHICH I'M EVERY EXCITED ABOUT. A LITTLE GOES A LONG WAY AND THEY ADD AN EXTRA DIMENSION TO THE ROSEMARY JUS.

Serves 4

150ml (1/4 pint) rapeseed oil

2 garlic cloves, crushed

1 fresh rosemary sprig

1 tsp Dijon mustard

4 x 150g (5oz) lamb rumps, trimmed

sea salt and freshly ground black pepper

50g (2oz) peeled broad beans (fresh or frozen)

100ml (3 1/2fl oz) rosemary jus (page 260)

wilted Cos lettuce (page 232), to serve

8 slices of red pepper polenta (page 237), to serve

pea purée (page 242), to serve

carrot purée (page 244), to serve

caramelised baby onions (page 235), to serve

smoked garlic foam (page 245), to garnish

To make the marinade, place the rapeseed oil, garlic, rosemary and Dijon mustard in a non-metallic container and mix well. Add in the lamb rumps and massage the oil mixture into the lamb. Cover with clingfilm and leave to marinate in the fridge for at least 2 hours, or overnight if possible.

Preheat the oven to 180°C (350°F/gas mark 4).

Remove the lamb from the fridge 20 minutes before you plan to cook it. Take the lamb out of the marinade, shaking off any excess. Heat an ovenproof frying pan over a medium heat and add 1 tablespoon of oil from the marinade. Season the lamb rumps and add to the heated frying pan. Cook for 2–3 minutes, turning regularly, until golden brown.

Transfer the lamb to the oven and cook for 8–10 minutes, until the lamb is still pink. If you prefer your meat more well done, leave it for another 8–10 minutes. Remove the lamb from the oven and cover loosely with tin foil. Set aside in a warm place for about 10 minutes to rest.

Blanch the broad beans in a pan of boiling salted water for 1–2 minutes, until just tender. Drain and quickly refresh under cold running water, then pop the beans out of their outer skins. Warm the rosemary jus in a small pan, then stir in the broad beans and allow to warm through. Keep warm.

To serve, spoon the wilted Cos into the centre of each warmed plate and arrange 2 pieces of red pepper polenta alongside. Add the pea purée, carrot purée and caramelised baby onions to each plate. Slice the lamb rumps in two and add to the plate cut side up, then pour over the rosemary jus with broad beans and finish with smoked garlic foam.

COOK AHEAD
The lamb can be marinated up to 2 days in advance.

WINE
Try a ripe New Zealand Pinot Noir with this dish. A Chianti Classico would also be a very good partner.

Assiette of Rare-breed Pork
(Caramelised Belly, Smoked Bacon-wrapped Fillet and Pork and Leek Sausage)

WE ALWAYS USE RARE BREED SADDLEBACK PORK, WHICH REALLY HAS THE MOST WONDERFUL FLAVOUR. THERE ARE LOTS OF CRAFT BUTCHERS NOW MAKING THEIR OWN SAUSAGES.

Serves 4

For the pork belly:

2 tbsp rapeseed oil

1.5kg (3lb) pork belly, boned and rolled and tied

2 carrots, cut into chunks

1 onion, roughly chopped

2 garlic cloves, peeled

1.2 litres (2 pints) beef stock (page 253)

600ml (1 pint) red wine

600ml (1 pint) freshly pressed apple juice

2 fresh thyme sprigs

2 fresh rosemary sprigs

sea salt and freshly ground black pepper

1 tsp softened butter

2 tbsp runny honey

2 tbsp dark soy sauce

For the pork fillet and sausages:

4 tbsp sun-dried tomato pesto (page 257)

350g (12oz) pork fillet, well trimmed

8–10 smoked bacon rashers, rinds removed and very thinly sliced

1 tbsp rapeseed oil

1 tsp softened butter

4 pork and leek sausages

carrot purée (page 244), to serve

apple gel (page 247), to garnish

apple chutney (page 249), to garnish

honey and clove sauce (page 259), to serve

smoked bacon foam (page 246), to garnish

Preheat the oven to 180°C (350°F/gas mark 4).

To prepare the pork belly, heat 1 tablespoon of the rapeseed oil in a large frying pan over a medium heat. Add the pork belly and brown all over, turning with tongs. Add the carrots, onion and garlic and cook for another 5 minutes, until golden brown.

Place the pork belly and vegetables in a casserole dish with a lid and pour in the stock, wine and apple juice. Add the herbs and season to taste, then cover with foil and the lid. Roast for 3 hours, until the pork is meltingly tender. When the pork belly is cooked, leave it to cool, then remove and cut off the string. Wrap tightly in a double sheet of tin foil, twisting the ends to form a good sausage shape. Place in the fridge overnight to firm up.

To prepare the pork fillet, smear the pesto all over the fillet, then wrap it in the smoked bacon. If it's not keeping together properly, roll it tightly in clingfilm. Leave to infuse overnight in the fridge.

The next day, preheat the oven to 180°C (350°F/gas mark 4). Cut the wrapped pork fillet into 4 portions and then carefully remove the clingfilm before cooking.

Heat a large ovenproof frying pan over a medium heat and add the oil and butter. Add the pork fillet portions and cook for 2–3 minutes, until golden, turning once. Transfer to a plate. Add the sausages to the same pan and cook for 5 minutes, until lightly golden, then return the pork fillet to the pan and transfer to the oven. Roast for 8–10 minutes, until the pork portions are cooked through and the sausages are tender and golden brown. Remove from the oven and leave to rest for 5 minutes in a warm place, then trim off the ends of the sausages to neaten.

Meanwhile, cut the braised pork belly into 4 x 2cm (3/4in) slices, trimming off the edges if necessary. Heat a large frying pan over a medium heat and add the remaining 1 tablespoon of oil and the butter. Add in the pieces of pork belly, skin side down, and cook for 1 minute on each side, until light golden. Drizzle over the honey and soy sauce, reduce the heat and simmer gently for 6–8 minutes, until caramelised and completely warmed through, turning and basting regularly.

To serve, place the carrot purée on each warmed plate and add a piece of caramelised pork belly, wrapped pork fillet and pork and leek sausage. Garnish each plate with the apple gel, apple chutney, honey and clove sauce and smoked bacon foam.

COOK AHEAD
The pork belly can be braised and shaped up to 2 days in advance and the pork fillet can be prepared ready to cook for the same amount of time. Remember to keep cooked and raw meats completely separate in the fridge.

WINE
A soft, juicy Cabernet Franc wine from Chinon or Bourgueil in the Loire Valley, France, or a ripe, spicy Zinfandel from California.

Fillet of Dry-aged Beef with Braised Blade and Celeriac Purée

BEEF IS OUR NUMBER ONE SELLER IN THE RESTAURANT AND WE SELL MORE FILLET THAN ANY OTHER CUT. HOWEVER, I'VE RECENTLY DISCOVERED THE BLADE OF BEEF, WHICH HAS AN EXCELLENT FLAVOUR AND OFFERS GREAT VALUE. FIRST WE BRAISE IT BEFORE SHAPING AND LEAVING OVERNIGHT TO FIRM UP, WHICH CREATES A LOVELY ROUND FOR PRESENTATION.

Serves 4

For the beef fillet:

4 x 175g (6oz) dry-aged beef fillets

1 tablespoon rapeseed oil

15g (1/2oz) butter

sea salt and freshly ground black pepper

For the braised blade:

4 tbsp rapeseed oil

400g (14oz) piece of beef blade, well trimmed

2 carrots, cut into chunks

1 onion, roughly chopped

2 garlic cloves, crushed

900ml (1 1/2 pints) beef stock (page 253)

300ml (1/2 pint) red wine

2 fresh thyme sprigs

2 fresh rosemary sprigs

sea salt and freshly ground black pepper

1 tsp softened butter

Preheat the oven to 180°C (350°F/gas mark 4).

To prepare the braised blade, heat 1 tablespoon of the oil in a large casserole dish with a lid. Add the beef blade and brown all over for 3–4 minutes, turning regularly with tongs. Transfer to a plate. Add another tablespoon of oil to the casserole, reduce the heat a little and add the carrots, onion and garlic. Cook for a further 5 minutes, stirring, until golden brown.

Return the beef blade and any juices to the casserole and pour over the beef stock and red wine. Add the herbs and season to taste, then bring to the boil. Cover tightly with foil and a lid. Cook for 3 hours, until the beef is meltingly tender. Carefully remove the beef from the braising juices and leave to rest on a warmed plate covered with foil.

Strain the braising juices into a clean pan and bring to the boil, then reduce the heat and simmer for 25–30 minutes, until reduced by half to a sauce consistency. Leave to cool and place in an airtight container in the fridge until needed.

When the beef blade has cooled slightly, shred it into pieces on a double layer of clingfilm, removing any fat, and make into a thick sausage shape. Roll up tightly to create a sausage shape about 5cm (2in) thick, tying the ends really tightly to make a good, firm shape. Place in the fridge overnight to firm up.

To prepare the garnishes, heat a large non-stick frying pan over a medium heat. When hot, add the bacon and cook until crisp and golden, turning once. Drain on kitchen paper and then dice very finely and place in a bowl. Next add the bread dice to the unwashed bacon pan and sauté until golden. Tip into the bowl with the bacon and add the chives, then mix well to combine. Set aside until needed.

Using a small melon baller (2cm/3/4in), make 8 balls of the carrot and 16 balls of the celeriac. Using a mandolin, cut the rest of the celeriac and carrot into thin slices and stamp out 8 x 2.5cm (1in) rounds from each. Place the carrot and celeriac balls in a pan of boiling salted water and cook for 4 minutes, adding the thin rounds for the last minute. Remove with a slotted spoon and drain, then quickly refresh under cold running water. Heat the butter in a frying pan over a medium heat and add the vegetable balls and rounds for 1–2 minutes, until heated through. Season to taste.

For the garnishes:

1 smoked streaky bacon rasher, rind removed

1 slice of white bread, crusts removed and very finely diced

1/2 tsp snipped fresh chives

1 large carrot

1/2 celeriac

1 tsp softened butter

sea salt and freshly ground black pepper

12 large spinach leaves

celeriac purée (page 244), to serve

4 tbsp mushroom foam (page 245), to garnish

Take a 2.5cm (1in) straight-sided cutter and stamp out 12 circles of spinach. Arrange on a plate and cover with clingfilm. Chill until needed. This will be used as a garnish for the beef.

To cook the beef fillets, allow them to come to room temperature. Meanwhile, preheat the oven to 200°C (400°F/gas mark 6).

Heat a large ovenproof frying pan over a medium heat and add the rapeseed oil and butter. Season the steaks and once the butter stops sizzling, add them to the pan. Sear for 2–3 minutes on each side, then transfer to the oven for 5 minutes for medium or 10–12 minutes for well done. Leave to rest in a warm place for at least 10 minutes.

Meanwhile, finish preparing the beef blade. Trim off the ends and then cut into 4 even-sized pieces that are each about 2cm (3/4in) and carefully remove the cling film. Heat a frying pan over a medium heat and add the remaining 2 tablespoons of the oil and the butter. Once the butter stops sizzling, add the pieces of beef blade to the pan and cook for 2 minutes on each side, until golden brown and crispy and completely warmed through.

Place a spoonful of the reserved bacon and crouton mixture on top of each beef blade piece and keep warm. Place the reserved reduced braising juices in a pan and allow to warm through for the sauce.

To serve, spoon some celeriac purée into the centre of each warmed plate and add a piece of the garnished beef blade and the beef fillet to each one. Garnish with the celeriac and carrot balls and rounds and the circles of spinach. Spoon over the sauce and mushroom foam.

COOK AHEAD
The braised beef blade can be made up to 2 days in advance but must be prepared at least 24 hours in advance to achieve a good shape. The sauce can also be prepared at the same time.

WINE
For a fillet of beef, choose the best bottle of Cabernet Sauvignon-based Claret from Bordeaux or a great bottle of Syrah from Hermitage, Rhône Valley.

FILLET OF DRY-AGED BEEF WITH BRAISED BLADE AND CELERIAC PURÉE

Peppered Steak with Gratin Potatoes and Whiskey Sauce

THIS IS THE ORIGINAL CLASSIC DISH THAT MY MUM HAS MADE FOR YEARS IN THE RESTAURANT. ALL OUR BEEF IS DRY AGED FOR 28 DAYS, GIVING A FABULOUS DEPTH OF FLAVOUR. IN MY OPINION IT'S IMPOSSIBLE TO BEAT THIS COMBINATION AND IT'S A DISH THAT I OFTEN DO WHEN I DO COOKERY DEMONSTRATIONS AROUND THE COUNTRY.

Serves 4

1 tbsp rapeseed oil

4 x 150g (5oz) sirloin or striploin steaks

1/4 tsp cracked black pepper

sea salt

gratin potatoes (page 230), to serve

watercress purée (page 244), to serve

fresh tiny watercress leaves, to garnish

For the whiskey sauce:

25g (1oz) butter

1 tbsp rapeseed oil

150g (5oz) button mushrooms, trimmed and sliced

1 shallot, finely chopped

120ml (4fl oz) Irish whiskey

150ml (1/4 pint) white wine

150ml (1/4 pint) beef stock (page 253)

150ml (1/4 pint) cream

1 tbsp Worcestershire sauce

good pinch of sugar

1 tbsp chopped fresh flat-leaf parsley

squeeze of fresh lemon juice

sea salt and freshly ground black pepper

Preheat the oven to 180°C (350°F/gas mark 4).

To make the sauce, heat a pan and add the butter and oil then swirl until the butter has melted and is foaming. Tip in the mushrooms and shallot and sauté for 2–3 minutes, until tender. Pour over the whiskey, then use a match or tilt up the pan to catch the flame. It will flare up for 5–10 seconds and then subside when the alcohol burns off. Add the white wine, stirring to combine, then simmer until reduced by half.

Stir the stock into the pan with the cream, Worcestershire sauce and sugar. Bring to the boil, then reduce the heat and simmer for 20–25 minutes, stirring occasionally, until thickened and reduced to a sauce consistency that will coat the back of a wooden spoon. Stir in the parsley and lemon juice and season to taste. Keep warm.

Heat the rapeseed oil in a heavy-based ovenproof frying pan over a high heat. Season the steaks with the black pepper and cook for 2 minutes on each side to seal in the juices, then transfer to the oven and cook the steak for another 5–10 minutes, turning once, depending on how rare you like your meat (5 minutes for rare, 7 for medium and 10 for well done).

To serve, transfer the cooked steak to warmed serving plates, season with salt and set aside in a warm place to rest while you assemble the dish. Pour any juices that run off the meat into your whiskey sauce for added flavour. Drizzle the whiskey sauce around the steaks and add the gratin potatoes and watercress purée. Garnish with the watercress leaves.

COOK AHEAD
Use the pepper sauce immediately or allow to cool down completely and store in a bowl covered with clingfilm in the fridge for up to 2 days. Reheat gently in a pan when needed.

WINE
A good-quality Malbec from Argentina or a Côtes du Rhône would match these robust flavours.

Roast Rib of Beef on the Bone with Yorkshire Puddings and Horseradish Cream

THIS DISH IS AN ALL-TIME SUNDAY LUNCH FAVOURITE IN THE RESTAURANT AND IS ALWAYS FIRST TO SELL OUT. THE KEY TO ITS SUCCESS IS TO START WITH A FANTASTIC PIECE OF BEEF THAT HAS BEEN HUNG FOR 21 DAYS TO IMPROVE THE FLAVOUR AND TEXTURE.

Serves 6–8

1 tsp dried thyme

1 tsp dried basil

1 tsp sweet paprika

1 tsp garlic salt

1/2 tsp cayenne pepper

1/2 tsp English mustard powder

2.25kg (5lb) piece of beef fore-rib (rib-eye), on the bone

2 tbsp Dijon mustard

3 tbsp olive oil

1 onion, roughly chopped

1 carrot, roughly chopped

1 leek, roughly chopped

sea salt and freshly ground black pepper

3 tbsp dripping (such as from a previous roast) or olive oil

150ml (1/4 pint) red wine

600ml (1 pint) beef stock (page 253)

horseradish cream (page 257), to serve

Yorkshire puddings (page 241), to serve

wilted spinach (page 233), to serve

Place the thyme, basil, paprika, garlic salt, cayenne and mustard powder in a bowl and mix to combine. Wipe the meat with damp kitchen paper, then spread a thin layer of the Dijon mustard all over the fat side of the joint. Sprinkle the spice powder on top, patting it down gently to help it stick. If you have time, wrap loosely in clingfilm and allow the beef to marinate overnight.

Preheat the oven to 200°C (400°F/gas mark 6) and allow the beef to come back to room temperature.

Pour the olive oil into a roasting tin and allow to heat in the oven for 5 minutes. Add the onion, carrot and leek, tossing to coat them in the oil. Season to taste and roast for 20 minutes, until lightly caramelised.

Increase the oven temperature to 230°C (450°F/gas mark 8). Heat a large, heavy-based frying pan over a medium heat. Add the dripping or olive oil, and when it's hot, quickly sear the beef for about 30 seconds on each side – be careful, as the spices will give off a strong aroma and can make your eyes water. Transfer the beef to the roasting tin, placing it on the bed of vegetables.

Add the red wine to the frying pan and allow it to bubble down to burn off the alcohol, then pour into the roasting tin with half of the stock. Roast the beef for 15 minutes, until well sealed, then reduce the oven temperature to 200°C (400°F/gas mark 6) once again and roast for 10 minutes per 450g (1lb) for rare, 12 minutes per 450g (1lb) for medium rare or 20–25 minutes per 450g (1lb) for well done. Baste the roast with the red wine and stock every 10 minutes or so during cooking. When it's done, remove the beef from the tin and place on a large dish. Allow to rest in a warm place for at least 10–15 minutes before carving.

To make the gravy, pour the remaining stock into the roasting tin and place directly on the hob to heat. Simmer for 5 minutes, stirring and scraping the bottom with a wooden spoon to release any sediment. Season and pour through a sieve into a gravy boat.

To serve, carve the beef into slices and arrange on warmed plates with a dollop of horseradish cream, the Yorkshire puddings and wilted spinach. Hand round the gravy boat separately.

COOK AHEAD
The beef can be marinated up to
2 days in advance.

WINE
Try a big, full-bodied Shiraz or Cabernet
Sauvignon from Alsace with this dish.

Stout-braised Shoulder of Pork with Potato and Apple Purée

THIS RECIPE TURNS A REASONABLY PRICED CUT OF PORK INTO SOMETHING SPECIAL. IT WOULD MAKE THE BASIS FOR A FANTASTIC DINNER PARTY OR SUNDAY LUNCH, LEAVING VERY LITTLE TO DO LAST MINUTE. IT WOULD ALSO BE DELICIOUS SERVED WITH CREAMED CABBAGE (PAGE 233).

Serves 6

For the caramelised shoulder:

2 tbsp rapeseed oil

900g (2lb) pork shoulder, boned and rolled and tied

2 carrots, diced

1 onion, diced

1.2 litres (2 pints) beef stock (page 253)

600ml (1 pint) stout

600ml (1 pint) freshly pressed apple juice

2 garlic cloves, crushed

2 fresh thyme sprigs

4 tbsp light soy sauce

4 tbsp clear honey

1 tsp freshly grated root ginger

apple and potato purée (page 229), to serve

smoked bacon foam (page 246), to garnish

For the stout jus:

2 tbsp balsamic vinegar

1 tsp dark brown sugar

1 tsp tomato purée

1 tsp chopped fresh thyme

sea salt and freshly ground black pepper

Preheat the oven to 160°C (325°F/gas mark 3).

To prepare the shoulder, heat 1 tablespoon of the rapeseed oil in a heavy-based frying pan. Add the pork shoulder and brown all over, turning regularly with tongs. Transfer to a casserole dish. Add the carrots and onion and cook for another 5 minutes, until golden brown, stirring regularly to ensure they cook evenly.

Tip the vegetables over the seared pork shoulder, then stir in the beef stock, stout, apple juice, garlic and thyme. Cover tightly with a lid or with foil and bake for 3 hours, until the pork shoulder is meltingly tender. Remove from the oven and leave to sit for 1 hour in the braising juices, then remove the pork from the tin, cut the string and wrap twice in tin foil. Strain the braising juices and reserve to add to the stout jus. All this is best done 24 hours in advance so that everything can be well chilled down in the fridge. Any excess fat can then be easily removed from the braising juices and discarded.

To make the stout jus, place the balsamic vinegar in a heavy-based pan with the brown sugar, tomato purée and thyme. Reduce by half, then add the reserved braising juice and simmer for 25–30 minutes, stirring occasionally, until reduced to a sauce consistency. Season to taste, then pass through a fine sieve into a clean pan and keep warm or reheat as needed.

Remove the foil from the cooked pork shoulder and trim off the ends to neaten, then slice into 6 pieces that are about 2.5cm (1in) thick. Heat the remaining 1 tablespoon of oil in an ovenproof pan over a low to medium heat and gently sear the pork for 2 minutes on each side, until golden brown and warmed through. Mix together the soy sauce, honey and ginger and pour it over the seared pork shoulder. Cook for another 4–5 minutes to caramelise and sweeten the pork.

Place a large spoonful of the apple and potato purée in the centre of each warmed bowl and carefully arrange the caramelised shoulder on top. Drizzle over the stout jus and garnish with the smoked bacon foam to serve.

COOK AHEAD
This dish must be made in advance and will keep happily in the fridge for up to 3 days.

WINE
An off-dry German Riesling is a great balance for the hint of sweetness with pork, while a red option is a Beaujolais from Fleurie or Moulin-à-Vent.

Loin of Venison with Quinoa and Spinach

WE USE ONE-YEAR-OLD DEER FROM FINNEBROGUE, WHICH IS ALWAYS TENDER BUT NEVER VERY STRONG IN TASTE. IT'S POPULAR WITH CUSTOMERS, AS IT'S CONSIDERED A LEAN AND HEALTHY OPTION, WHICH IS WHY I'VE CHOSEN TO SERVE IT WITH SOME QUINOA. THIS NUTTY FLAVOURED SUPERFOOD IS THE MOST COMPLETE PROTEIN OF ANY GRAIN AND A FANTASTIC SOURCE OF MAGNESIUM.

Serves 4

4 x 100g (4oz) venison loins, well trimmed

sea salt and freshly ground black pepper

1 tbsp rapeseed oil

1 tsp softened butter

12 spinach leaves

quinoa (page 239), to serve

beetroot purée (page 245), to serve

spinach purée (page 244), to serve

8 sweet potato fondants (page 231), to serve

apple gel (page 247), to garnish

mushroom foam (page 245), to garnish

Preheat the oven to 180°C (350°F/gas mark 4).

Season the venison all over. Heat a large ovenproof frying pan until very hot. Add the oil until smoking and then cook the venison loins for 2 minutes on each side, until browned. Add the butter to the venison and allow to melt, then transfer to the oven and cook for another 6–8 minutes for medium, turning once (leave it a little longer if you prefer your meat more well done). Remove from the oven and keep warm while leaving to rest for at least 5 minutes, then carve each one in half lengthways.

Meanwhile, using a straight-sided cutter, stamp out 2.5cm (1in) circles from the spinach and set aside until needed.

To serve, shape quenelles of the quinoa on each warmed plate. Add the beetroot and spinach purées with the sweet potato fondants. Add the spinach circles and then arrange the venison on top. Add the apple gel and spoon over the mushroom foam.

WINE
Barolo or Barbaresco, made from Nebbiolo grapes in north-west Italy, are great partners with venison. A good-quality Tempranillo wine from northern Spain would also work well.

Vegetables
Celeriac and Baby Carrot Risotto with Sherry Vinegar Caramel and Crispy Potato Rosti

RISOTTO IS ALWAYS A POPULAR DISH IN THE RESTAURANT AND WE USUALLY HAVE A VERSION ON THE MENU. THE SHERRY VINEGAR CARAMEL WORKS WELL WITH THE VEGETABLES AND CRISPY POTATO ROSTI. IT'S A COMBINATION I FIRST TRIED ON A TRIP TO ROME WITH MY CHEFS. THEY SAVE UP ALL THE TIPS AND USE THEM TO EAT IN SOME OF THE BEST RESTAURANTS IN THE WORLD.

Serves 4

8 baby carrots, peeled and cut into 1cm (1/2in) slices

3 tbsp rapeseed oil

2 fresh thyme sprigs

sea salt and freshly ground black pepper

300g (11oz) celeriac, peeled and finely diced

850ml (1 pint 9fl oz) vegetable stock (page 252)

1 large shallot, finely diced

1 garlic clove, crushed

200g (7oz) risotto rice, such as Arborio or Carnaroli

100ml (3 1/2fl oz) dry white wine

25g (1oz) freshly grated Parmesan cheese

2 tbsp mascarpone cheese

1 tbsp snipped fresh chives

1 tbsp chopped fresh flat-leaf parsley

sherry vinegar caramel (page 260), to serve

Parmesan foam (page 246), to garnish

4 crispy potato rosti (page 228)

fresh micro salad leaves, to garnish

Preheat the oven to 180°C (350°F/gas mark 4).

Place the carrots on a small baking sheet that will take the vegetables in one even layer and drizzle with 1 tablespoon of the oil. Scatter over the thyme sprigs and season to taste, then roast for 5 minutes. Add the celeriac to the carrots and cook for another 10–15 minutes, until all the vegetables are cooked through and lightly coloured, tossing them occasionally to ensure they cook evenly.

Meanwhile, pour the vegetable stock into a pan and bring to a gentle simmer. Keep warm.

Heat a non-stick sauté pan over a medium heat and add the remaining 2 tablespoons of the oil. Tip in the shallot and garlic and sauté for about 5 minutes, until well softened and lightly coloured. Stir in the risotto rice and cook for another 2 minutes. Add the white wine and allow to bubble down and reduce, stirring constantly.

Add a ladleful of the warm vegetable stock and cook gently until all the liquid has almost been absorbed, stirring regularly with a wooden spoon. Continue adding stock in this way until the rice is al dente – this should take about 20 minutes depending on the type of rice you use. The risotto should be quite thick rather than soupy and each grain of rice should be holding its shape.

Remove the risotto from the heat and stir in the Parmesan, mascarpone and herbs. Season to taste, then fold in the roasted carrot and celeriac, discarding the thyme sprigs.

To serve, place a 7.5cm (3in) cooking ring on warmed plates and fill with the risotto, pressing it down gently with a spoon. Carefully remove the ring and drizzle around the sherry vinegar caramel. Spoon over the Parmesan foam and arrange a potato rosti on top of each risotto. Garnish with the micro salad.

COOK AHEAD
Prepare and weigh out all the ingredients up to 1 hour before cooking, but it's best to leave the celeriac until the last minute, as it tends to oxidise.

WINE
A warm and ripe south of France Chardonnay or a New Zealand Pinot Noir.

Open Lasagne with Roasted Vegetables

THIS DISH IS ALWAYS HUGELY POPULAR WHEN WE PUT IT ON THE MENU. I LIKE TO MAKE IT WHEN MEDITERRANEAN VEGETABLES, PARTICULARLY TOMATOES, ARE AT THEIR BEST, WHICH IS IN THE LATE SUMMER/EARLY AUTUMN. WE NORMALLY MAKE OUR OWN FRESH PASTA, BUT YOU CAN USE THE READY-MADE VARIETIES, WHICH ARE NOW WIDELY AVAILABLE.

Serves 4

3 red onions, trimmed and cut into wedges (keeping roots intact)

2 large courgettes, cut into 2.5cm (1in) chunks

2 yellow peppers, cored and cut into chunks

1 small aubergine, trimmed and cut into chunks

4 tbsp rapeseed oil

sea salt and freshly ground black pepper

4 ripe tomatoes, quartered

3 garlic cloves, finely chopped

1 tbsp balsamic vinegar

6 fresh pasta sheets (page 241 or shop bought)

red pepper purée (page 243), to serve

basil purée (page 243), to serve

8 tbsp basil pesto (page 256)

fresh micro herbs, to garnish

Preheat the oven to 200°C (400°F/gas mark 6).

Place the red onions, courgettes, peppers and aubergine into a large roasting tin. Drizzle over 3 tablespoons of the rapeseed oil, season generously and roast for 30 minutes, until the vegetables are almost tender but not charred.

Remove the vegetables from the oven and stir in the tomatoes, garlic and balsamic vinegar. Roast for another 15 minutes, until all the vegetables are completely tender and lightly charred.

Bring a large pan of water with a tight-fitting lid to the boil and add a good pinch of salt and the remaining tablespoon of oil. Cut the pasta sheets in half across the width. Add the pasta to the boiling water and cook until just tender but with a slight bite, then drain well. The drained pasta needs to be used straight away.

To serve, drizzle the warmed plates with the red pepper and basil purées, then place a piece of cooked pasta on top. Spoon over half of the roasted vegetables, then drizzle 1 tablespoon of pesto over each serving. Repeat with another sheet of pasta and cover with the rest of the roasted vegetables, spooning over any remaining juices from the roasting tin. Drizzle over the remaining pesto, then cover with the last sheets of pasta and garnish with the micro herbs.

COOK AHEAD

The vegetables can be roasted before adding the tomatoes up to 4 hours in advance and kept at room temperature until you're ready to finish cooking them. Simply pop them back into the oven for a couple of minutes to warm through before adding the tomatoes, garlic and vinegar. The pasta can be blanched very briefly and kept in a bowl of iced water until needed. When ready to serve, make an emulsion with 2 tablespoons vegetable stock and 2 teaspoons softened butter in a sauté pan and slip in the pasta sheets to just warm through.

WINE

Try an Italian red Chianti or Valpolicella with this dish. For a white option, Pinot Grigio would also be good.

Avocado Spring Roll with Red Pepper Polenta

THIS IS A FANTASTIC VEGETARIAN OPTION, WHICH WE OFTEN HAVE ON THE MENU AS WE ALWAYS GET SUCH POSITIVE COMMENTS FROM CUSTOMERS ABOUT IT. IT HAS AN EXCELLENT BALANCE OF FLAVOURS AND TEXTURES AND THE POLENTA REALLY FILLS YOU UP.

Serves 4

100g (4oz) sun-dried tomatoes, diced

1 small red onion, diced

1 garlic clove, crushed

1 tbsp basil pesto (page 256)

3 small, firm, ripe avocados

1 tbsp sweet chilli sauce

3 tbsp chilli jam (page 248)

1 tbsp chopped fresh mixed herbs (such as basil and flat-leaf parsley)

4 spring roll wrappers, thawed if frozen (each 25cm (10in) square)

egg wash (made with 1 egg and 1 tbsp milk), to seal

groundnut oil, for deep-frying

balsamic gel (page 247), to serve

basil purée (page 243), to serve

red pepper purée (page 243), to serve

12 red pepper polenta discs (page 237), to serve

12 oven-dried cherry tomato halves (page 237), to serve

fresh micro coriander, to garnish

fresh baby pea shoots, to garnish

Place the sun-dried tomatoes, onion, garlic and pesto in a small pan. Stir well to combine, then cook gently for 3 minutes, until softened. Remove from the heat.

Meanwhile, cut the avocados in half and remove the stone, then peel away the skin and cut the flesh into cubes. Stir into the warm pesto mixture with the sweet chilli sauce, 1 tablespoon of the chilli jam and the herbs. Season to taste and leave to completely cool.

To fill the spring rolls, lay out the spring roll wrappers and brush with the egg wash just on one side. Place a quarter of the avocado mixture across the diagonal in the centre of the wrapper and shape into a cylinder shape about 2.5cm (1in) thick. Fold two of the opposite diagonal corners of the wrapper into the centre so that they can cover the avocado mixture, then roll tightly to form a sausage shape. Do not overfill or they will split.

When ready to serve, heat the groundnut oil in a deep-sided pan or in a deep-fat fryer to 180°C (350°F). Deep-fry the spring rolls for 3–4 minutes, until golden brown, turning them once with a tongs to ensure they cook evenly. Remove from the oil and place on kitchen paper to drain off any excess oil.

To serve, drizzle each warmed plate with the remaining chilli jam, balsamic gel, basil purée and red pepper purée. Add the red pepper polenta discs and top with the oven-dried cherry tomatoes. Trim off the ends, then cut each spring roll into 3 pieces. Arrange on the plate and garnish with the micro coriander and pea shoots.

COOK AHEAD
The spring roll filling can be made the night before and these can be filled 3–4 hours ahead and kept in the fridge. However, they must be deep-fried to order.

WINE
A good-quality Casablanca Sauvignon Blanc from Chile or an Italian Dolcetto would work here.

Pappardelle Pasta with Vegetables and Parmesan Foam

THIS IS A VERY QUICK SUPPER THAT'S ALSO DELICIOUS WITH CHICKEN IF YOU'RE CATERING FOR ANYONE WHO ISN'T VEGETARIAN. USE THE BEST-QUALITY EGG PAPPARDELLE YOU CAN FIND. AS A GENERAL RULE, THE MORE EXPENSIVE, THE BETTER! ALWAYS READ THE COOKING INSTRUCTIONS ON THE PACKET, AS THE TIMINGS CAN VARY CONSIDERABLY DEPENDING ON WHAT TYPE YOU USE.

Serves 4

2 tbsp rapeseed oil

1 large aubergine, trimmed and chopped into 2.5cm (1in) pieces

1 large red pepper, cored and cut into squares

1 large yellow pepper, cored and cut into squares

1 large courgette, cubed

2 garlic cloves, crushed

1 small red chilli, seeded and finely chopped (optional)

sea salt and freshly ground black pepper

350g (12oz) pappardelle pasta

finely grated rind and juice of 1/2 lemon

2 tbsp torn fresh basil

4 tbsp sun-dried tomato pesto (page 257)

basil purée (page 243), to serve

Parmesan foam (page 246), to serve

fresh tiny basil sprigs, to garnish

fresh micro herbs, to garnish

Heat the oil in a large pan over a medium heat. Add the aubergine and sauté for about 5 minutes, until tender. Add the peppers, courgette, garlic and chilli, if using. Season to taste, then sauté for another 10 minutes, until all the vegetables are completely tender.

Meanwhile, cook the pappardelle pasta in a large pan of boiling salted water for 8–10 minutes or according to packet instructions, until tender but still al dente, with a little bite.

Drain the pasta, quickly refresh under cold running water and then return to the pan. Add the cooked vegetable mixture along with the lemon rind and juice, stirring to combine. Fold in the basil and enough of the sun-dried tomato pesto to coat. Season to taste.

To serve, divide the pasta among warmed wide-rimmed bowls and add the basil purée and Parmesan foam. Garnish with the basil sprigs and micro herbs.

COOK AHEAD
The vegetable mixture can be made up 2 hours in advance and kept at room temperature, then reheated gently to order.

WINE
Try a Verdejo from Rueda in Spain or a dry Tempranillo rosé, also from Spain.

Warm Potato Pancakes with Leeks and Wild Mushrooms

THESE WARM POTATO PANCAKES SERVED WITH LEEKS AND A NICE SELECTION OF WILD MUSHROOMS IS A USEFUL RECIPE FOR VEGETARIANS AND ALSO MAKES GREAT USE OF LEFTOVER POTATOES. IT'S ALSO A DELICIOUS STARTER SERVED IN SMALLER PORTIONS.

Serves 4

For the potato pancakes:

125g (4 1/2oz) self-raising flour

pinch of salt

2 eggs

225ml (8fl oz) milk

75g (3oz) cooked mashed potato (leftovers are fine)

2 tbsp chopped fresh mixed herbs (such as flat-leaf parsley and chives)

sea salt and freshly ground black pepper

rapeseed oil, for frying

crème fraîche, to serve

Mushroom and leek topping:

50g (2oz) butter

225g (8oz) mixed mushrooms, sliced (such as chestnut, shiitake and button)

4 baby leeks, trimmed and sliced on the diagonal

1 bunch spring onions, trimmed and thinly sliced

sea salt and freshly ground black pepper

Preheat the oven to 180°C (350°F/gas mark 4) and put in a large non-stick baking sheet to heat up.

To make the pancakes, sieve the flour and a pinch of salt into a bowl. Make a well in the centre and break the eggs into the well. Gradually pour in the milk, beating continuously. Add the cooked mashed potato and the herbs. Season to taste and mix well to form a smooth batter similar in consistency to single cream. Cover with clingfilm and chill in the fridge until needed.

Heat a thin film of oil in a large heavy-based frying pan over a medium heat. Ladle in a quarter of the potato pancake batter and cook for about 1 minute on each side. Using a fish slice, transfer to the baking sheet and cook in the oven for another 6–8 minutes, until risen and set, while you cook the remainder. Keep warm.

Meanwhile, to make the mushroom and leek topping, add the butter to the pan that you've cooked the potato pancakes in, then tip in the mushrooms, leeks and spring onions. Sauté over a low heat for 5 minutes, until just tender and cooked through, then season to taste.

To serve, spoon the mushroom mixture into the centre of warmed serving plates. Place a warm pancake on top of each one and spoon around small dollops of crème fraîche to serve.

COOK AHEAD
The potato pancake batter can be made 2 hours in advance and kept covered with clingfilm in the fridge, then cooked to order. The vegetables can also be prepared ready to cook in advance.

WINE
A ripe and fruity New Zealand Sauvignon Blanc or a juicy Beaujolais-Villages will match these flavours.

Satay Vegetable Noodles

STIR-FRYING IS A TRADITIONAL CHINESE COOKING TECHNIQUE THAT'S VERY EASY TO MASTER. TO CHECK IF THE VEGETABLES ARE COOKED, PIERCE THEM WITH THE TIP OF A KNIFE – THE VEGETABLES SHOULD FEEL AS SOFT AS BUTTER. WE OFTEN MAKE THIS FOR A STAFF DINNER WHEN WE'RE LOOKING FOR SOMETHING SPEEDY BUT TASTY. FEEL FREE TO USE DIFFERENT VEGETABLES DEPENDING ON WHAT YOU HAVE IN THE FRIDGE. YOU COULD ALWAYS ADD SOME COOKED PEELED PRAWNS OR DICED COOKED CHICKEN IF YOU'RE NOT LOOKING FOR SOMETHING VEGETARIAN.

Serves 4–6

275g (10oz) fine egg noodles

1 tbsp rapeseed oil

175g (6oz) baby corn, cut in half lengthways

100g (4oz) fine green beans, trimmed

100g (4oz) sugar snap peas

1 large red pepper, cored and thinly sliced

2 garlic cloves, crushed

400g can coconut milk

100g (4oz) crunchy peanut butter

2 tbsp dark soy sauce

2 tbsp sweet chilli sauce

1 tsp light brown sugar

juice of 1/2 lime

sea salt and freshly ground black pepper

chopped fresh coriander, to garnish

Place the fine egg noodles in a pan of boiling water and cook for 3–4 minutes, until tender, or according to the packet instructions.

Heat a wok until very hot. Add the oil and swirl it around the edges, then tip in the baby corn, green beans, sugar snap peas, red pepper and garlic and stir-fry for 3–4 minutes, until the vegetables are tender, sprinkling over 1 tablespoon water if the mixture is getting too dry.

Add the coconut milk, peanut butter, soy sauce, chilli sauce and sugar, then squeeze in the lime juice. Stir-fry for another 2–3 minutes, until all of the ingredients are piping hot and the sauce has reduced a little.

Drain the noodles and fold into the satay vegetables until evenly combined. Season to taste.

To serve, divide among warmed plates or bowls and scatter over the coriander.

COOK AHEAD
The vegetables can be prepared and the other ingredients can be weighed out and left ready to cook to order up to 2 hours in advance.

WINE
Try a spicy Austrian Gruner Veltliner or an off-dry German Riesling to match the Asian flavours.

Aubergine and Potato Dhansak

WE SERVE THIS DELICIOUS LENTIL-BASED CURRY AS A STAFF MEAL WITH PILAU RICE OR OCCASIONALLY I PUT IT ON OUR VEGETARIAN MENU. IF YOU CAN'T FIND LIQUID COCONUT CREAM (SOLD IN TETRA PAK CARTONS), USE CREAMED COCONUT (SOLD IN A SOLID BLOCK FORM) INSTEAD. SIMPLY FOLLOW THE INSTRUCTIONS ON THE PACKET TO MAKE UP TO THE REQUIRED QUANTITY – IT WORKS JUST AS WELL.

Serves 4–6

2 tbsp rapeseed oil

4 whole cloves

1 cinnamon stick

2 tsp black mustard seeds

2 tsp cumin seeds

1 onion, finely chopped

2 garlic cloves, crushed

5cm (2in) fresh root ginger, peeled and finely grated

400g can chopped tomatoes

225g (8oz) waxy potatoes, cut into bite-sized pieces

75g (3oz) red lentils

1 small aubergine, trimmed and cut into bite-sized pieces

1 tbsp ground cumin

1 tbsp ground coriander

1 tbsp ground turmeric

1 tbsp sweet paprika

1 tsp chilli powder

200ml (7fl oz) carton coconut cream

900ml (1 1/2 pints) vegetable stock (page 252)

sea salt and freshly ground black pepper

275g (10oz) small cauliflower florets

75g (3oz) baby spinach leaves

2 tbsp chopped fresh coriander, plus extra leaves to garnish

plain boiled or pilau rice, to serve

plain natural yoghurt, to garnish

Heat the oil in a large pan over a medium heat, then add the cloves, cinnamon stick, mustard and cumin seeds and allow to sizzle for 20 seconds. Reduce the heat to low and add the onion, garlic and ginger. Cook for 10 minutes, stirring occasionally, until softened but not browned.

Add the tomatoes, potatoes, lentils, aubergine, ground cumin, ground coriander, turmeric, paprika and chilli powder to the onion mixture. Pour in the coconut cream and 600ml (1 pint) of the stock, season to taste and bring slowly to the boil. Reduce to a simmer for 20–25 minutes, stirring occasionally, until the lentils are quite soft and have almost disintegrated into the sauce and the vegetables are just beginning to soften.

Add the cauliflower and the remaining stock, cover and simmer for another 15–20 minutes, until all the vegetables are tender. Stir the spinach into the curry and cook for 1–2 minutes, until just wilted. Stir in the fresh chopped coriander.

To serve, arrange the aubergine and potato dhansak on warmed plates with the rice and garnish each one with a dollop of natural yoghurt and the coriander leaves.

COOK AHEAD
This curry's flavour actually improves as it sits, so it's best made 24 hours in advance and kept covered with clingfilm in the fridge until needed. Place in a pan and warm through very gently to serve.

WINE
An Australian Riesling will cut through the curry flavours. A Syrah from the south of France would be a good contrast.

Mediterranean Vegetable and Boilíe Pizza Tart

A WONDERFUL VEGETARIAN TART THAT IS REALLY LIGHT AND FULL OF FLAVOUR. IT USES BOILÍE CHEESE, WHICH IS AVAILABLE IN JARS FROM ALL SUPERMARKETS AND IS MADE IN THE FIVEMILETOWN DAIRY NOT FAR FROM US HERE AT BLACKLION. TRY TO SOURCE AN ALL BUTTER PUFF PASTRY IF YOU CAN, OR YOU COULD ALWAYS MAKE YOUR OWN…

Serves 4

425g (15 oz) packet ready-rolled frozen puff pastry, thawed

a little plain flour, for dusting

1 large red pepper

1 large yellow pepper

3 tbsp rapeseed oil

100g (4oz) aubergine, cut into 2cm (3/4in) dice

1 small courgette, cut into 2cm (3/4in) dice

1 small red onion, cut into 2cm (3/4in) dice

sea salt and freshly ground black pepper

2 tbsp basil pesto (page 256)

20 Boilíe goat's cheese balls, drained (from jars)

egg wash (made with 1 egg and 1 tbsp milk), for glazing

balsamic and port syrup (page 260), to serve

red pepper purée (page 243), to serve

basil purée (page 243), to serve

2 tbsp toasted pine nuts

fresh micro basil, to garnish

Unroll the two pieces of puff pastry and place on a lightly floured board. Cut out 4 x 15cm (6in) circles and place on baking sheets lined with parchment paper, then chill for 30 minutes.

Meanwhile, preheat the oven to 200°C (400°F/gas mark 6) and preheat the grill.

Rub the peppers with 1 tablespoon of the rapeseed oil and roast them under a very hot grill for about 20 minutes, turning regularly, until the skins are blackened and blistered. Transfer to a bowl and cover with clingfilm, then leave to cool. Peel, core and cut into 0.5cm (1/4in) dice.

Prick the inner circle of pastry all over many times to prevent it from puffing up, making a slight dip for the topping. Lay another sheet of parchment paper over the pastry circles and cover with a second baking sheet. This will prevent them from rising too much and will make them extra crispy and golden brown. Bake for 10–15 minutes, until slightly puffed up and light golden, swapping the baking sheets around on the oven shelves halfway through to ensure they cook evenly.

While the pastry is baking, heat the remaining 2 tablespoons of the rapeseed oil in a frying pan over a medium heat and sauté the aubergine, courgette and red onion on a medium heat for 8–10 minutes, until the vegetables are beginning to soften and catch colour. Season to taste and stir in the roasted diced peppers and basil pesto.

Divide the sautéed vegetable mixture evenly among the pastry cases, spreading them out to the rim using the back of a spoon. Arrange 5 Boilíe goat's cheese balls on top of each one then brush the rim with the egg wash. Return to the oven for 8–10 minutes, until the tarts have completely warmed through.

To serve, arrange the pizza tarts on warmed plates and drizzle around the balsamic and port syrup, red pepper purée and basil purée. Scatter over the pine nuts and garnish with the micro basil.

COOK AHEAD
The pastry circles can be cooked 24 hours in advance and kept in an airtight container. You'll find they freshen up nicely once they're put back in the oven with the toppings.

WINE
A ripe, juicy Italian red like Barbera or a Nebbiolo would be best with this dish.

DESSERTS

The Orchard
(Apple Panna Cotta with Apple Jelly, Glazed Apple Tart, Apple Crumble and Apple Parfait)

THIS IS OUR SIGNATURE DESSERT AND A GREAT WAY TO PRESENT APPLES WHEN THEY'RE IN SEASON. THE IDEA IS TO TAKE YOUR TASTE BUDS ON A JOURNEY OF LOTS OF DIFFERENT TEXTURES AND FLAVOURS. WE CALL IT THE ORCHARD AFTER CO. ARMAGH.

Serves 6

For the apple jelly:

2 gelatine leaves

200ml (7fl oz) apple coulis (page 264)

For the apple panna cotta:

2 gelatine leaves

200ml (7fl oz) cream

100ml (3 1/2fl oz) milk

50g (2oz) caster sugar

1 vanilla pod, split in half and seeds scraped out

50ml (2fl oz) apple coulis (page 264)

For the glazed apple tarts:

100g (4oz) ready-rolled puff pastry, thawed if frozen

a little plain flour, for dusting

1 small eating apple, such as Granny Smith

50g (2oz) caster sugar

50g (2oz) butter

1 tbsp apricot jam

To make the apple jelly, soak the gelatine in a bowl of water for 10 minutes to soften, then gently squeeze dry. Heat the apple coulis in a small pan and stir in the gelatine. Mix well until the gelatine has dissolved. Divide among 6 x 200ml (7fl oz) pudding basins. Place in the fridge for at least 1 hour to set, or overnight is fine.

Once the jellies are set, make the panna cotta. Soak the gelatine leaves in a bowl of water for 10 minutes to swell, then gently squeeze dry. Place the cream, milk, sugar and vanilla seeds in a pan. Bring to the boil, then take the pan off the heat and stir in the squeezed gelatine and apple coulis. Strain the mixture into a jug. Leave to cool, then pour on top of the set apple jellies in the pudding basins. Cover with clingfilm. Place on a tray and chill for at least 2 hours, or overnight is best.

To make the tarts, preheat the oven to 190°C (375°F/gas mark 5). Unroll the pastry on a lightly floured work surface and cut into six 8.5cm x 3.5cm x (3 1/2in x 1 1/2in) rectangles. Prick with a fork, then place on a baking sheet lined with parchment paper.

Cut the apple into quarters and remove the core. Slice each apple quarter very thinly and arrange on the puff pastry rectangles in an overlapping layer, leaving a small border around the edge of each one so that they're able to rise. Sprinkle evenly with the caster sugar and place a small knob of butter in the centre of each one. Bake for 10–12 minutes, until the pastry is golden brown. Just before the apple tarts are ready, heat the apricot jam in a small pan or in the microwave. Remove the cooked tarts from the oven and quickly brush each one with a little of the jam. Set aside at room temperature until needed.

For the crumble:

50g (2oz) plain flour

30g (1 1/4 oz) butter

4 tbsp caster sugar

1 Bramley apple, peeled, cored and diced

2 tbsp freshly pressed apple juice

apple parfait (page 266), to serve

salted butterscotch sauce (page 262), to serve

apple gel (page 247), to serve

spun sugar curls (page 268), to decorate

dried split vanilla pods, to decorate

Meanwhile, to make the apple crumble, preheat the oven to 200°C (400°F/gas mark 6). Place the flour in a bowl and rub in the butter until it resembles breadcrumbs, then stir in 2 tablespoons of the sugar. Place the diced apple into a small pan over a medium heat with the apple juice and sprinkle over the remaining 2 tablespoons sugar. Allow to cook for 2–3 minutes, until the apple is just tender. Divide the poached apples among 6 x 20ml ovenproof dishes and sprinkle the crumble on top. Bake for 8–10 minutes, until bubbling and golden brown.

To serve, dip the panna cotta and jelly moulds in a bowl of warm water for 5–10 seconds to help them unmould. Invert onto a plate with the apple tart, apple crumble and apple parfait. Drizzle with the salted butterscotch sauce and apple gel, then decorate with the spun sugar curls and dried vanilla pods.

COOK AHEAD
This is definitely a dessert that you can have prepared well ahead. The panna cotta can be made up to 2 days in advance and the apple tarts can be made up to 24 hours in advance if you toss the apples in a little lemon juice to prevent them from browning. You can have the apples poached and the crumble topping prepared 24 hours in advance. However, it's best to assemble to order so that the crumble doesn't lose any of its crunch and become soggy.

THE ORCHARD (APPLE PANNA COTTA
WITH APPLE JELLY, GLAZED APPLE TART,
APPLE CRUMBLE AND APPLE PARFAIT)

Warm Chocolate and Pecan Brownie with Boozy Fudge Sauce

WHO DOESN'T LIKE A GOOD CHOCOLATE BROWNIE? THE PECAN NUTS ADD EXTRA TEXTURE AND BITE. IF THE BROWNIES HAVE GONE COLD AND YOU WANT TO HEAT THEM UP IN A HURRY, POUR OVER SOME OF THE FUDGE SAUCE AND FLASH THEM UNDER A HOT GRILL UNTIL BUBBLING. ANY LEFTOVERS CAN BE FROZEN AND USED TO MAKE AN ICE CREAM SUNDAE OR TO FLAVOUR ICE CREAM.

Serves 8

For the brownie:

400g (14oz) plain chocolate, finely chopped (at least 70% cocoa solids)

225g (8oz) butter

4 eggs

275g (10oz) caster sugar

100g (4oz) self-raising flour

75g (3oz) cocoa powder

100g (4oz) pecan nuts, roughly chopped

For the fudge sauce:

150ml (1/4 pint) cream

25g (1oz) butter

1 tbsp caster sugar

175g (6oz) plain chocolate, finely chopped (at least 70% cocoa solids)

50ml (2fl oz) Coole Swan Dairy Cream Liqueur

crème anglaise (page 263), to serve

Malteser ice cream (page 265), to serve

spun sugar curls (page 268), to decorate

Preheat the oven to 160°C (325°F/gas mark 3).

Place 100g (4oz) of the chocolate in a heatproof bowl with the butter and set over a pan of simmering water until melted, then stir to combine. Remove from the heat and leave to cool a little.

Meanwhile, whisk the eggs in a bowl until stiff and holding their shape, then whisk in the sugar until you have achieved a stiff sabayon that can hold a trail of the figure eight. Sift the flour and cocoa powder into the sabayon and lightly fold in. Add the melted chocolate mixture along with the remaining finely chopped chocolate and the nuts and continue folding gently until all the ingredients are just combined. Pour the chocolate mixture into a deep-sided 30cm x 25cm (12in x 10in) baking tin lined with parchment paper. Bake for 35–40 minutes, until the top is crusty but the centre is still a little soft. Remove the brownies from the oven and allow to cool in the tin for about 5 minutes, then remove from the tin and peel off the parchment paper.

Meanwhile, make the fudge sauce. Place the cream in a pan with the butter and sugar and bring to the boil, stirring. Reduce the heat and simmer gently for a few minutes, until thickened and toffee-like, stirring occasionally to prevent the mixture from catching. Remove from the heat and leave to cool.

Place the chocolate in a heatproof bowl set over a pan of simmering water until melted. Whisk into the sauce until smooth and well combined. Leave to cool completely, then transfer to a bowl and stir in the Coole Swan liqueur. Cover with clingfilm and keep in the fridge until needed. It should keep happily for up to 1 week.

When ready to serve, transfer the fudge sauce to a pan and gently heat through, or pierce the clingfilm and heat in the microwave and pour into a squeezy bottle. Cut the brownies into 7cm (2 3/4in) circles using a straight-sided cutter. Arrange on warmed plates and drizzle over the hot fudge sauce followed by a little of the crème anglaise. Add quenelles of the Malteser ice cream to each plate and decorate with the spun sugar curls.

COOK AHEAD
These brownies can be made up to 2 days in advance and kept in the fridge until needed. Remove from the fridge and preheat the oven to 140°C (275°F/gas mark 1) for 10–15 minutes to warm through before serving. The fudge sauce will keep for 1 week in the fridge – just reheat gently to serve.

MacNean Cheesecake with Raspberries and White Chocolate

IN THE RESTAURANT WE SERVE THIS CHEESECAKE WITH A JAMMIE DODGER (PAGE 221) AND SOMETIMES A NICE QUENELLE OF RASPBERRY SORBET (PAGE 266) OR RASPBERRY RIPPLE ICE CREAM. THE CHEESECAKE ITSELF IS REALLY LIGHT, AS WE USE A LIGHT CREAM CHEESE FROM JANE AND KIERAN CASSIDY, WHO RUN KILBEG DAIRY DELIGHTS IN KELLS, CO. MEATH. LOOK OUT FOR THEIR PRODUCTS, AS THEY REALLY DO HAVE THE MOST WONDERFUL RANGE OF SOFT CHEESES AND YOGHURT. I LIKE TO DECORATE THE PLATE WITH DRIED RASPBERRIES AND BABY MALTESERS, BOTH OF WHICH ARE AVAILABLE FROM GOOD CATERING SUPPLIERS.

Serves 8

400g (14oz) cream cheese

100g (4oz) icing sugar

1 vanilla pod, split in half and seeds scraped out

finely grated rind and juice of 1/2 lemon

200g (7oz) white chocolate, broken into squares

200ml (7fl oz) cream

8 shortbread biscuits, finely broken up (page 220)

white chocolate curls (page 269), to decorate

dried raspberries (shop bought), to decorate

baby Maltesers (shop bought), to decorate

spun sugar (page 268), to decorate

fresh mint sprigs, to decorate

8 jammie dodgers (page 221), to serve

For the poached raspberries:

300ml (1/2 pint) red wine

2 tbsp crème de cassis

75g (3oz) caster sugar

1 cinnamon stick

1 star anise

1/2 vanilla pod, split in half and seeds scraped out

400g (14oz) raspberries, plus extra to decorate

Using an electric mixer, beat the cream cheese, icing sugar, vanilla seeds and the lemon rind and juice for about 5 minutes, until smooth and light.

Melt the white chocolate in a heatproof bowl set over a pan of simmering water. Remove from the heat and set aside to cool a little. Meanwhile, place the cream in a separate bowl and whip until stiff.

Fold the melted chocolate into the cream cheese mixture and then carefully fold in the whipped cream. Transfer to a piping bag fitted with a 1cm (1/2in) plain nozzle and place in the fridge until needed.

To poach the raspberries, place the red wine and crème de cassis in a pan with the sugar, cinnamon stick, star anise and vanilla pod and seeds and bring to the boil. Reduce the heat and simmer for 15 minutes, until reduced by half and slightly thickened. Place the raspberries in a heatproof bowl and pour over the wine mixture through a fine sieve, discarding the cinnamon stick, star anise and vanilla pod. Stir to combine and leave to cool.

To assemble the cheesecake, divide the poached raspberries among martini glasses and crumble the shortbread biscuits on top. Pipe the cheesecake mixture right up to the rim of the glasses and decorate with raspberries, white chocolate curls, dried raspberries, baby Maltesers, spun sugar and mint sprigs.

To serve, arrange the cheesecakes on plates with a jammie dodger.

COOK AHEAD

The poached raspberries will keep in the fridge for up to 5 days. All the other elements can be prepared 24 hours in advance and assembled just before serving.

Toasted Coconut and Malibu Parfait with Pineapple Carpaccio and Coconut Sorbet

A GREAT SUMMER DESSERT THAT REMINDS ME OF THE TROPICS AND IS BEAUTIFULL TO LOOK AT. THE PARFAIT IS ACTUALLY INCREDIBLY LIGHT AND WONDERFULLY REFRESHING WHEN SERVED WITH THE PINEAPPLE CARPACCIO.

Serves 8

For the parfait:

rapeseed oil, for greasing

50g (2oz) caster sugar

3 egg yolks

200ml (7fl oz) cream

50ml (2fl oz) Malibu rum

1 tbsp toasted desiccated coconut

For the pineapple carpaccio

50g (2oz) caster sugar

1 vanilla pod, seeds only

1 lemon grass stalk, cut in half

1 star anise

finely grated rind and juice of 1 lime

2 passion fruit

1 large ripe pineapple

2 tbsp finely shredded mint leaves

coconut sorbet (page 266), to serve

8 lime meringues (page 160), to decorate

fresh mint sprigs, to decorate

mango gel (page 247), to decorate

To make the parfait, brush 10 x 40g (1 1/2oz) cone moulds or a 450ml (3/4 pint) non-stick loaf tin with rapeseed oil and set aside until needed.

Place the sugar and 50ml (2fl oz) water in a heavy-based pan and simmer gently until the sugar has dissolved. Bring to the boil, then continue to boil without stirring until the mixture has reached 116°C (240°F), or the soft ball stage, which means that when you drop a bit of it into cold water to cool it down, it will form a soft ball.

Meanwhile, whisk the egg yolks in a separate bowl until they look pale yellow in colour and have become thick and creamy in consistency. When the sugar has reached the correct temperature, quickly whisk it into the egg yolks and continue to whisk until the mixture is cold.

Pour the cream into another bowl and whisk to soft peaks. Mix the Malibu and toasted coconut into the cooled egg yolk mixture and gently fold in the whipped cream. Pour into the prepared moulds or loaf tin, then cover with clingfilm and freeze for at least 4 hours, or preferably overnight, until solid.

To make the pineapple carpaccio, pour 120ml (4fl oz) water into a small heavy-based pan. Add the sugar, vanilla seeds, lemon grass, star anise and lime juice and bring to a gentle simmer for 2–3 minutes, stirring until the sugar has dissolved. Remove from the heat. Cut the passion fruits in half and scoop out the seeds, then stir the seeds into the sugar syrup and leave to cool. When the sugar syrup has cooled, stir in the lime rind and mint.

Meanwhile, slice the top and bottom off the pineapple, sit it upright on a board and slice away the skin and all the little brown 'eyes'. Using an apple corer, remove the core and then using a very sharp knife, slice the pineapple as thinly as possible.

To serve, carefully remove the parfait from the moulds, or if you've used a loaf tin, use a sharp knife dipped in boiling water to cut it into slices. Arrange on plates with the pineapple carpaccio in an attractive layer around it and drizzle the syrup over the pineapple. Place a scoop of coconut sorbet to the side. Drizzle over a little of the carpaccio syrup and decorate with the lime meringues, fresh mint sprigs and mango gel.

COOK AHEAD
The pineapple keeps well covered with clingfilm and set aside at room temperature for 2 hours. Any longer and the mint beings to blacken. The parfait can be made well in advance and can be frozen for up to 1 month.

Lime Meringues with Fresh Fruit and Cream

I LIKE TO USE THESE MERINGUES AS AN ACCOMPANIMENT TO MY TOASTED COCONUT AND MALIBU PARFAIT (PAGE 158). I ALSO LIKE TO BREAK THEM UP FOR ICE CREAM SUNDAE. OF COURSE, YOU CAN PIPE THEM INTO ANY SHAPE YOU LIKE – SMALL DISCS ALSO LOOK GREAT, OR MAKE THEM LARGER FOR A MORE SUBSTANTIAL DESSERT.

Serves 6–8 (makes about 100)

2 egg whites

1 vanilla pod, split in half and seeds scraped out

75g (3oz) caster sugar

finely grated rind of 1 lime

500ml (18fl oz) cream

450g (1lb) small strawberries

2 kiwi fruit, peeled and cut into slices, then halved again

1 mango, peeled, stone removed and pared into thin slices

icing sugar, to dust

fresh tiny mint sprigs, to decorate

Preheat the oven to 100°C (200°F/gas mark 1/4).

To make the meringues, whisk the egg whites in a spotlessly clean, dry, large bowl until stiff. Add the scraped out vanilla seeds, then gradually whisk in the sugar a tablespoon at a time, until the meringue holds its shape and is shiny and glossy. Fold half of the lime rind into the meringue mixture.

Transfer the mixture to a piping bag fitted with a 0.5cm (1/4in) nozzle. Pipe 5cm (2in) lengths of the meringue mixture onto baking sheets lined with non-stick parchment paper and sprinkle over the remaining lime rind. You should end up with about 100 meringues in total. Cook on the lowest shelf in the oven for 1–1 1/2 hours, until the meringue is crisp but not coloured. Leave the oven door slightly ajar and leave to cool completely in the oven – this helps to prevent them from cracking.

To serve, whip the cream in a bowl, then use to fill a piping bag fitted with a 0.5cm (1/4in) plain nozzle. Arrange the fruit in an attractive layer on plates and pipe on small swirls of the cream. Decorate the swirls of the cream with the lime meringues in a criss-cross fashion. Dust with the icing sugar and decorate with mint sprigs.

COOK AHEAD
The meringues keep well in an airtight container for up to 1 week.

Roasted Pineapple and Coconut Rice Pudding

RICE PUDDING IS EXCELLENT COMFORT FOOD AND I'M SURE ON MOST PEOPLE'S LISTS OF FAVOURITE CHILDHOOD DESSERTS. THIS IS A DESSERT THAT IS OFTEN ASKED FOR BY SOME OF OUR OLDER GUESTS ALTHOUGH CHILDREN REALLY SEEM TO ENJOY IT TOO. TO CHECK THAT A PINEAPPLE IS RIPE, GIVE IT A GOOD SNIFF – IT SHOULD SMELL FRAGRANT – AND THEN TRY TO GENTLY PULL OUT ONE OF THE CENTRE LEAVES – IF IT COMES AWAY EASILY, THE PINEAPPLE IS DEFINITELY RIPE.

Serves 6

1 small fresh pineapple, peeled, cored and cut into wedges

For the caramel pineapple sauce:

225g (8oz) caster sugar

150ml (1/4 pint) pineapple juice

1/2 vanilla pod, split and seeds scraped out

For the rice pudding:

300ml (1/2 pint) milk

200ml (7fl oz) cream

400g can coconut milk

100g (4oz) pudding rice (short grain)

75g (3oz) caster sugar

25g (1oz) butter

finely grated rind of 1 orange

1/2 vanilla pod, split

Preheat the oven to 150°C (300°F/gas mark 2).

To make the caramel pineapple sauce, place the sugar in a small heavy-based pan with 150ml (1/4 pint) cold water and cook until the sugar has dissolved, then simmer gently, without stirring, until you have achieved a golden caramel. This should take no more than 15 minutes in total.

Stir the pineapple juice and vanilla seeds into the caramel and cook for another 2 minutes, stirring to combine with a wooden spoon. It will splutter and create plenty of steam, so be careful. Remove from the heat and leave to cool, then pour into a jug and chill until needed.

Arrange the pineapple wedges in a baking tin and drizzle over 3 tablespoons of the pineapple caramel sauce, then stir until well coated. Roast for 15–20 minutes, until the pineapple is roasted and lightly golden, tossing the tray occasionally to prevent it from catching and burning – if in doubt, drizzle over 1 tablespoon water.

To make the rice pudding, place the milk and cream in a pan and bring to a simmer. Stir in the coconut milk, rice, sugar, butter, orange rind and vanilla pod and bring to the boil, stirring until the sugar has dissolved. Reduce the heat to the lowest setting and cook for 45 minutes, stirring frequently, until the rice is tender and creamy. Remove the vanilla pod from the pan.

To serve, spoon the roasted pineapple wedges into the centre of warmed plates. Spoon the rice pudding to one side and then drizzle around the remaining caramel sauce.

COOK AHEAD
The roast pineapple will keep in the fridge for 2–3 days, covered with clingfilm.

Coconut Floating Islands with Coole Swan Crème Anglaise, Raspberries and Spun Sugar Basket

A MODERN TWIST ON A CLASSIC FRENCH DESSERT CONSISTING OF MERINGUE FLOATING ON A CRÈME ANGLAISE (VANILLA CUSTARD) FLAVOURED WITH COOLE SWAN DAIRY CREAM LIQUEUR. THE MERINGUES ARE PREPARED FROM WHIPPED EGG WHITES, SUGAR AND VANILLA EXTRACT, THEN QUICKLY POACHED. THERE IS OFTEN CONFUSION ABOUT THE ORIGINS OF THE NAME. IN FRENCH CUISINE, THE TERMS ŒUFS À LA NEIGE (EGGS IN SNOW) AND ÎLE FLOTTANTE (FLOATING ISLAND) ARE SOMETIMES USED INTERCHANGEABLY.

Serves 4

2 medium egg whites

100g (4oz) caster sugar

50g (2oz) desiccated coconut, toasted

600ml (1 pint) milk

Coole Swan crème anglaise (page 263), to serve

1 tbsp toasted flaked almonds, to serve

2 tbsp raspberry coulis (shop bought), to serve

4 spun sugar baskets (page 268), to serve

fresh raspberries, to decorate

fresh tiny mint sprigs, to decorate

To make the floating islands, whisk the egg whites in a spotlessly clean, dry, large bowl until stiff. Add the sugar 1 tablespoon at a time, whisking well after each addition, until glossy and stiff. Fold in the coconut until well combined.

Place the milk in a large, deep frying pan and bring to the boil, then reduce the heat to a gentle simmer. Using 2 dessertspoons, shape the coconut meringue into a quenelle and drop into the milk, then repeat until you have 5 or 6 quenelles cooking in total. Poach for 4 minutes, turning once, until lightly set. Remove from the pan using a slotted spoon and plunge into a large bowl of iced water to cool down quickly and then drain on kitchen paper. Repeat until all the mixture is used up – there should be 12 meringues.

To serve, pour the Coole Swan crème anglaise onto plates and carefully arrange 3 poached meringues on top. Sprinkle over the flaked almonds and drizzle with the raspberry purée. Carefully top each one with a spun sugar basket and decorate with the fresh raspberries and mint sprigs.

COOK AHEAD
The spun sugar basket will keep in an airtight container for 2–3 days.

Baked Alaska

THIS IS MY TWIN BROTHER DAVID'S FAVOURITE DESSERT. WHENEVER HE COMES TO THE RESTAURANT, WE ALWAYS MAKE THIS FOR HIM AND IT OFTEN GRACES THE TABLE AT CHRISTMAS. YOU'RE GOING TO BE USING BOUGHT ICE CREAM AND CAKE, SO IT'S WORTH SPENDING A LITTLE TIME MAKING A PERFECT SHAPE FOR THE MERINGUE TO PIPE ON.

Serves 4

16 slices of Madeira cake, each about 2cm (3/4in) thick (shop bought)

600ml (1 pint) block vanilla ice cream (shop bought)

4 egg whites

squeeze of lemon juice

1 vanilla pod, split in half and seeds scraped out

100g (4oz) caster sugar

chocolate fudge sauce (page 263), to serve

crème anglaise (page 263), to serve

fresh raspberries, to decorate

Using a 5cm (2in) straight-sided cutter, stamp out discs from each slice of cake (you need 12 discs). Using the same cutter, punch out 4 discs of ice cream and then cut each one into 3 slices across the equator so that you end up with 12 discs of ice cream in total.

Working quickly so that the ice cream doesn't melt, place 4 discs of cake on a baking sheet lined with parchment paper and put an ice cream disc on top. Cover with another cake disc and then put an ice cream disc on top. Finally, cover with the rest of the cake discs and put in the freezer to firm up for at least 30 minutes. If you want to prep ahead, you'll need to wrap them individually in clingfilm so they don't dry out.

Whisk the egg whites in a spotlessly clean, dry, large bowl with a squeeze of lemon juice and the vanilla seeds until they're almost forming stiff peaks. Add the sugar a tablespoon at a time, whisking until stiff and shiny after each addition.

Fill a piping bag fitted with a 1cm (1/2in) plain nozzle with meringue and start to pipe in rows from the bottom to the top of each cake and ice cream tower. Decorate the top with little peaks of meringue. Place in the freezer for at least 2 hours to firm up.

Using a blowtorch, cook the meringue until it's golden brown but the ice cream is still frozen in the middle. This can also be done in an oven preheated to 200°C (400°F/gas mark 6) for 6–8 minutes, but I find it works best with the blowtorch.

To serve, carefully lift the baked Alaskas off the baking sheet with a fish slice and put on plates. Drizzle around the chocolate fudge sauce and crème anglaise and decorate with the raspberries.

COOK AHEAD

These baked Alaskas can be made up to 2 days in advance – any longer and they will get freezer burn. If they are wrapped individually in clingfilm before the meringue goes on, they will be fine for up to 1 week.

Classic Tiramisu

TO BRING THIS DESSERT UP TO DATE, I LIKE TO SERVE IT IN MARTINI GLASSES, BUT YOU COULD ALWAYS JUST LAYER IT UP IN ONE SINGLE GLASS DISH IF YOU PREFER, AS I'VE SUGGESTED HERE. MASCARPONE IS A RICH, CREAMY CHEESE ORIGINATING FROM LODI IN THE LOMBARDY REGION OF ITALY. IT HAS A SWEETENED TASTE AND IS FAMOUSLY USED IN TIRAMISU.

Serves 8-10

4 large eggs

100g (4oz) caster sugar

250g mascarpone cheese

250m (9fl oz) cream

250ml (9fl oz) freshly brewed strong espresso coffee (left to cool)

150ml (1/4 pint) Tia Maria liqueur

30-40 sponge fingers

cocoa powder, to dust

Separate the eggs, putting the yolks in one bowl with the sugar and the egg whites in another.

Using an electric whisk, beat the egg yolks and sugar until pale and creamy, then mix in the mascarpone cheese until well combined. Whip the cream in a seperate bowl until soft peaks form, then fold into the egg and mascarpone mixture.

Using spotlessly clean beaters, whisk the egg whites until soft peaks form, then fold this into the mascarpone cream. Spoon a third of this mixture into a 32.5cm x 23cm (13in x 9in) dish that is at least 6cm (2 1/2in) deep.

Pour the coffee into a shallow dish and stir in the Tia Maria. Dip in enough of the sponge fingers to make an even layer on top of the mascarpone mixture. It's important to only dip the sponge fingers in as you go along so they don't soak for long and become difficult to handle.

Cover the layer of soaked sponge fingers with another third of the mascarpone cream, then add the rest of the soaked sponge fingers in an even layer on top. Spoon over the remaining mascarpone cream to completely cover the layer of sponge fingers, then cover with clingfilm and chill overnight to allow the flavours to develop and the dessert to settle.

To serve, give the tiramisu an even dusting of cocoa powder and place in the middle of the table so that everyone can help themselves.

COOK AHEAD
This dessert can be made up to 2 days in advance.

Rhubarb and Strawberry Pudding

DEPENDING ON THE TIME OF YEAR, YOU CAN VARY THE FRUIT, OR TRY USING A BAG OF MIXED FROZEN SUMMER BERRIES. WE OCCASIONALLY MAKE THIS IN THE RESTAURANT FOR THE KITCHEN STAFF FOR A SPECIAL TREAT OR IN INDIVIDUAL PORTIONS AS PART OF A MORE COMPLICATED DESSERT PLATE.

Serves 4–6

275g (10oz) fresh rhubarb stalks, trimmed and cut into chunks

225g (8oz) large strawberries, hulled and quartered

275g (10oz) caster sugar

1 piece of stem ginger, drained and finely chopped (optional)

175g (6oz) plain flour

1 tsp baking powder

175g (6oz) butter, at room temperature

3 eggs

1 tsp vanilla extract

crème anglaise (page 263), to serve

Preheat the oven to 160°C (325°F/gas mark 3).

Arrange the rhubarb and strawberries in a large pie dish and sprinkle over 100g (4oz) of the sugar and the stem ginger, if using.

Sieve the flour into a bowl with the baking powder. Place the butter in a separate bowl with the remaining sugar and beat until light and fluffy. Beat in the eggs and vanilla extract, then fold in the sieved flour mixture.

Carefully spread the cake mixture over the fruit and bake for 45–50 minutes, until the sponge is well risen and golden and an inserted skewer comes out clean. Spoon into warmed serving bowls and pour over some crème anglaise to serve.

COOK AHEAD

Prepare this pudding before your guests arrive and then leave at room temperature until needed. Flash in the oven to warm through to serve. However, as it only takes minutes to make, it's best prepared to order.

Passion Fruit and Orange Jelly with Vanilla Yoghurt and Granita

A REFRESHING PALATE CLEANSER IN THE RESTAURANT, BUT EQUALLY GOOD AS A DESSERT SERVED WITH A YOGHURT ICE CREAM – YOU CAN'T BEAT JELLY AND ICE CREAM. IF YOU'RE SERVING THEM AS A PRE-DESSERT, PUT 50ML (2FL OZ) OF THE JELLY INTO 75ML (3FL OZ) SHOT GLASSES. FEEL FREE TO EXPERIMENT WITH OTHER FLAVOURS, SUCH AS CRANBERRY AND ORANGE, APPLE AND VANILLA OR MANGO. THE GRANITA CAN BE FLAVOURED WITH GINGER BEER, RASPBERRY COULIS OR STRAWBERRY COULIS AND CHAMPAGNE. THE PASSION FRUIT COULIS IS AVAILABLE IN GOOD COOK SHOPS OR ONLINE IN POUCHES AND HAS AN EXCELLENT SHELF LIFE IF IT HASN'T BEEN OPENED.

Serves 4

For the passion fruit and orange jelly:

3 gelatine leaves

300ml (1/2 pint) freshly squeezed orange juice

150ml (1/4 pint) passion fruit coulis (shop bought)

25g (1oz) caster sugar

For the passion fruit granita:

250g (9oz) passion fruit coulis (shop bought)

125g (4 1/2oz) caster sugar

For the vanilla yoghurt:

200g (7oz) plain natural yoghurt

1 vanilla pod, half in half and seeds scraped out

passion fruit seeds, to decorate

fresh tiny mint sprigs, to decorate

To prepare the jelly, place the gelatine leaves in a bowl and cover with cold water. Set aside for 10 minutes to soften.

Place the orange juice in a pan with the passion fruit coulis and sugar. Bring to the boil, then take the soaked gelatine out of the water and gently squeeze dry. Add to the orange and passion fruit mixture and stir until the gelatine is completely dissolved. Set aside to cool.

Pour the cooled jelly into 4 x 200ml (7fl oz) glasses, leaving a 2.5cm (1in) space at the top. Place in the fridge to set for at least 2 hours, or overnight is best.

To make the passion fruit granita, place the passion fruit coulis, sugar and 100ml (3 1/2fl oz) water in a pan and bring gently to the boil to dissolve the sugar. Remove the passion fruit mixture from the heat and pass through a sieve into a rigid plastic container. Leave to cool completely, then place in the freezer. Whisk or stir the granita every 20 minutes to break up the ice crystals until the granita is set. This will take 2–3 hours in total.

To make the vanilla yoghurt, mix together the yoghurt and vanilla in a bowl, then transfer to a squeezy bottle. Chill until needed.

To serve, add a layer of the yoghurt on top of the set jelly and spoon some passion fruit granita on top of each one. Decorate with the passion fruit seeds and mint sprigs.

COOK AHEAD

The jellies can be made 2 days in advance and the granita will keep in the freezer for 4–5 days. The yoghurt can also be flavoured 2 days in advance.

Summer Fruit Crumble

I JUST LOVE MAKING THIS IN THE AUTUMN, WHEN THERE ARE STILL PLENTY OF BERRIES AROUND. THE WALNUTS GIVE GREAT TEXTURE, BUT BLANCHED HAZELNUTS COULD BE USED INSTEAD OF THE ALMONDS IF YOU PREFER. THE CRUMBLE MIXTURE WORKS WELL ON TOP OF ANY FRUIT AND THE LIGHT BROWN SUGAR GIVES THE CRUMBLE ITS FAMOUS CRUNCHINESS. TO MAKE A LARGE ONE, SIMPLY COOK FOR 45–50 MINUTES, DEPENDING ON THE SIZE OF THE DISH. WE GET OUR SUMMER BERRIES FROM PAT CLARKE IN CO. MEATH. HE'S THE BEST SOFT FRUIT GROWER IN IRELAND AND HE PICKS ALL HIS STRAWBERRIES BY HAND, WHICH ENSURES THE FRUIT DOESN'T GET BRUISED. WHATEVER HE PICKS IN THE MORNING IS ON SUPERMARKET SHELVES WITHIN 24 HOURS, WHICH IS AS FRESH AS YOU COULD EVER HOPE FOR.

Serves 4

100g (4oz) caster sugar

250ml (9fl oz) red wine

2 whole star anise (optional)

1/2 vanilla pod, split in half and seeds scraped out

1 tbsp fresh lemon juice

450g (1lb) mixed summer berries, such as strawberries, raspberries, blueberries and blackberries

citrus mascarpone cream (page 264), to serve

salted butterscotch sauce (page 262), to serve

For the crumble:

75g (3oz) plain flour

50g (2oz) butter

50g (2oz) light brown sugar

25g (1oz) whole blanched almonds, finely chopped

25g (1oz) shelled walnuts, finely chopped

1/2 tsp ground cinnamon

Preheat the oven to 180°C (350°F/gas mark 4).

To prepare the berries, place the sugar in a heavy-based pan with the red wine, star anise, if using, vanilla seeds and lemon juice. Bring to the boil, then reduce the heat and simmer for 5 minutes, until slightly thickened and syrup-like. Stir in the summer berries, then remove from the heat and leave to cool.

To make the crumble, place the flour in a bowl and rub in the butter until the mixture resembles fine breadcrumbs. Stir in the sugar, almonds, walnuts and cinnamon until well combined.

Remove the star anise and spoon the berry mixture into four individual ovenproof dishes or large ramekins. Sprinkle over the crumble mixture and arrange on a baking sheet, then bake for about 20 minutes, until the crumble topping is golden brown and bubbling around the edges.

To serve, arrange the summer fruit crumbles on plates and spoon some of the citrus mascarpone cream on the side, then drizzle with the salted butterscotch sauce. The remainder of the caramel sauce can be served separately in a jug on the table.

COOK AHEAD

The berries can be poached up to 2 days in advance and the crumble mix can be made up to 2 days in advance and kept covered with clingfilm in the fridge or frozen. However, you need to assemble and bake the crumbles to order.

The Raspberry Plate
(Baked Raspberry Shortcake, Buttermilk Mousse, Raspberry and White Chocolate Parfait and Raspberry Sorbet)

THIS IS A SIGNATURE DESSERT THAT HAS BEEN ON THE MENU FOR YEARS BUT IS CONSTANTLY EVOLVING. IT WAS ORIGINALLY GIVEN TO ME BY MY GOOD FRIEND NEIL MCFADDEN. I JUST LOVE THE COMBINATION OF SHORTCAKE AND COLD BUTTERMILK PUDDING AND IT'S A GREAT DESSERT FOR ENTERTAINING, AS THERE IS A LOT THAT CAN BE DONE IN ADVANCE. IN THE AUTUMN WE USE BLACKBERRIES INSTEAD OF RASPBERRIES AND AT THE HEIGHT OF SUMMER WE SOMETIMES USE A MIXTURE OF BERRIES DEPENDING ON WHAT IS AT ITS BEST. IRISH SOFT FRUIT IS NOW AVAILABLE SEVEN MONTHS OF THE YEAR, FROM THE END OF MAY RIGHT THROUGH UNTIL NOVEMBER. LOOK OUT FOR SUPPLIERS LIKE THE WONDERFUL PAT CLARKE FROM CO. MEATH.

Serves 6

For the buttermilk mousse:

2 gelatine leaves

200ml (7fl oz) cream

100ml (3 1/2fl oz) buttermilk

50g (2oz) caster sugar

1 vanilla pod, split in half with the seeds scraped out

For the pastry cream:

150ml (1/4 pint) milk

1/2 vanilla pod, split in half

2 egg yolks

25g (1oz) caster sugar

1 tbsp plain flour

18 shortbread biscuits (page 220)

255g (9oz) raspberries

icing sugar, for dusting

raspberry gel (page 247), to decorate

fresh tiny mint sprigs, to decorate

dried raspberries (shop bought), to decorate

raspberry and white chocolate parfait (page 267), to serve

raspberry sorbet (page 266), to serve

To make the buttermilk mousse, put the gelatine into a bowl of cold water and leave to soak for about 10 minutes. Put the cream, buttermilk, caster sugar and vanilla into a pan and slowly bring up to the boil, then take the pan off the heat. Gently squeeze out the gelatine leaves to remove excess water. Add the gelatine to the buttermilk mixture and stir continuously until the gelatine is dissolved. Strain the mixture through a sieve into a measuring jug. Rinse off the vanilla pod and cut into quarters, then reserve for decoration. Divide the mixture equally between 6 x 50ml (2fl oz) dariole moulds or espresso cups, then place them on a baking sheet and leave to set in the fridge for at least 3 hours, or up to 2 days is fine.

To make the pastry cream, place the milk in a pan with the vanilla pod and seeds. Bring to the boil and remove from the heat. Meanwhile, using a hand-held mixer, beat the egg yolks in a bowl with the sugar and flour until thick and pale and leaving a trail.

Remove the vanilla pod from the milk and rinse well, then cut in half and reserve for decoration. Carefully pour the heated milk onto the egg yolk mixture, stirring to combine. Transfer to a clean pan and cook over a very low heat for 2–3 minutes, stirring continuously, until very thick. Do not allow to boil or it will curdle. Pour into a clean bowl and place a piece of clingfilm directly on the surface to prevent a skin from forming. Leave to cool completely, then chill until needed.

To assemble, preheat the oven to 180°C (350°F/gas mark 4). Place one of the shortbread biscuits on a baking sheet lined with parchment paper. Spoon 1 tablespoon of the pastry cream into the centre and arrange some raspberries around the edge. Top with another shortbread biscuit and repeat the cream and raspberry layer. Finish with a third shortbread biscuit and dust liberally with icing sugar. Repeat with the remaining ingredients to make 6 shortcake stacks in total. Flash through the oven for 3–4 minutes to just warm through.

To serve, dip the buttermilk mousse moulds in hot water for 5–10 seconds and carefully invert one onto each plate. Remove the warm shortcake stacks from the oven and add one to each plate, then decorate with the raspberry gel, mint sprigs and dried raspberries. Add a slice of the raspberry and white chocolate parfait and a scoop of the raspberry sorbet, decorating with the reserved vanilla pods and more mint sprigs.

COOK AHEAD
A lot of this can be prepared at least 2 days in advance, which makes it much easier for serving. Then it's only a matter of assembly on the day. The shortcake stacks can be made ready to go into the oven up to 2 hours before you intend using them; any longer and they might start going a little soft.

Vanilla Crème Brûlée
with Poached Irish Apple Compote

A FRENCH CLASSIC, A REALLY CREAMY AND DELICIOUS WAY TO END A MEAL. IN THE RESTAURANT WE LIKE TO VARY THE FLAVOURS BY USING COCONUT MILK, PASSION FRUIT OR COOLE SWAN DAIRY CREAM LIQUEUR. I HAVE MY DEAR FRIEND LÉA LINSTER TO THANK FOR THIS RECIPE. I NORMALLY USE A BLOWTORCH FOR THIS RECIPE, BUT YOU DO NEED TO BE CAREFUL WITH THEM AND THEY ARE DEFINITELY NOT FOR THE FAINT HEARTED. ALTERNATIVELY, PLACE THE BRÛLÉES UNDER A HOT GRILL, BUT WATCH THEM LIKE A HAWK BECAUSE THEY BURN VERY EASILY. WHEN GLAZED, THEY SHOULD BE A NICE MAHOGANY BROWN COLOUR.

Serves 6

For the crème brûlée:

8 egg yolks

150g (5oz) caster sugar

1 vanilla pod, split in half and seeds scraped out

600ml (1 pint) cream

300ml (1/2 pint) milk

spun sugar (page 268), to decorate

For the poached apple compote:

300ml (1/2 pint) freshly pressed apple juice

25g (1oz) caster sugar

1 cinnamon stick

1 star anise

1/2 vanilla pod, split in half

2 Bramley apples, cored and finely diced

1 tsp fresh tiny mint leaves

Preheat the oven to 115°C (240°F/gas mark 1/4).

To make the crème brûlée, place the egg yolks in a large bowl with 125g (4 1/2oz) of the sugar and the vanilla seeds. Whisk for about 5 minutes, until pale and fluffy and the mixture holds a trail of the figure eight.

Meanwhile, place the cream and milk in a pan with the scraped out vanilla pod, then simmer gently until the mixture just comes to the boil. Remove the vanilla pod, then slowly pour the hot milk and cream into the yolk mixture, whisking continuously. Pass through a sieve into a clean bowl.

Using a ladle, divide the mixture into 6 x 120ml (4fl oz) small dishes or ramekins set in a baking tin filled with enough boiling water to come halfway up the sides of the ramekins (this is called a bain-marie). Cover tightly with foil and bake in the oven for 1 hour, until just set but still with a slight wobble in the middle. Remove from the oven and leave in the bain-marie, still covered with foil, for another 30 minutes before removing and allowing to cool completely. Transfer to the fridge and allow to set for at least 6 hours, or preferably overnight.

To prepare the poached apple compote, place the apple juice, sugar, cinnamon, star anise and vanilla pod in a pan and bring to the boil, stirring until the sugar has dissolved. Reduce the heat and simmer for 2–3 minutes to allow the flavours to combine, then add the apples and cook for another 4–5 minutes, until the apples are tender but still holding their shape. Remove from the heat and leave to cool completely. Transfer to a rigid plastic container and chill until needed, allowing the apples to come back to room temperature before using.

To finish the brûlées, sprinkle the remaining 25g (1/2 oz) of the caster sugar over the baked custard in an even layer and use a blowtorch to melt and glaze the sugar until caramelised. Arrange on plates. Stir the mint into the poached apples, then divide among small dishes and place alongside the brûlées. Decorate with the spun sugar.

COOK AHEAD
This can be made up to 2 days in advance and kept covered in the fridge until needed. The sugar for the brûlées just needs to be caramelised at the last minute.

Sticky Toffee Pudding and Salted Whiskey Butterscotch Sauce

IN THE RESTAURANT WE SOMETIMES SERVE INDIVIDUAL STICKY TOFFEE PUDDINGS FOR LUNCH. IT'S DERIVED FROM A RECIPE MY MUM OFTEN MADE FOR SUNDAY LUNCH AND IS STILL A FIRM FAVOURITE WITH OUR FAMILY. I JUST LOVE THE COMBINATION OF HOT PUDDING AND SAUCE AGAINST THE COLD ICE CREAM. STICKY TOFFEE PUDDING IS A CLASSIC. WHEN I MADE IT ON TV FOR HOME CHEF, I REALLY NOTICED HOW MANY PEOPLE IN THE RESTAURANT ASKED FOR IT. IT'S TRADITIONALLY THOUGHT OF AS A HEAVY DESSERT, BUT THIS IS A LIGHT VERSION. I LIKE TO USE MEDJOOL DATES. THEY'RE MORE EXPENSIVE BUT WORTH IT FOR THIS DESSERT. I LOVE THEIR STICKY CARAMEL TEXTURE AND TASTE.

Serves 8

200g (7oz) butter, at room temperature

175g (6oz) self-raising flour, plus extra for dusting

175g (6oz) Medjool dates, stoned and roughly chopped

1 tbsp dark rum

1 tsp bread soda

175g (6oz) light brown sugar

1/2 vanilla pod, split in half and seeds scraped out

2 eggs, beaten

1 tsp vanilla extract

salted whiskey butterscotch sauce (page 262), to serve

caramel foam (page 246), to serve

vanilla ice cream (page 265), to serve

toasted chopped pecan nuts, to serve

melted plain chocolate, to decorate

fresh raspberries, to decorate

fresh mint sprigs, to decorate

Preheat the oven to 180°C (350°F/gas mark 4).

Melt 50g (2oz) of the butter in a small pan or in the microwave and use to brush the insides of 8 x 200ml (7fl oz) small pudding bowls, then lightly dust with a little flour, shaking out any excess. Set aside until needed.

Place the dates in a pan with 300ml (1/2 pint) water and the rum. Bring to the boil, then reduce the heat to a simmer and cook for about 5 minutes, until the dates are soft. Add the bread soda to the date mixture, which will cause it to foam up, then set aside to cool a little. Place the date mixture in a food processor and blend for 2 minutes. Pour into a bowl.

Meanwhile, cream the sugar, the remaining 150g (5oz) of the butter and the vanilla seeds together in a bowl for about 10 minutes, until light and fluffy. Add 1 tablespoon of the flour to the butter and sugar mixture, then slowly add the eggs and beat well to combine. Add the blended date mixture with the remaining flour and the vanilla extract and combine everything gently to give a smooth dropping consistency.

Pour the pudding batter into the prepared bowls and arrange on a baking sheet, then bake for 35–40 minutes, until slightly risen and firm to the touch.

To serve, leave the puddings to settle for a minute or two before turning out onto warmed plates. Spoon over the salted whiskey butterscotch sauce and finish with the caramel foam. Add a scoop of ice cream to each one with a little of the chopped pecans underneath to prevent the ice cream from slipping around the plate. Decorate with the melted chocolate, raspberries and mint sprigs.

COOK AHEAD
The puddings can be made up to 2 days in advance once they have been cooked and kept covered in the fridge until needed. To serve, just warm them through in the oven for about 10 minutes. This sauce will keep for 2 weeks in the fridge.

Trio of Chocolate
(Warm Fondant, Delice and Opera Cake)

ONE OF OUR SIGNATURE DISHES, THIS HAS ALL THE ELEMENTS OF CHOCOLATE. IT'S ON THE PRESTIGE MENU IN THE RESTAURANT. STEPHEN, MY HEAD PASTRY CHEF, TAKES GREAT PRIDE IN HIS CHOCOLATE WORK AND THIS DESSERT REALLY SHOWCASES IT.

Serves 10

For the opera cake roulade:

4 eggs, separated

100g (4oz) caster sugar

25g (1oz) cocoa powder, sieved

For the Italian buttercream:

1 egg

1 egg yolk

1 tsp instant coffee granules

50g (2oz) caster sugar

250g (9oz) unsalted butter, softened

1/2 vanilla pod, split in half and seeds scraped out

For the chocolate ganache:

250g (9oz) plain chocolate, broken into squares (at least 70% cocoa solids)

250ml (9fl oz) cream

50ml (2fl oz) Coole Swan Dairy Cream Liqueur

To prepare the chocolate roulade for the opera cake, preheat the oven to 190°C (375°F/gas mark 5). Mix the egg yolks with 70g (2 3/4oz) of the sugar and the cocoa powder in a bowl. In a separate clean, dry bowl, whisk the egg whites until stiff, then gradually add the remaining 30g (1 1/4oz) sugar and beat until stiff and glossy. Gently fold the meringue into the yolk mixture, then spread on a non-stick baking tin lined with parchment paper and bake for 10 minutes. Remove from the tin and allow to cool.

To prepare the Italian buttercream, place the egg, egg yolk and coffee granules into a bowl and whisk to sabayon stage. Put the caster sugar and 2 tablespoons water in a heavy-based pan and cook until it reaches the soft ball stage – 116°C (240°F). At this stage, add the hot sugar to the egg mix and mix until it begins to go cold (feel the outside of the bowl – this will indicate the mixture going cold). Gradually add the butter to the mixture in the bowl, beating all the time. When the mixture is soft and fluffy, add the vanilla seeds. Cover with clingfilm and set aside until needed.

To prepare the ganache, melt the chocolate in a heatproof bowl set over a pan of simmering water. Bring the cream to the boil in a heavy-based pan, then stir in the melted chocolate along with the Coole Swan and mix together to combine. Transfer to a bowl and leave to cool completely, stirring occasionally to ensure it stays smooth.

To assemble the opera cake, using a square bread tin or flan mould, cut the roulade in three to fit into the tin. For the first layer, spread over the cooled chocolate ganache and leave to set in the fridge, then spread over a layer of the Italian buttercream, cover with the roulade and leave to set. Repeat the layers two more times until you have three layers of each and all the mixtures have been used up. This will keep in the fridge or you can store it in the freezer until you need it.

For the fondants:

100g (4oz) butter, plus a little extra

100g (4oz) plain chocolate, broken into squares (at least 70% cocoa solids)

125g (4 1/2oz) caster sugar

2 eggs

2 egg yolks

50g (2oz) plain flour, sieved, plus a little extra for dusting

30 plain chocolate drops

10 chocolate delice portions (page 182)

vanilla ice cream (page 265), to serve

chocolate fudge sauce (page 263), to serve

Meanwhile, to prepare the chocolate fondants, grease 10 x 50ml (2fl oz) dariole moulds that are 15cm (6in) square with a little butter and then dust with plain flour. Place in the freezer to set for at least 10 minutes.

Melt the butter and chocolate in a heatproof bowl set over a pan of simmering water. Remove from the heat and leave to cool a little. Whisk the sugar, eggs and egg yolks in a large bowl until light and fluffy. Beat the chocolate mixture into the egg mixture, then gently fold in the flour.

Pipe or spoon the chocolate mixture into the prepared dariole moulds until each one is no more than about one-third full, gently tapping to remove any air bubbles. Place 3 chocolate drops into the centre of each dariole mould, then add the remaining chocolate mixture until the chocolate drops are completely covered but the dariole moulds are no more than halfway full. Place in the fridge for 2 hours, until firm but still a little sticky to the touch.

To cook the chocolate fondants, preheat the oven to 180°C (350°F/gas mark 5). Arrange the prepared fondants on a baking sheet and bake for 8 minutes, until just cooked but still soft in the centre. Leave to rest for a minute or two.

To serve, arrange a chocolate delice on each plate and place a piece of the opera cake alongside. Add the chocolate fondant and a scoop of vanilla ice cream and chocolate sauce to each one.

COOK AHEAD

All the components of this dish can be made 2–3 days in advance. The opera and delice can be frozen and the fondant can also be frozen and baked just before serving.

TRIO OF CHOCOLATE (WARM FONDANT, DELICE AND OPERA CAKE)

Chocolate Delice

THIS CHOCOLATE DELICE CONSISTS OF A LAYER OF CHOCOLATE SPONGE SOAKED WITH COFFEE SYRUP AND CHOCOLATE FILLING. IT'S COMPLETELY DELICIOUS SERVED ON ITS OWN OR AS PART OF THE TRIO OF CHOCOLATE DESSERT (PAGE 178).

Serves 4–6 (makes 10 portions)

For the chocolate filling:

2 gelatine leaves

50ml (2fl oz) liquid glucose

200g (7oz) plain chocolate, broken into squares (at least 70% cocoa solids)

300ml (1/2 pint) cream

100ml (3 1/2fl oz) Coole Swan Dairy Cream Liqueur

For the chocolate sponge:

2 eggs

50g (2oz) caster sugar

50g (2oz) plain flour

25g (1oz) cocoa powder, plus extra for dusting

For the coffee syrup:

25g (1oz) caster sugar

50ml (2fl oz) strong espresso coffee

50ml (2fl oz) Kahlúa liqueur

chocolate fudge sauce (page 263), to serve

crème anglaise (page 263), to serve

Malteser ice cream (page 265), to serve (optional)

fresh raspberries, to decorate (optional)

To make the chocolate filling for the delice, place the gelatine in a bowl of cold water and set aside for 10 minutes to soften. Heat 5 tablespoons water in a heavy-based pan with the glucose. Gently squeeze out the gelatine and add to the pan, then gently warm through, stirring well until the gelatine is dissolved. Remove from the heat and leave to cool.

Place the plain chocolate in a heatproof bowl set over a pan of simmering water and allow to melt. Stir until very smooth and leave to cool a little, then fold into the gelatine mixture. Whip the cream in a bowl and fold into the chocolate mixture. Finally, fold in the Coole Swan liqueur.

To make the sponge for the delice, preheat the oven to 190°C (375°F/gas mark 5) and line a 18cm (7in) square non-stick tin with parchment paper. Whisk the eggs and caster sugar in a bowl until light and fluffy. Sieve the flour and cocoa powder into the egg mixture and gently fold in until just combined. Pour into the prepared tin and bake for 15 minutes, until just cooked.

To make the coffee syrup, place 200ml (7fl oz) water in a heavy-based pan with the sugar, coffee and Kahlúa liqueur. Bring to the boil, then reduce the heat and simmer for a couple of minutes, until the sugar has dissolved. Remove from the heat and leave to cool completely.

To assemble the chocolate delice, place the chocolate sponge on a lined tray and brush all over with the coffee stock syrup. Spoon over the chocolate filling and spread evenly with a palette knife and leave to set, then cut into 4cm (1 1/2in) circles with a straight-sided cutter and dust with cocoa powder.

To serve, arrange on plates with the chocolate fudge sauce, crème anglaise and Malteser ice cream. Decorate with the raspberries or use the individual portions as required.

COOK AHEAD

This can be made up to 3 days in advance and kept on a tray covered with clingfilm in the fridge. It can also be frozen.

Dessert Wine Matches

Crème brûlée/crème caramel
SAUTERNES OR BARSAC FROM FRANCE OR A SWEET OLOROSO SHERRY

Fresh fruit
MUSCAT DE BEAUMES DE VENISE OR LATE HARVEST GERMAN RIESLING

Chocolate
SWEET RED BANYULS FROM SOUTH-WEST FRANCE OR A LATE
BOTTLED VINTAGE (LBV) PORT

Cheesecake
TOKAJI, HUNGARY, OR SAUTERNES, FRANCE

Ice cream
PEDRO XIMÉNEZ SWEET SHERRY

Tiramisu
ITALIAN VIN SANTO OR A SWEET MADEIRA

Sticky toffee pudding
AUSTRALIAN LATE HARVEST 'STICKY'

Apple based
A SWEET WINE FROM ANJOU IN THE LOIRE VALLEY, FRANCE

Citrus based
A SWEET MUSCAT FROM FRANCE OR AUSTRALIA

PETITS FOURS

Coconut and Malibu Marshmallows

NORMALLY MARSHMALLOWS ARE LIGHTLY DUSTED WITH CORNFLOUR TO PREVENT THEM FROM STICKING TOGETHER, BUT I USE TOASTED DESICCATED COCONUT INSTEAD BECAUSE I LOVE THE TEXTURE. THESE PETIT FOURS WOULD ALSO MAKE A GREAT GIFT FOR SOMEONE SPECIAL IN YOUR LIFE! TRY USING A PASSION FRUIT OR SMOOTH RASPBERRY COULIS INSTEAD OF THE MALIBU IF YOU WANT TO SERVE THEM TO CHILDREN AS WELL.

Makes about 100

400g (14oz) granulated sugar

1 tbsp liquid glucose

9 gelatine sheets

2 large egg whites

100ml (3 1/2fl oz) Malibu rum

1 tsp vanilla extract

75g (3oz) desiccated coconut

Put the granulated sugar, glucose and 200ml (7fl oz) water into a heavy-based pan. Bring to the boil and continue cooking until it reaches 127°C (260°F) on a sugar thermometer.

Meanwhile, soak the gelatine in cold water for about 10 minutes, until softened. Beat the egg whites in a separate clean, dry bowl until stiff. When the syrup is up to 127°C (260°F), drain the gelatine leaves and squeeze dry, then carefully slide into the syrup. Remove the syrup from the heat and stir until the gelatine has dissolved.

Pour the gelatine and syrup mixture into a metal jug. Continue to beat the egg whites while pouring in the hot syrup from the jug. The mixture will become shiny and start to stiffen. Add the Malibu and vanilla extract and continue whisking for about 15 minutes, until the mixture is stiff and thick enough to hold its shape and the outside of the bowl is cooled.

Line a 30cm x 23cm (12in x 9in) Swiss roll tin that is 2.5cm (1in) deep with parchment paper. Preheat the grill and sprinkle the desiccated coconut on a separate sturdy baking sheet. Place under the grill until lightly toasted, stirring occasionally to ensure it cooks evenly.

Add a thin even layer of the toasted desiccated coconut to the lined Swiss roll tin, then pour in the marshmallow mixture and smooth it out with a palette knife. Leave to set in the fridge for 1 hour. Using a sharp knife that has been dipped in hot water and wiped, trim off the ends from the marshmallow to make precise squares. Cut the trimmed down marshmallow into 2.5cm (1in) square pieces and toss in the rest of the coconut. Arrange on plates or use as required.

COOK AHEAD
These will keep in an airtight container in the fridge for 4–5 days.

MacNean Chocolate Orange Truffles

THIS IS ON OUR PETITS FOURS SECTION IN THE RESTAURANT AND WE TEND TO CHANGE THE FLAVOUR ON A WEEKLY BASIS, MUCH TO THE DELIGHT OF OUR CUSTOMERS. IF YOU WOULD LIKE TO EXPERIMENT WITH DIFFERENT FLAVOURS, HERE IS A SELECTION THAT WE SERVE IN THE RESTAURANT: TRY ADDING 2 TABLESPOONS OF COOLE SWAN DAIRY CREAM LIQUEUR INSTEAD OF THE COINTREAU OR THE SAME AMOUNT OF CRÈME DE MENTHE ALSO WORKS WELL. FOR A 4TH OF JULY CELEBRATION, FOLD IN 1 TABLESPOON CRUNCHY PEANUT BUTTER TO THE CHOCOLATE TRUFFLE MIXTURE AND ROLL THEM IN FINELY CHOPPED ROASTED PEANUTS.

Makes about 35

125ml (4 1/2fl oz) cream

finely grated rind of 1 orange

250g (9oz) plain chocolate, broken into squares (at least 70% cocoa solids)

125g (4 1/2oz) butter

4 tbsp Cointreau liqueur

For the coating:

225g (8oz) plain chocolate, broken into squares (at least 70% cocoa solids)

cocoa powder, for dusting

Place the cream and orange rind in a pan and bring to the boil. Reduce the heat, then whisk in the chocolate and butter until smooth and melted. Stir in the Cointreau and transfer to a bowl. Leave to cool completely, whisking every 20 minutes so that the butter is evenly distributed. Cover the bowl with clingfilm and chill for 2–3 hours, until set firm, stirring occasionally to present a skin from forming.

When the mixture is cold and set, use a melon baller to scoop it into 1.75cm (3/4in) balls. Make sure to dip the melon baller in hot water to give the chocolate mixture a better shape. Arrange on a baking sheet lined with non-stick parchment paper.

To make the coating, melt the chocolate in a heatproof bowl set over a pan of simmering water or in the microwave. Leave to cool a little, then dip the truffles in the melted chocolate and quickly roll in the cocoa powder. Place in the fridge to set.

To serve, arrange the truffles on a plate and hand around to guests while they are enjoying their coffee.

COOK AHEAD
These truffles will keep well in the fridge for up to 1 week in an airtight container. They can also be frozen very successfully, but should always be left at room temperature to thaw out completely.

Madeleines

I HAVE LÉA LINSTER TO THANK FOR THIS RECIPE. SHE IS THE ONLY FEMALE CHEF TO WIN THE BOCUSE D'OR (BEST CHEF IN THE WORLD COMPETITION) AND PEOPLE TRAVEL FAR AND WIDE TO TASTE HER MADELEINES. FOR THESE SHELL-SHAPED TREATS YOU DO NEED A MADELEINE TIN 7.5CM (3IN) LONG X 3CM (1 1/4IN) WIDE, AVAILABLE FROM SPECIALIST KITCHEN SHOPS OR BY MAIL ORDER. THE SAME GOES FOR THE HAZELNUT PASTE, WHICH I NORMALLY BUY FROM A COMPANY CALLED MSK (SEE PAGE 270 FOR DETAILS).

Makes 48

125g (4 1/2oz) butter, plus extra melted butter for greasing

50g (2oz) plain flour, plus extra for dusting

8 large egg whites, at room temperature

125g (4 1/2oz) icing sugar

50g (2oz) ground almonds

50g (2oz) hazelnut paste

50g (2oz) finely chopped hazelnuts, toasted

Lightly grease 2 x 24 mini madeleine tins with melted butter, then dust with flour, shaking off any excess. Place the tins in the fridge for at least 2 hours, but overnight is best.

Preheat the oven to 200°C (400°F/gas mark 6).

Place the butter in a small pan and allow to brown slightly. Remove from the heat and leave to cool.

Sift the flour into a large bowl. Add the egg whites, icing sugar, ground almonds and hazelnut paste. Using an electric mixer, beat until well combined and smooth. Slowly add the cooled melted brown butter and mix slowly for 5 minutes, until smooth and thickened.

Spoon the mixture into the prepared tins so that it's about level with the tops, leaving a little room for rising, and sprinkle over the toasted hazelnuts. Bake for 7 minutes, until well risen, golden and springy to the touch. Remove from the oven and leave to rest in the tin for 2 minutes, then ease out of the tins with a palette knife and leave to cool slightly on a wire rack.

To serve, arrange on plates and enjoy with coffee or a cup of tea.

VARIATION
Pistachio Madeleines
Use pistachio paste instead of the hazelnut paste and sprinkle over 50g (2oz) finely chopped toasted pistachio nuts instead of the hazelnuts before they go into the oven.

COOK AHEAD
Madeleines don't keep particularly well so are best on the day that they are made, but the raw mixture will keep well in the fridge for 1 week, so you can make them as you need them. The tins are also best prepared 24 hours in advance and kept in the fridge until needed.

White Chocolate and Pistachio Fudge

THIS DELICIOUSLY CREAMY FUDGE MAKES A LOVELY GIFT – JUST WRAP IT IN CELLOPHANE, THEN FINISH WITH A STYLISH RIBBON. IT'S ALSO DELICIOUS MADE WITH SOME GOOD-QUALITY PLAIN OR MILK CHOCOLATE, DEPENDING ON YOUR PREFERENCE. I GOT THIS RECIPE FROM THE AMSTEL HOTEL IN AMSTERDAM, WHICH HAS A TWO MICHELIN STAR RESTAURANT, WHEN I DID A STAGE THERE IN JANUARY 2012. I BUY THE PISTACHIO PASTE FROM A COMPANY CALLED MSK (SEE PAGE 270 FOR DETAILS).

Makes about 64 squares

475g (1lb 1oz) white chocolate, broken into squares

50g (2oz) butter

50g (2oz) liquid glucose

100ml (3 1/2fl oz) cream

2 tbsp pistachio paste

3 tbsp finely chopped toasted pistachio nuts

Melt the chocolate in a heatproof bowl set over a pan of simmering water, then remove from the heat and leave to cool a little.

Cream together the butter and glucose in a bowl. Place the cream in a heavy-based pan and bring to the boil, then add the pistachio paste and melted chocolate.

Transfer to a mixer using a spade attachment and mix until it all comes together. Pour into a 18cm (7in) square baking tin that is at least 2.5cm (1in) deep and that has been lined generously with parchment paper, leaving enough paper coming up the sides so that you can use it to help you lift the set fudge out. Place in the fridge to set for at least 1 hour.

Remove the set fudge from the baking tin. Dip a sharp knife into boiling water and then wipe clean. Use to cut the fudge into 2cm (3/4in) squares, then dip the tops of each square into the toasted chopped pistachio nuts.

To serve, arrange on a plate or use as required.

COOK AHEAD
This will keep very happily for at least 1 week in the fridge stored in an airtight container. The fudge also freezes very well, but needs to be dipped in the pistachio nuts just before serving or they will go soft.

Vanilla Macaroons with Chocolate and Peanut Butter Cream

I GOT THIS RECIPE FROM ONE OF MY PASTRY CHEFS, OLIVIA RAFTERY, WHO GOT IT WHILE SHE WAS WORKING IN LOS ANGELES. THERE ARE SO MANY RECIPES FOR MACAROONS, BUT THIS IS THE BEST I'VE USED BY FAR. FEEL FREE TO EXPERIMENT WITH DIFFERENT FLAVOURS. IF YOU PREFER, THE PEANUT GANACHE CAN ALSO BE MADE IN A COFFEE, PISTACHIO AND CHOCOLATE FLAVOUR.

Makes about 120

150g (5oz) granulated sugar

110g egg whites

168g icing sugar, sifted

168g ground almonds

1 vanilla pod, split in half and seeds scraped out

1 tbsp vanilla extract

For the ganache:

100g (4oz) plain chocolate, finely chopped (at least 70% cocoa solids)

100ml (3 1/2fl oz) cream

2 tbsp smooth peanut butter

Preheat the oven 135°C (270°F/gas mark 1).

Place 200ml (7fl oz) water in a heavy-based pan with the granulated sugar and bring to the boil, stirring gently, until the temperature reaches 100°C (210°F) on a sugar thermometer placed in the pan.

Place 55g of the egg whites in a mixer and beat on high speed until slightly foamy. When the sugar syrup reaches 110°C (230°F) and the egg mixture is foamy, remove the syrup from the heat. Slowly and carefully add the syrup in a steady stream to the whipping egg whites. Continue to beat the meringue for 8–10 minutes, until cool to the touch.

Meanwhile, place the icing sugar and ground almonds in a separate bowl. Mix to combine, then add the rest of the egg whites with the vanilla seeds and extract and a little of the meringue mixture. Mix well with a spatula, then gently fold in the remaining meringue until it runs like a batter, not too runny and not too stiff. The mixture should have a shine to it.

Transfer the prepared mixture to a piping bag fitted with a 1cm (1/2in) nozzle. Pipe out circles of meringue about 1.75cm (3/4in) in diameter onto baking sheets lined with parchment paper. Bake for 12–16 minutes – after 12 minutes, check the meringue every 2 minutes to see if they are done. You know when they are done when you touch the top of the meringue and they barely move. When cooked, leave to cool at room temperature on a wire rack.

To prepare the ganache, place the chocolate, cream and peanut butter in a small pan and cook gently until melted, stirring occasionally. Transfer to a bowl and leave to cool, then lightly whip.

To serve, place the ganache in a piping bag fitted with a 1cm (1/2in) plain nozzle and pipe onto half of the macaroons. Sandwich together and arrange on plates to serve.

COOK AHEAD

The macaroons can be made up to 1 week in advance and kept in an airtight container until needed. The buttercream can be made 2–3 days in advance.

Brandy Snaps with Chilli and Passion Fruit Cream

THIS IS A SIMPLE, LIGHT DESSERT THAT MY MOTHER ALWAYS HAD ON OUR DESSERT TROLLEY IN THE RESTAURANT. THIS IS MY TWIST ON HER RECIPE. THE PASSION FRUIT MAKES THEM VERY REFRESHING AND THE LITTLE CHILLI KICK IS A NICE AFTER NOTE. ONCE THE BATTER IS MADE, THEY TAKE VERY LITTLE TIME TO PREPARE.

Makes about 16

100g (4oz) butter

100g (4oz) caster sugar

4 tbsp golden syrup

100g (4oz) plain flour, sieved

1 1/2 tsp freshly grated root ginger

finely grated rind and juice of 1 lime

250ml (9fl oz) cream

2 passion fruits, halved and pulp scooped out

2 tbsp sifted icing sugar

pinch of hot chilli powder

Preheat the oven to 180°C (350°F/gas mark 4).

Melt the butter with the caster sugar and golden syrup. Remove from the heat and gently fold in the flour, ginger, lime rind and juice. Leave to cool down completely.

Drop large tablespoons of the mixture (about 20g/3/4oz) onto heavy-based non-stick baking sheets. The mixture is enough for about 16 brandy snaps in total. Make sure that you keep the mixture well spaced apart, as it will spread out while cooking. Cook for about 8 minutes, until the brandy snaps are golden and lacy.

Remove the brandy snaps from the oven and leave to cool for a couple of minutes on the baking sheet, then carefully remove using a palette knife and lift each one gently onto a rolling pin that is about 2.5cm (1in) thick. Quickly roll a circle, with the join underneath. Press the join lightly together to seal, then slide the brandy snap off and leave it to firm up on the wire rack, again with the join underneath. If any of the circles on the sheet harden too much to work with, put them back in the oven for a few seconds to soften again. Repeat until all the snaps have been formed.

Whip the cream in a bowl until you have achieved soft peaks, then fold in the passion fruit pulp, icing sugar and chilli powder. Scoop into a piping bag with a 2.5cm (1in) fluted nozzle and leave in the fridge until you're ready to serve.

To serve, pipe each snap with the chilli and passion fruit cream and arrange on a plate.

COOK AHEAD

The brandy snap mixture can be made in advance and kept for up to 1 week in the fridge. However, it's best to bake them the day ahead and keep in an airtight container, then fill with the flavoured cream at the last minute.

BREADS, CAKES
AND BISCUITS

MacNean Wheaten Bread

EVERYONE CLAIMS TO HAVE A GREAT FAMILY RECIPE FOR WHEATEN BREAD. I'VE EXPERIMENTED WITH A LOT OF RECIPES OVER THE YEARS AND THIS IS DEFINITELY THE BEST I'VE TASTED TO DATE. IT HAS A LOVELY SWEET FLAVOUR BUT IS STILL VERY MUCH A SAVOURY BREAD.

Makes 2 x 900ml (1 1/2 pint) loaves

500g (1lb 2oz) coarse wholemeal flour

125g (4 1/2oz) plain flour, plus extra for dusting

1 tsp bread soda

1 tsp salt

600ml (1 pint) buttermilk, plus a little extra if necessary

1 tbsp light brown sugar

1 tbsp melted butter, plus extra butter for greasing and serving

1 tbsp golden syrup

1 tbsp porridge oats

Preheat the oven to 200°C (400°F/gas mark 6) and grease 2 x 900ml (1 1/2 pint) loaf tins.

Sift the flours, bread soda and salt into a bowl. Make a well in the centre of the dry ingredients and add the buttermilk, brown sugar, melted butter and golden syrup. Using a large spoon, mix gently and quickly until you have achieved a nice dropping consistency. Add a little bit more buttermilk if necessary, until the mixture binds together without being sloppy.

Divide the mixture equally between the prepared loaf tins and sprinkle over the porridge oats. Bake for 1 hour, until cooked through and each one has a slightly cracked crusty top, checking halfway through that the loaves aren't browning too much. If they are, reduce the temperature or move the loaves down in the oven.

To check that the loaves are properly cooked, tip each one out of the tin and tap the base. It should sound hollow. If it doesn't, return it to the oven for another 5 minutes. Tip out onto a wire rack and leave to cool completely.

To serve, place the brown wheaten bread on a breadboard and cut into slices at the table. Hand around with a separate pot of butter for spreading.

COOK AHEAD
The beauty of this bread is that it takes so little time to prepare, but you could have everything weighed out and ready to go beforehand, though it's hardly necessary. However, it can be frozen very successfully.

Rosemary and Cranberry Soda Bread

THIS IS AN INTERESTING TWIST ON OUR BEAUTIFUL SODA BREAD. LOOK FOR DRIED CRANBERRIES IN THE LARGER SUPERMARKETS OR ANY HEALTH FOOD SHOP SHOULD STOCK THEM. THIS IS MY FAVOURITE BREAD THAT WE SERVE AS PART OF OUR BREAD SELECTION IN THE EVENING.

Makes 1 loaf

450g (1lb) plain flour, plus extra for dusting

1 tsp bread soda

1 tsp salt

100g (4oz) dried cranberries

4 fresh rosemary sprigs, leaves stripped and finely chopped

350ml (12fl oz) buttermilk, plus a little extra if necessary

butter, to serve

Preheat the oven to 220°C (425°F/gas mark 7).

Sift the flour, bread soda and salt into a bowl. Stir the cranberries and rosemary through and make a well in the centre. Add the buttermilk and using a large spoon, mix gently and quickly until you have achieved a nice soft dough. Add a little bit more buttermilk if necessary, until the dough binds together without being sloppy.

Knead the dough very lightly on a lightly floured surface and then shape into a round that is roughly 15cm (6in) in size. Place on a non-stick baking sheet and cut a deep cross in the top.

Bake for 15 minutes, then reduce the temperature to 200°C (400°F/gas mark 6) and bake for another 20–25 minutes, until the loaf is evenly golden and crusty. To check that the bread is properly cooked, tap the base – it should sound hollow. If it doesn't, return it to the oven for another 5 minutes.

Transfer the cooked soda bread to a wire rack and leave to cool for about 20 minutes. This bread is best eaten while it's still warm.

To serve, place the soda bread on a breadboard and cut into slices at the table. Have a dish of butter to hand for spreading.

COOK AHEAD
This bread is best made fresh, but it can be made in advance and frozen.

Pizza Bread

CHILDREN AND ADULTS LOVE THIS PIZZA BREAD THAT WE SERVE IN THE RESTAURANT. IT'S ALSO GREAT FOR A BARBECUE AND IS JUST THAT LITTLE BIT DIFFERENT. FEEL FREE TO VARY THE TOPPINGS DEPENDING ON WHAT YOU FANCY.

Makes one 30cm x 23cm (12in x 9in) flat loaf

450g (1lb) strong white flour, plus extra for dusting

1 tsp salt

2 tsp fast action dried yeast (7g/1/4oz sachet)

225ml (8fl oz) tepid water

1 tbsp rapeseed oil, plus extra for greasing

For the topping:

200g (7oz) tomato sauce (page 255)

75g (3oz) mature Cheddar cheese, grated

125g (4 1/2oz) basil pesto (page 256)

2 tbsp chilli jam (page 248)

Sieve the flour into a large bowl with the salt and stir in the yeast. Make a well in the centre and pour in the tepid water and the oil. Mix to a smooth dough.

Turn the dough out onto a lightly floured surface and knead for 5–10 minutes, pushing and stretching until smooth and elastic. Alternatively, use a food mixer with the dough hook attached and set on a low speed – it saves quite a bit of elbow grease. Place in a large lightly oiled bowl. Cover with a clean cloth and leave in a warm place for 1 hour, until it has doubled in size.

Preheat the oven to 200°C (400°F/gas mark 6).

Knock the risen dough back, punching it lightly to knock out large air bubbles, and knead briefly on a lightly floured surface. Roll out the dough into a large rectangular shape with a rolling pin and place onto a Swiss roll tin that is 30cm x 23cm (12in x 9in) and preferably non-stick – if it isn't, you'll need to oil it lightly.

Leave to rise in a warm place for another 10 minutes, until doubled in size, then using a palette knife, spread over the tomato sauce. Bake the pizza bread for 15 minutes, until cooked through and golden brown.

Preheat the grill to a medium heat. Sprinkle the Cheddar cheese over the cooked pizza bread and place under the grill for about 5 minutes, until the cheese is melting and bubbling. Drizzle over the pesto and chilli jam and flash under the grill for another minute to just warm through. Carefully remove from the Swiss roll tin onto a breadboard and leave to cool a little.

To serve, cut the warm pizza bread into squares and arrange in a bread basket.

COOK AHEAD
The bread base covered with the tomato sauce can be baked and frozen in the tin. Simply defrost at room temperature for a couple of hours and then add the toppings and proceed as above.

Tomato and Parmesan Twister Bread Rolls

THESE BREAD ROLLS ARE REALLY VERY EASY TO MAKE. WE SERVE THEM AT THE BEGINNING OF MEALS IN THE RESTAURANT. YOUNG PEOPLE IN PARTICULAR LOVE THEM. YOU CAN VARY THE FLAVOURINGS, BUT GO LIGHT ON THEM OR THE FILLING MAY BURN WHILE THEY'RE COOKING.

Makes 20 rolls

450g (1lb) strong white flour, plus extra for dusting

1 tsp salt

2 tsp fast action dried yeast (7g/1/4oz sachet)

225ml (8fl oz) tepid water

1 tbsp rapeseed oil, plus extra for greasing

200g (7oz) tomato sauce (page 255)

125g (4 1/2oz) basil pesto (page 256)

75g (3oz) freshly grated Parmesan

egg wash (made with 1 egg and 1 tbsp milk), for brushing

Sieve the flour into a large bowl with the salt and stir in the yeast. Make a well in the centre and pour in the tepid water and the oil. Mix to a smooth dough.

Turn the dough out onto a lightly floured surface and knead for 5–10 minutes, pushing and stretching until smooth and elastic. Alternatively, use a food mixer with the dough hook attached and set on a low speed – it saves quite a bit of elbow grease. Place in a large lightly oiled bowl. Cover with a clean cloth and leave in a warm place for 1 hour, until it has doubled in size.

Preheat the oven to 200°C (400°F/gas mark 6) and lightly oil 2 x 12 hole muffin tins.

Knock the risen dough back, punching it lightly to knock out large air bubbles, and knead briefly on a lightly floured surface. Roll out the dough into a large rectangular shape approximately 55cm (22in) long and 35cm (14in) wide with a rolling pin. Using a palette knife, spread over the tomato sauce, then spread the pesto on top. Sprinkle over the Parmesan, then gently roll the dough into a long Swiss roll shape – with the dough on the work surface with short ends on either side, pick up the long end closest to you and roll it away from you. Don't worry if it sticks a little, just gently coax it up a bit at a time with floured fingers until it reaches the other side, then press the seam together to stick.

Cut the rolled-up dough into 4cm (1 1/2in) thick slices and place one into 20 of the muffin holes, one of the cut sides down. Brush the tops lightly with egg wash and leave to rise in a warm place for 10 minutes, until doubled in size.

Bake the twister bread rolls for 20–25 minutes, swapping the tins around on the oven shelves halfway through, until cooked through and golden brown. Leave for a couple of minutes in the tin before loosening the bread rolls from the muffin tins with a knife and sliding out onto a wire rack. Serve warm or leave to cool completely.

COOK AHEAD

These bread rolls can frozen in the tin before baking. Defrost at room temperature for a couple of hours and then bake as described above.

Irish Tea Bread

THIS KEEPS VERY WELL WRAPPED IN CLINGFILM AND TIN FOIL. THE LEFTOVERS CAN BE MADE INTO BREAD AND BUTTER PUDDINGS WITH A DASH OF BAILEYS OR EVEN JUST A SIMPLE FRENCH TOAST WORKS WELL.

Makes 1 loaf

100g (4oz) sultanas

100g (4oz) currants or raisins

50g (2oz) glacé cherries, chopped

50g (2oz) cut mixed peel

300ml (1/2 pint) strong hot tea

good splash of Irish whiskey

225g (8oz) light brown sugar

a little rapeseed oil, for greasing

275g (10oz) self-raising flour

good pinch of freshly ground nutmeg

1 egg, beaten

1 tbsp clear honey

butter, to serve

Place the sultanas, currants or raisins, glacé cherries and mixed peel in a large bowl. Pour over the tea and whiskey and stir in the sugar until dissolved. Cover with a plate and leave overnight to allow all the fruit to plump up.

Preheat the oven to 150°C (300°F/gas 2). Lightly grease a 900ml (1 1/2 pint) non-stick loaf tin with rapeseed oil and then base line with parchment paper.

Sieve the flour and nutmeg into a bowl, then stir into the soaked fruit mixture with the egg until evenly combined. Turn into the prepared tin and level the surface. Bake for 1 1/2 hours, until well risen and firm to the touch. A fine skewer inserted into the centre should come out clean.

Allow the tea bread to cool in the tin for about 10 minutes before turning out. Brush the top with the honey and then leave to cool completely on a wire rack.

To serve, cut the tea bread into slices and spread with butter, then arrange on a plate.

COOK AHEAD
Wrapped tightly in clingfilm and then in tin foil, this will then keep happily for 3–4 days.

Sesame and Poppy Seed White Bread

THIS IS THE BREAD THAT WE NORMALLY SERVE AT THE BEGINNING OF EVERY MEAL. THE DOUGH CAN BE FLAVOURED WITH 1 TABLESPOON CHOPPED FRESH HERBS, SUCH AS THYME OR ROSEMARY, OR FOR A MORE PRONOUNCED TASTE ADD IN UP TO 10 TABLESPOONS CHOPPED FRESH MIXED HERBS, SUCH AS A MIXTURE OF FLAT-LEAF PARSLEY, BASIL AND CHIVES, OR TRY ADDING 4 TABLESPOONS SUN-DRIED TOMATO PESTO (PAGE 257) WITH 1 TEASPOON FENNEL SEEDS.

Makes 2 loaves

675g (1 1/2lb) strong white flour, plus extra for dusting

2 x 7g (1/4oz) sachets fast action dried yeast (about 1 tbsp in total)

1 tsp salt

about 450ml (3/4 pint) hand-hot water

egg wash (made with 2 egg yolks and 1 tbsp milk), to glaze

2 tsp white sesame seeds

1 tsp black poppy seeds

butter, to serve

Place the flour in the bowl of a food mixer fitted with a dough attachment if you have one. Add the yeast, salt and hand-hot water. Switch on the machine and mix until you have a very sloppy dough. Knead on medium speed for 6–8 minutes, until you have a slightly sticky but pliable dough.

You can also do this by hand – mix with your fingers for 2–3 minutes, then knead to incorporate the flour, scraping the sides of the bowl and folding the dough over itself until it gathers into a rough mass. Turn the dough out onto a well-floured surface and lightly flour your hands. Knead for 6–8 minutes, until the dough is smooth and pliable. The dough will be very sticky at first; keep your hands and the work surface lightly floured, using a dough scraper if necessary to prevent it from sticking and building up on the work surface. As you continue kneading, the dough will become more elastic and easier to handle.

Either way, divide the dough into 2 pieces and knead each one into a long sausage shape, each about 35cm (14in) long and 5cm (2in) wide. Carefully transfer to a large non-stick baking sheet well spaced apart and slot a piece of parchment paper between them to ensure that they don't stick together. Leave to prove for 1 hour, until doubled in size.

Meanwhile, preheat the oven to 200°C (400°F/gas mark 6).

Brush the tops of the loaves with the egg wash and sprinkle over the sesame and poppy seeds. Bake for 45 minutes, until the loaves are a deep golden brown and sound hollow when tapped on the bottom. Leave to cool for 5 minutes in the tin, then transfer to a wire rack and leave to cool completely before slicing.

To serve, cut the bread into slices and arrange in a breadbasket with a separate pot of butter to serve.

COOK AHEAD
Bread is always best served on the day it's made, but these loaves do keep well for up to 24 hours. They also freeze well.

Goat's Cheese and Red Onion Focaccia with Rosemary

THIS IS ONE OF THE BREADS THAT WE LIKE TO SERVE BEFORE THE STARTERS ARRIVE IN THE RESTAURANT. BOILÍE GOAT'S CHEESE ALSO MAKES A FANTASTIC TOPPING, AS IT'S WONDERFULLY CREAMY YET HAS A MILD FLAVOUR. THIS IS BEST WARM, BUT IT ALSO REHEATS WELL OR IS FINE WHEN COLD.

Makes one 27.5cm x 18cm (11in x 7in) flat loaf

450g (1lb) strong white flour, plus extra for dusting

1 tsp fast action dried yeast

1 1/4 tsp sea salt

225ml (8fl oz) tepid water

7 tbsp olive oil, plus a little extra for greasing

1 large red onion, halved and cut into slices (keeping them attached at the root)

1 tbsp balsamic vinegar

1 tsp brown sugar

2 tbsp basil pesto (page 256)

2 fresh rosemary sprigs, leaves stripped

12 Boilíe goat's cheese balls, drained (from a jar)

50g (2oz) freshly grated Parmesan

Mix together the flour, yeast and 1/4 teaspoon salt in a large bowl. Make a well in the centre and pour in the tepid water and 5 tablespoons of the olive oil. Mix well to achieve a soft dough.

Turn the dough out onto a clean surface and knead for 10 minutes, until smooth and elastic. Place in an oiled bowl, cover with oiled clingfilm and leave to rise in a warm place for about 1 hour, until doubled in size.

Turn the dough out onto a clean surface and knock it back, then knead for another 2–3 minutes and roll out to a large rectangle about 1cm (1/2in) thick. Place in an oiled, lined baking tin that is 27.5cm (11in) x 18cm (7in) and at least 4cm (1 1/2in) deep. Cover with oiled clingfilm. Leave to rise again for 30 minutes, until it looks soft and pillowy.

Meanwhile, preheat the oven to 220°C (425°F/gas mark 7).

Heat 1 tablespoon of the olive oil in a small pan over a low heat and toss in the red onion, vinegar and sugar. Gently cook for 12–15 minutes, until the onion is completely softened and caramelised.

Prick the risen dough all over with a fork. Spread over the pesto, then arrange the red onions on top. Stick the rosemary into the dough and arrange the goat's cheese balls in rows, then sprinkle over the Parmesan with the remaining 1 teaspoon salt. Drizzle with the remaining 1 tablespoon of olive oil and bake for about 30 minutes, until risen, cooked through and golden brown. Leave in the tin for a few minutes, then transfer to a wire rack to cool. Drizzle with a little extra olive oil to keep the crust softened.

To serve, transfer the focaccia to a breadboard and cut into chunks. Arrange in a breadbasket to serve.

COOK AHEAD
This focaccia keeps relatively well because of its high oil content. It can be reheated on a baking sheet in a preheated oven (180°C/350°F/gas mark 4) for 6–8 minutes, until warmed through. It also freezes well.

Sun-dried Tomato Gluten-free Bread

IT ALWAYS AMAZES ME THE AMOUNT OF COELIAC CUSTOMERS THAT COME TO THE RESTAURANT. I HAVE MY GOOD FRIEND NOLEEN BOYLE, A WONDERFUL PASTRY CHEF FROM DONEGAL, TO THANK FOR THIS RECIPE AND WE ALWAYS MAKE SURE THAT WE HAVE SOME AVAILABLE FOR ANYONE WHO REQUESTS IT. SUPERMARKETS ARE GETTING MUCH BETTER AT STOCKING GLUTEN-FREE PRODUCTS SO YOU SHOULD BE ABLE TO GET THE TRITAMYL FLOUR AND RICE BRAN FROM THEIR SPECIALIST SECTION. OTHERWISE, ANY HEALTH FOOD SHOP SHOULD HAVE BOTH.

Makes 2 x 1.2 litre (2 pint) loaves

olive oil, for greasing

600g (1lb 5oz) tritamyl flour (gluten-free flour)

2 tsp bread soda

1/2 tsp salt

325g (11oz) rice bran

150g (5oz) light brown sugar

700ml (1 1/4 pints) buttermilk

100ml (3 1/2fl oz) sun-dried tomato pesto (page 257)

3 eggs

2 tbsp chopped sun-dried tomatoes

1 tbsp sesame seeds

1 tbsp sunflower seeds

butter, for spreading

Preheat the oven to 180°C (350°F/gas mark 4). Lightly grease 2 x 1.2 litre (2 pint) loaf tins.

Sieve the flour into a large bowl with the bread soda and salt, then stir in the rice bran and sugar. Place the buttermilk, sun-dried tomato pesto, eggs and chopped sun-dried tomatoes in a jug, mixing well to combine.

Make a well in the centre of the flour and pour in the buttermilk mixture, stirring to combine. Spoon the mixture into the greased loaf tins and smooth the surface using the back of a spoon. Sprinkle the sesame and sunflower seeds on top.

Bake the bread loaves for 1 hour, until golden brown and crusty on top. Leave in the tin for 5 minutes, then transfer to a wire rack and allow to cool completely.

To serve, place the cooled bread on a breadboard and cut into slices at the table. Hand around a separate pot of butter for spreading.

COOK AHEAD

This bread can be baked, cut into slices and frozen in zip-lock bags. When using, just defrost at room temperature and toast under the grill.

Brioche

THE PERFECT BRIOCHE HAS A DELICIOUS RICH, BUTTERY FLAVOUR, YET IT DOESN'T LEAVE A TRACE OF BUTTER ON YOUR FINGERTIPS OR AN AFTERTASTE ON THE PALATE. THIS IS ANOTHER RECIPE GIVEN TO ME BY MY GOOD FRIEND LÉA LINSTER.

Makes 1 loaf

15g (1/2oz) fresh yeast

70ml (2 1/2fl oz) warm milk

15g (1/2oz) salt

500g (1lb 2oz) strong white flour, plus extra for dusting

6 eggs

355g (12 1/2oz) unsalted butter, softened, plus extra for greasing

60g (2 1/4oz) sugar

For the glaze:

1 egg yolk

1 tbsp milk

Grease a large brioche mould that is 24cm (9 1/2in) at the top and 11cm (4 1/2in) wide at the base.

Place the yeast and warm milk in the bowl of an electric food mixer. Lightly beat with a wire whisk, then beat in the salt. Add the flour and whole eggs and knead the dough with the dough hook for about 10 minutes, until it's smooth and elastic. Alternatively, you can combine all the ingredients in a large bowl and beat with a wooden spoon or knead with your hands for about 20 minutes, until the dough is smooth and elastic.

In a separate bowl, beat the softened butter and sugar until creamy. Switch on the mixer at a low speed and add this mixture to the dough a little at a time, making sure it's completely amalgamated each time before adding more. If you're working by hand, squeeze the butter into the dough. Continue to mix for about 5 minutes in the mixer or 15 minutes by hand, until the dough is perfectly smooth. It should be glossy, shiny and fairly elastic.

Cover the bowl with a damp tea towel and leave in a warm place for about 2 hours, until the dough has doubled in size.

Knock back the dough by flicking it over with your fingertips no more than 3 times. Return the dough to the bowl, cover as before and chill for several hours but no more than 24 hours in total.

Preheat the oven to 220°C (425°F/gas mark 7).

Remove the chilled dough from the fridge and place on a lightly floured surface, then shape into a large bowl.

To prepare the glaze, beat the egg yolk in a small dish with the milk. Lightly glaze the brioche working from the outside in, being careful not to let any run into cracks in the dough or edges of the mould, as this will prevent the dough from rising properly.

Leave the brioche to rise again in a warm, draught-free area until it has almost doubled in size, then give it another light glaze. Using a scissors dipped in cold water, snip around the edge. Bake for 40–45 minutes, until it's golden brown and sounds hollow when tapped underneath. Unmould immediately and leave to cool completely on a wire rack. Cut into slices and use as required.

COOK AHEAD
Brioche dough can be frozen, wrapped in freezer wrap, after the knocking back stage. To bake, leave the dough to thaw gradually in the fridge for 4–5 hours, then proceed as described above. Alternatively, you may bake the loaf as normal and then wrap and freeze.

Prune and Armagnac Tart

A SUMPTUOUS AND EXTRAVAGANT TART THAT MY MOTHER-IN-LAW EILEEN JUST ADORES. THIS IS A FANTASTIC DINNER
PARTY DESSERT THAT YOUR GUESTS WILL FIND IRRESISTIBLE. ANY LEFTOVER ARMAGNAC SYRUP IS DELICIOUS DRIZZLED
OVER ICE CREAM.

Serves 6

For the prunes:

15g (1/2oz) caster sugar

50ml (1 3/4fl oz) Armagnac

2 star anise

1 vanilla pod, split in half

1 cinnamon stick

150g (5oz) pitted Agen prunes

For the pastry:

175g (6oz) plain flour, plus extra for
dusting

150g (5oz) butter, diced and chilled

50g (2oz) caster sugar

1 egg yolk

1/2 tbsp cream

For the frangipane filling:

150g (5oz) butter, at room
temperature

100g (4oz) icing sugar, sifted

100g (4oz) ground almonds

25g (1oz) plain flour

2 eggs, lightly beaten

1 vanilla pod, split in half and seeds
scraped out

large pinch of ground cinnamon

3 tbsp apricot jam

softly whipped cream, to serve

caramel ice cream (page 265), to
serve

The prunes need to be prepared a day or two in advance. Place the sugar, Armagnac
and 5 tablespoons water into a pan. Bring to the boil, then reduce the heat and add
the star anise, vanilla pod and cinnamon stick. Simmer for 2 minutes, then add in the
prunes. Return to the boil, then remove from the heat. Pour into a non-metallic bowl
and set aside at room temperature for at least 24 hours, though a couple of days is best.

To make the pastry, place the flour in a food processor with the butter and sugar and
pulse until just blended. Add the egg yolk and cream, then blend again briefly. Wrap
with clingfilm and chill in the fridge for 1 hour to rest.

To make the filling, place the butter and the icing sugar in a large bowl and beat until
light and fluffy using an electric hand beater. Beat in the ground almonds and flour,
then gradually beat in the eggs, vanilla seeds and cinnamon. Continue to beat for 5
minutes, until light and fluffy.

Preheat the oven to 190°C (375°F/gas mark 5).

Roll out the pastry on a lightly floured work surface and use to line a 23cm (9in) loose-
bottomed flan tin. Chill again for 15 minutes to allow the pastry to rest.

Drain the prunes from the Armagnac syrup and cut each one in half. Spread the
almond filling in the rested pastry case and carefully arrange the prunes on top in a
fan shape, then gently press the prunes down into the filling. Bake the tart for 25–30
minutes, until the pastry is cooked through and golden brown.

Remove from the flan tin and transfer to a plate. Melt the apricot jam in a pan or in
the microwave and brush over the tart.

To serve, cut the tart into wedges and serve warm or cold on plates with a good dollop
of whipped cream and a scoop of caramel ice cream.

COOK AHEAD
The prunes need to be left for up to 2 days to plump up and the pastry and the filling
can also be made 2 days in advance and kept covered in the fridge until needed.

Lemon and Sultana Scones

THIS IS MY BASIC SCONE RECIPE, WHICH HAS A LOVELY LEMON FLAVOUR. THE SCONES COOK IN ABOUT 15 MINUTES AND WE MAKE THEM FRESH IN THE RESTAURANT EVERY DAY. OMIT THE LEMON AND SULTANAS IF YOU PREFER THEM PLAIN.

Makes about 12

450g (1lb) self-raising flour, plus extra for dusting

generous pinch of salt

pinch of baking powder

50g (2oz) caster sugar

110g (4 1/4oz) unsalted butter, diced

1 egg, lightly beaten

50ml (2fl oz) cream

200ml (7fl oz) milk

50g (2oz) sultanas

finely grated rind of 1 lemon

butter, whipped cream and raspberry jam, to serve

Preheat the oven to 180°C (350°F/gas mark 4).

Sift the flour into a bowl with the salt and baking powder, then stir in the sugar. Using your fingertips, rub in the butter until the mixture resembles fine breadcrumbs.

Make a well in the centre and add the egg, cream and enough milk to moisten, then stir in the sultanas and lemon rind. Using a tablespoon, gently and quickly stir the liquid into the flour. It should be soft but not sticky.

Lightly flour the work surface. Turn the dough out onto it and pat into a circle about 2.5cm (1in) thick. Cut into triangles with a sharp knife or stamp out 5cm (2in) rounds with a cutter.

Arrange the scones on a non-stick baking sheet and bake for 15–20 minutes, until well risen and golden brown. Leave to cool for at least 10 minutes on a wire rack.

These scones are best served warm and straight out of the oven. Serve with butter for spreading and small pots of whipped cream and raspberry jam.

COOK AHEAD
These scones are best served on the day they are made, but will keep in an airtight container for 2–3 days and then toasted lightly to serve. They can also be frozen quite successfully.

Oaty Chocolate Chip Cookies

THESE COOKIES MAKE A DELICIOUS ACCOMPANIMENT TO TEA OR COFFEE. MAKE THEM ON A RAINY AFTERNOON AND EAT THEM WHILE STILL WARM FROM THE OVEN. WE SERVE THEM IN OUR BEDROOMS FOR OVERNIGHT GUESTS.

Makes 18-20

250g (9oz) butter, at room temperature

100g (4oz) soft brown sugar

50g (2oz) caster sugar

200g (7oz) self-raising flour

175g (6oz) porridge oats

100g (4oz) plain or milk chocolate drops

100g (4oz) chopped nuts, such as walnuts or almonds, or use a mixture

Preheat the oven to 180°C (350°F/gas mark 4).

Cream together the butter and both sugars in a large bowl until light and fluffy. Beat in the flour, then fold in the porridge oats, chocolate drops and nuts. Mix well to combine.

Using your hands, form the mixture into 18–20 small balls, then flatten them slightly with a fork. Place them on baking sheets lined with parchment paper, leaving enough room for the cookies to spread out.

Bake in the oven for 15–20 minutes. When they are done, remove from the oven and allow to settle and harden for a minute or two, then transfer to a wire rack with a fish slice and leave to cool completely. Store in an airtight container and serve on plates as required.

COOK AHEAD
If there are any cookies left, they can be stored in an airtight tin for up to 1 week.

Oatmeal Cookies

THIS RECIPE WAS GIVEN TO ME BY MARY FLAHAVAN AND I LIKED IT SO MUCH THAT WE NOW MAKE IT UP IN BATCHES AND KEEP THEM IN KILNER JARS IN OUR ROOMS FOR GUESTS IN CASE THEY'RE FEELING A BIT PECKISH AFTER A LONG JOURNEY BUT DON'T WANT TO RUIN THEIR DINNER!

Makes about 36

275g (10oz) Flahavan's Progress Oatlets

225g (8oz) butter, at room temperature

150g (5oz) caster sugar

100g (4oz) plain flour, plus a little extra for dusting

1/2 tsp bread soda

Blend the oatlets in a food processor until quite fine. Add the butter, sugar, flour and bread soda and blend again until the dough just comes together.

Divide the dough into 3 pieces and roll each one into a long sausage shape that is 15cm (6in) long and 4cm (1 1/2in) wide. Wrap in clingfilm and chill in the fridge for 1 hour to firm up.

Preheat the oven to 200°C (400°F/gas mark 6).

Using a sharp knife, trim the ends from each cookie roll and cut each roll into about 12 cookies – each one should be about 1cm (1/2in) thick. Arrange the oatmeal cookies well spaced apart on parchment-lined baking sheets. Bake for 15–20 minutes, until pale golden and slightly firm. Remove from the oven and leave to cool for 1 minute, then transfer to a wire rack and leave to cool completely.

To serve, put into Kilner jars or arrange on a plate.

COOK AHEAD
The cookie rolls keep well in the fridge for up to 1 week or can be frozen and defrosted at room temperature before using. The baked cookies keep well in an airtight container for up to 1 week.

Shortbread Biscuits

THESE SHORTBREAD BISCUITS ARE CRUCIAL FOR MY BAKED RASPBERRY SHORTCAKES (PAGE 172), WHICH IS PART OF THE RASPBERRY PLATE, AND I ALSO USE THEM BROKEN UP IN THE MACNEAN CHEESECAKE WITH RASPBERRIES AND WHITE CHOCOLATE (PAGE 156). HOWEVER, THEY ARE ALSO A DELICIOUS ACCOMPANIMENT TO ANY CREAMY DESSERT OR JUST WITH A CUP OF TEA!

Makes 32

275g (10oz) butter, diced, at room temperature, plus extra for greasing

150g (5oz) icing sugar, sieved, plus extra to decorate

275g (10oz) plain flour, plus extra for dusting

150g (5oz) cornflour

Place the butter and icing sugar in a bowl, then sieve the flour and cornflour on top. Using a hand-held beater, mix until you have achieved a smooth dough, adding 1 tablespoon cold water to help bring the mixture together if necessary. Cover with clingfilm. Place in the fridge to rest for at least 1 hour and preferably overnight.

Roll out the shortbread on a lightly floured work surface until it's 3mm (1/8in) thick. Stamp out discs using a 5cm (2in) fluted cutter. Place on a greased baking sheet and leave to rest again in the fridge for 10 minutes – this will help to stop them from shrinking.

Preheat the oven to 180°C (350°F/gas mark 4).

Bake the cookies for 10–12 minutes, until golden brown. Using a fish slice, transfer to a wire rack to cool.

To serve, arrange on a plate or use as required.

COOK AHEAD
These biscuits keep well in an airtight container for 2–3 days. Alternatively, the dough can be frozen for up to 2 weeks.

Jammie Dodgers

WHO DIDN'T LOVE THESE AS A CHILD? I CERTAINLY DID, WHICH IS WHY I DEVELOPED THIS RECIPE, WHICH I LIKE TO SERVE WITH THE MACNEAN CHEESECAKE WITH RASPBERRIES AND WHITE CHOCOLATE (PAGE 156). THEY'RE NOT ONLY A BIT OF FUN, BUT ALSO TASTE DELICIOUS AND THERE'S NO DOUBT THAT CHILDREN WILL ABSOLUTELY ADORE THEM. YOU CAN USE ANY JAM YOU LIKE, BUT I FIND THAT THE VIBRANT COLOUR OF RASPBERRY JAM IS FANTASTIC.

Makes 16–18

For the shortcake:

75g (3oz) plain flour, plus extra for dusting

25g (1oz) icing sugar, plus extra for dusting

finely grated rind of 1 lime

50g (2oz) butter, softened

For the jam filling:

100g (4oz) raspberry jam

1 tbsp crème de cassis

1/4 tsp vanilla extract

To make the shortcake, sift the flour and icing sugar into a bowl. Stir in the lime rind, then beat in the butter with a wooden spoon until it forms rough crumbs. Bring the mixture together with your hands to form a soft, smooth dough. Wrap in clingfilm and chill for at least 30 minutes, though up to 3 days is fine.

To make the jam filling, place the raspberry jam, crème de cassis and vanilla extract in a pan and simmer over a low heat for 8–10 minutes, until melted and slightly thickened. Leave to cool completely, then place in a bowl. Cover with clingfilm and chill if keeping for any length of time.

Preheat the oven to 190°C (375°F/gas mark 5).

Roll out the dough on a lightly floured surface to a 3mm (1/8in) thickness. Stamp out 32–36 rounds using a 4cm (1 3/4in) fluted cutter and arrange on baking sheets lined with parchment paper. Using a piping bag nozzle (a metal rather than plastic one is best for this) with a 1cm (1/2in) wide head, press the nozzle into the centre of half of the rounds to stamp out a hole (which will allow you to see the jam later). Bake for 8–10 minutes, until crisp and lightly golden.

To assemble, spoon a teaspoon of jam mixture into the centre of each uncut shortcake. Dust the remaining shortcakes with icing sugar and then place on top, pressing down lightly so the jam just squeezes out through the hole a little.

To serve, arrange on a plate or use as required.

COOK AHEAD

These are best eaten on the day of assembly. If making in advance, keep the shortcakes in an airtight container and fill with the jam just before serving. The jam filling can be stored in your fridge, covered with clingfilm, for up to 1 month.

The MacNean Celebration Cake

THIS CAKE IS A VERY SPECIAL TREAT AND IS GREAT FOR ALL MANNER OF OCCASIONS. WE GET SO MANY CUSTOMERS CELEBRATING BIRTHDAYS AND ANNIVERSARIES IN THE RESTAURANT. I LOVE THE LIGHTNESS OF THE CHOCOLATE SPONGE WITH THE SLIGHTLY SALTY PEANUT FROSTING. OF COURSE, YOU CAN USE ANY FLAVOUR OF CHOCOLATE TRUFFLES YOU FANCY. I BUY CRISPY FEUILLETINE FROM B.D. FOODS OR PALLAS FOODS (SEE PAGE 270 FOR DETAILS), BUT YOU COULD ALWAYS USE CRUMBLED TUILE BISCUITS, THIN WAFERS, CHOPPED NUTS OR TOASTED FLAKED ALMONDS INSTEAD.

Serves 8

For the cake:

175g (6oz) butter, softened, plus extra for greasing

175g (6oz) caster sugar

1 tbsp cocoa powder

1 tsp vanilla extract

200g (7oz) self-raising flour

1 tsp baking powder

100ml (3 1/2fl oz) milk

3 eggs

For the peanut frosting:

100g (4oz) cream cheese

200g (7oz) icing sugar

120g (4 1/2oz) unsalted butter, at room temperature

2 tbsp crunchy peanut butter

1 tsp vanilla extract

For the ganache:

200g (7oz) plain chocolate, broken into squares (at least 70% cocoa solids)

250ml (9fl oz) cream

1 tbsp liquid glucose

75g (3oz) pecans, toasted and chopped

100g (4oz) crispy feuilletine

fresh raspberries, to decorate

chocolate orange truffles (page 189), to decorate

melted white chocolate, for drizzling

plain and white chocolate curls, (page 269), to decorate

Preheat the oven to 180°C (350°F/gas mark 4). Butter 2 x 18cm (7in) non-stick sandwich tins and set aside until needed.

Place the butter in a large bowl with the sugar, cocoa powder and vanilla, then beat with an electric mixer until soft and fluffy. Slowly add the flour, baking powder, milk and eggs, beating continuously until creamy.

Transfer the cake mixture into the prepared tins for 25–30 minutes, until risen and firm to the touch. Leave to cool in the tins for a few minutes, then turn out onto a wire rack and leave to cool completely.

Meanwhile, make the peanut frosting. Place the cream cheese in a bowl and sift in the icing sugar, then add the butter, peanut butter and vanilla extract. Using an electric mixer, beat until pale and fluffy.

To make the ganache, melt the chocolate in a heatproof bowl set over a pan of simmering water. Bring the cream and glucose to the boil in a separate pan, then pour over the melted chocolate. Mix well until smooth, then leave until thickened and cool.

Using a bread knife, split the cooled cakes into 2 even-sized sections. Choose the flattest top and set it aside. Set the remaining 3 layers out on a clean work surface and spread over the peanut frosting, then sprinkle the pecan nuts on top and place the layers back on top of each other. Cover with the top layer of the cake and place on a wire rack set over a plastic tray.

To decorate, pour the ganache over the cake and use a palette knife to help spread and smooth it down the sides. Leave to set for about 5 minutes, then carefully press some crispy feuilletine around the outside of the cake. Decorate with the raspberries, chocolate truffles, drizzles of melted white chocolate and the plain and white chocolate curls.

To serve, carefully transfer the finished cake to a cake stand and cut into slices, then arrange on plates.

COOK AHEAD
The chocolate sponge, peanut frosting and ganache can all be made 24 hours in advance. Keep the sponge wrapped tightly in clingfilm; the frosting and ganache need to be kept covered with clingfilm in the fridge. To use, simply reheat in the microwave for 30 seconds. The cake itself needs to be assembled at the last minute.

Sophie's Chocolate Biscuit Cake

THIS RECIPE WAS GIVEN TO ME BY JEAN DIX FROM HOWTH, CO. DUBLIN. SHE DEVISED IT FOR HER DAUGHTER SOPHIE'S BIRTHDAY, WHO WAS THE CRITICAL TASTER. IT'S A BRILLIANT ONE TO DO WITH CHILDREN, AS THERE IS NO COOKING INVOLVED. UNLIKE MANY OTHER CHOCOLATE BISCUIT CAKE RECIPES, IT CUTS BEAUTIFULLY EVEN STRAIGHT OUT OF THE FRIDGE AND KEEPS WELL WRAPPED IN CLINGFILM FOR AT LEAST 2 WEEKS.

Makes 1 loaf

250g (9oz) milk chocolate

100g (4oz) unsalted butter

5 tbsp whipping cream

1 tbsp golden syrup

400g (14oz) packet digestive biscuits

100g (4oz) white chocolate (optional)

Break the chocolate into squares and place in a heatproof bowl with the butter. Set over a pan of simmering water and allow to melt. Remove from the heat and mix in the cream and golden syrup by hand, which will take a few minutes.

Break the digestive biscuits into large chunks and gently fold into the chocolate mixture so as not to break up the biscuits too much. Using a spatula, transfer to a 900ml (1 1/2 pints) loaf tin that has been double lined with clingfilm, as this makes the cake much easier to lift out. Chill for at least 2 hours, though overnight is best.

To serve, turn out the chocolate biscuit cake onto a platter. Break the white chocolate into squares, if using, and melt in a heatproof bowl over a pan of simmering water. Drizzle all over the chocolate biscuit cake and leave at room temperature to set for about 20 minutes before cutting into slices and arranging on plates.

COOK AHEAD

This cake is best made overnight and keeps very well for 2–3 days wrapped tightly in the fridge with clingfilm and then a layer of tin foil.

BASIC RECIPES

Potato Sides

Crispy Potato Rosti

Serves 4

1 large baking potato, preferably
Maris Piper

sea salt

3 tbsp rapeseed oil

Peel the potato, then grate the flesh
using the coarse side of a grater, a
mandolin or a Benriner mandolin
slicer, which I find is the best of all (see
page 272 for details). Squeeze out all
the excess water and place the grated
potato in a bowl, then season with salt.

Heat 4 x 10cm (4in) blini pans (or
use a straight-sided cutter placed
on a frying pan). Add a good film
of oil to the pan. Divide the potato
mixture into 4 portions and using
2 forks, spread each portion evenly
into the pans, separating out the
strands of potatoes. Cook over a low
heat for 5–6 minutes, until golden
brown, turning regularly and using
the forks to separate out the strands
as necessary.

Drain the crispy potato rostis on
kitchen paper and use as required.

COOK AHEAD

The rosti can be made up to 6 hours in
advance and left at room temperature
until ready to use. To reheat, place
the rosti on a cooling rack and place
the cooling rack on a baking sheet in a
preheated oven (140°C/275°F/gas mark 1)
for 10–12 minutes. Alternatively, you can
reheat the rosti under a medium grill for a
couple of minutes on each side.

Potato Purée

Serves 6

1.5kg (3lb) floury potatoes, cut into
even-sized chunks

about 120ml (4 fl oz) milk and/or
cream

75g (3oz) butter

sea salt and freshly ground white
pepper

Place the potatoes in a large pan of
salted water. Bring to the boil, cover
and simmer for 15–20 minutes, until
the potatoes are tender without
breaking up. Drain and return to the
pan over a low heat to dry out. Mash
the potatoes or pass them through a
potato ricer or vegetable mouli if you
want a really smooth finish.

Heat the milk and/or cream in a small
pan. Using a wooden spoon, beat the
butter into the potatoes until melted
and then beat in enough of the hot
milk until you have achieved smooth,
creamy purée. Season to taste. Use as
required.

COOK AHEAD

This will keep warm in a very cool oven
(120°C/250°F/gas mark 1/2) for up to
1 hour. Alternatively, leave to cool and
transfer to a bowl. Cover with clingfilm
and chill for up to 24 hours. Reheat gently
in a small pan to order using a little more
butter and a splash of milk.

Apple and Potato Purée

Serves 6

1.5kg (3lb) floury potatoes, cut into even-sized chunks

4 spring onions, finely chopped

1 eating apple, peeled, cored and finely chopped

120ml (4 fl oz) milk

75g (3oz) butter

sea salt and freshly ground white pepper

Place the potatoes in a large pan of salted water. Bring to the boil, cover and simmer for 15–20 minutes, until the potatoes are tender without breaking up. Drain and return to the pan over a low heat to dry out.

Just before the potatoes are ready, place the spring onions, apple and milk in a small pan. Simmer gently until the spring onions have softened in the milk, then remove from the heat.

Mash the potatoes or pass them through a potato ricer or vegetable mouli if you want a really smooth finish. Using a wooden spoon, beat the butter into the potatoes until melted and then beat in the milk and spring onion mixture until you have achieved a smooth, creamy purée. Season to taste and use as required.

VARIATIONS

Once mastered, this recipe can be adapted for different results. Try replacing a couple of tablespoons of the milk with crème fraîche or cream for a richer version. A couple of tablespoons of chopped chives or a good dollop of Dijon mustard can also work well, depending on what you are serving with the purée.

COOK AHEAD

This will keep warm in a very cool oven (120°C/250°F/gas mark 1/2) for up to 1 hour. Alternatively, leave to cool and transfer to a bowl. Cover with clingfilm and chill for up to 24 hours. Reheat gently in a small pan to order using a little more butter and a splash of milk.

Roast Potatoes

Serves 8–10

1.5kg (3lb) potatoes, cut into even-sized pieces

sea salt

about 100ml (3 1/2 fl oz) rapeseed oil, dripping or duck fat

2 fresh rosemary sprigs

Place the potatoes in a saucepan of cold water with a pinch of salt, then cover and bring to the boil. Reduce the heat and simmer for 7–8 minutes. Drain the potatoes and leave in the colander to cool slightly, then give them a good shake to fluff up the edges.

Meanwhile, preheat the oven to 220°C (425°F/gas mark 7). Put a roasting tin in the oven with a 1cm (1/2in) depth of rapeseed oil, dripping or duck fat for a few minutes, until just smoking. Carefully tip the potatoes and the rosemary into the hot oil, basting the tops. Roast for 35–45 minutes, turning occasionally, until crisp and golden.

To serve, drain the roast potatoes of any excess oil and season with salt, then use as required.

Potato Gratin

Serves 8

400ml (14 fl oz) milk

300ml (1/2 pint) double cream

4 garlic cloves, crushed

good pinch freshly grated nutmeg

8 rindless smoked streaky bacon rashers (optional)

900g (2lb) potatoes, cut into wafer-thin slices

sea salt and freshly ground black pepper

butter, for greasing

100g (4oz) mature Cheddar cheese, grated

Preheat the oven to 160°C (325°F/gas mark 3).

Pour the milk and cream into a pan and add the garlic and nutmeg. Season to taste and just heat through but do not allow the mixture to boil, then quickly remove from the heat.

Meanwhile, preheat the grill if using the bacon rashers. Arrange the bacon rashers on a grill rack and cook for about 5 minutes, until crisp and lightly golden, turning once. Drain on kitchen paper and when cool enough to handle, snip into pieces with a scissors.

Arrange a third of the potatoes in a greased ovenproof dish that is about 23cm (9in) x 18cm (7in) and at least 5cm (2in) deep. Season to taste and scatter over half of the bacon, if using, then add another third of the potatoes in an even layer, season to taste and scatter over the remaining bacon. Arrange the rest of the potatoes on top in an attractive overlapping layer and carefully pour over the milk mixture.

Cover the potato gratin with a piece of foil and sit the dish on a baking sheet. Bake for 1 hour 15 minutes, until cooked through. Compress the gratin every 20 minutes or so with a fish slice to make sure it's compact.

If serving straight away, sprinkle over the Cheddar and return to the oven for another 10 minutes, until the Cheddar is bubbling and golden brown. Remove the gratin from the oven and leave to settle for 5 minutes, then cut into portions and serve immediately.

Alternatively, leave the gratin to cool completely. Chill for at least 6 hours, though overnight is best to firm it up. Cut into portions or use a 5cm (2in) straight-sided cutter to make rounds and arrange on a non-stick baking sheet. When almost ready to serve, preheat the oven to 160°C (325°F/gas mark 3). Place the potato gratin rounds in the oven for about 15 minutes, until warmed through, then remove and carefully scatter over the cheese. Flash under the grill for a few minutes, until bubbling and golden. Use as required.

COOK AHEAD

This can be made up to 2 days in advance and kept covered with clingfilm in the fridge until needed. Reheat as described above.

Potato Gnocchi

Serves 12 (makes about 60 pieces)

350g (12oz) potatoes, washed (such as Maris Piper)

100g (4oz) plain flour, plus extra for dusting

75g (3oz) freshly grated Parmesan cheese

1 egg yolk

2 tbsp ricotta cheese

1 tbsp snipped fresh chives

sea salt and freshly ground white pepper

1 tbsp rapeseed oil

25g (1oz) butter

Preheat the oven to 200°C (400°F/ gas mark 6).

Boil or steam the potatoes in their skins until just cooked through. Drain and quickly peel them while they are still hot, wearing gloves.

Cut each potato into quarters and place on a baking sheet. Place in the oven for about 5 minutes to dry them out, then mash until smooth – a potato ricer is best for this.

Mix the mashed potato with the flour, Parmesan, egg yolk, ricotta and chives and season to taste. Do not overmix or the gnocchi will be tough. Place the potato mixture on a plate and cover loosely with clingfilm and chill for at least 1 hour, until firm.

Dust the work surface with flour. Using your hands, roll out the potato mixture into long cigar shapes about 1cm (1/2in) thick, then cut into 2.5cm (1in) lengths – you should end up with about 60 pieces in total.

Bring a large pan of water to the boil, then add the gnocchi in batches and simmer for 2–3 minutes, until they have risen to the top and are cooked through. Remove with a slotted spoon and transfer to a bowl of iced water while you cook the rest. This step is important for the texture of the gnocchi. When all the gnocchi are cooked, drain on kitchen paper.

Heat a frying pan with the oil over a medium heat. Add the butter and once it's foaming and lightly browned, add the gnocchi. Cook for a few minutes on each side, until light golden, turning regularly. Season lightly with salt and keep warm. Use as required.

COOK AHEAD

The potato gnocchi can be made 24 hours in advance and even blanched, then left to cool completely and arranged on a plate lined with kitchen paper. Cover with clingfilm and chill until needed. Pan-fry as described, remembering that they will take a little longer if they've come straight from the fridge. They also freeze well.

Sweet Potato Fondants

THIS HAS TO BE ONE OF MY FAVOURITE ACCOMPANIMENTS AT THE RESTAURANT, WHERE I OFTEN SERVE IT WITH DUCK OR LAMB. I NORMALLY USE A 5CM (2IN) STRAIGHT-SIDED COOKING RING AS A CUTTER, WHICH CREATES PERFECT LITTLE SWEET POTATO TOWERS EVERY TIME!

Makes 4

2 sweet potatoes, each at least 8cm (3in) long and 4cm (1 1/2in) across

25g (1oz) butter

1 tsp rapeseed oil

sea salt and freshly ground black pepper

300ml (1/2 pint) chicken stock (page 253)

2 fresh thyme sprigs

Peel the sweet potatoes and trim down until they are 8cm (3in) long so you are left with cylindrical sections. Place these on your chopping board and cut each one into 2cm (3/4in) slices, then use a straight-sided cutter to stamp out 8 x 4cm (1 1/2in) rounds.

Heat a frying pan over a medium heat and add the butter and oil. Add the sweet potato discs and cook for 2–3 minutes on each side, until golden. Season to taste and pour in enough stock to come three-quarters of the way up the sweet potatoes.

Add the thyme sprigs to the fondants, then increase the heat and bring to the boil. Reduce the heat and simmer gently for 10–12 minutes without moving the potatoes, until all of the stock mixture has gone and the potatoes are tender when pierced with the tip of a sharp knife. Turn the discs over carefully with a spatula. You will notice that the bottoms have started to brown and caramelise. Cook for 3–4 minutes, until browned and completely tender.

COOK AHEAD

Make the sweet potato fondants up to 2 days in advance and keep covered in the fridge until needed. Reheat on a baking sheet at 180°C (350°F/gas mark 4) for 10 minutes. They also keep well in a cool oven.

Vegetable Sides

Wilted Cos Lettuce

Serves 4

1 smoked streaky bacon rasher, rind removed

1 tsp rapeseed oil

1 head Cos lettuce, trimmed down and separated into leaves (about 150g /5oz)

sea salt and freshly ground black pepper

Heat a frying pan over a medium heat and cook the smoked streaky bacon until golden brown in colour, turning regularly. Drain on kitchen paper and chop very small. Set aside until needed.

In a separate pan, heat the rapeseed oil over a medium heat and toss in the Cos lettuce leaves. Cook for 2 minutes, until the lettuce has wilted. Add the bacon and season (being careful with the salt). Use as required.

COOK AHEAD

The bacon can be cooked in advance and kept in a bowl covered with clingfilm in the fridge until needed. The Cos leaves can be separated up to 12 hours in advance, but everything needs to be cooked to order.

Wilted Spinach

Serves 6

100g (4oz) butter

550g (1lb 4oz) spinach, tough stalks removed

pinch of caster sugar

sea salt and freshly ground black pepper

Heat a pan over a medium heat and add the butter. Once it has stopped foaming, quickly sauté the spinach with the sugar until soft and wilted. Season to taste and drain well on kitchen paper to remove the excess moisture. Return to the pan and keep warm. Use as required.

COOK AHEAD

This can be made up to 24 hours in advance, then cooled and kept on kitchen paper on a plastic tray covered with clingfilm in the fridge until needed. Place in a pan and reheat gently, stirring occasionally.

Creamed Spinach

Serves 4

100ml (3 1/2fl oz) cream

2 tsp softened butter

1 garlic clove, crushed

200g (7oz) spinach leaves, washed and tough stalks removed

sea salt and freshly ground black pepper

Heat the cream and butter for 30 seconds in a large heavy-based pan over a medium heat. Add the garlic, then tip in the spinach. Cook for 1 minute, until just wilted, stirring constantly. Season to taste and use as required.

Creamed Savoy Cabbage

Serves 4–6

1 tbsp rapeseed oil

100g (4oz) carrot, finely diced

75g (3oz) celeriac, finely diced

2 tbsp softened butter

350g (12oz) Savoy cabbage, tough stalks removed and finely sliced

200ml (7fl oz) cream

sea salt and freshly ground black pepper

Heat a pan over a medium heat. Add the oil and gently sweat the carrot and celeriac for 3–4 minutes. Add the butter and once it has melted, tip in the cabbage and cook for 2–3 minutes, until the cabbage is wilted. Pour in the cream, stirring to combine, then allow to simmer and reduce until slightly thickened. Season to taste and use as required.

COOK AHEAD

This can be made up to 12 hours in advance, then cooled and kept covered with clingfilm in a bowl in the fridge until needed. Place in a pan and reheat gently, stirring occasionally.

Creamed Leeks

Serves 6

1 tbsp rapeseed oil

knob of butter

2 leeks, trimmed and finely chopped (about 150g (5oz) in total)

175ml (6fl oz) cream

salt and freshly ground black pepper

Heat a pan over a medium heat and add the oil and butter. Tip in the leeks and sauté for 2–3 minutes, until softened. Pour in the cream and cook for another 4–5 minutes, until the cream has reduced and the leeks are completely softened. Season to taste and use as required.

COOK AHEAD

This can be made up to 12 hours in advance, then cooled and kept covered with clingfilm in a bowl in the fridge until needed. Place in a pan and reheat gently, stirring occasionally.

Braised Red Cabbage

Serves 6–8

1 tbsp rapeseed oil

1 small head red cabbage, finely chopped in a food processor

300ml (1/2 pint) red wine

300ml (1/2 pint) freshly pressed apple juice

4 tbsp light brown sugar

2 tbsp balsamic vinegar

2 cooking apples, peeled, cored and chopped

1 tsp ground cinnamon

1 tsp mixed spice

1 tsp ground cloves

sea salt and freshly ground black pepper

Heat the oil in a heavy-based pan over a high heat. Stir in the cabbage. Reduce the heat and cook for 15 minutes, stirring occasionally, until the cabbage is well cooked down, adding a tablespoon or two of water if the cabbage starts to catch on the bottom.

Add the red wine, apple juice, brown sugar and vinegar to the cabbage mixture. Give it a good stir, then cover with a lid and simmer for 1 hour over a low heat, stirring occasionally. Stir in the apples and spices and cook gently for another 30 minutes, again stirring occasionally. Season to taste and use as required.

COOK AHEAD

This will keep for up to 1 week in the fridge covered with clingfilm in a non-metallic bowl. It can also be frozen very successfully.

Dried Cauliflower

Serves 20

1/2 small cauliflower

Cut off the florets from the cauliflower, then using a Japanese mandolin, cut into wafer-thin slices.

Put the slices in a food dehydrator (see page 271 for more details) set at 65°C (150°F) for 3–4 hours, until crisp and dry. Remove and use as required.

COOK AHEAD

This can be made up to 2 days in advance and kept in an airtight container until needed.

Caramelised Baby Onions

Serves 4–6

1 tbsp clear honey

1 tsp softened butter

12 baby onions, peeled

sea salt and freshly ground white pepper

Place the honey and butter in a small pan over a medium heat and add 1 tablespoon water. Add the onions and cook for 3 minutes, until lightly caramelised and well coated. Season to taste and use as required.

COOK AHEAD

If you have any difficulty finding baby onions, use the pickled ones from a jar and rinse them well before using.

Onion Tart Tatin

Serves 8 (makes 4)

1 large onion, peeled

100g (4oz) caster sugar

100g (4oz) butter

200g (7oz) ready-rolled puff pastry, thawed if frozen

Cut the onion into 4 x 1cm (1/2in) rings, discarding the ends. Take away enough outer rings so that each one will neatly sit in the bottom of a 10cm (4in) blini pan.

Sprinkle the sugar over the base of the blini pans. Put two cubes of butter into the base of each one and place a slice of onion on top of each one. Stamp or cut out 4 x 10cm (4in) rounds from the puff pastry and place on top of the onion, carefully tucking down the edges to create a rim. Place in the fridge to rest for at least 10 minutes.

Preheat the oven to 190°C (375°F/gas mark 5).

Place the blini pans directly on the hob on a medium heat and cook for 4–5 minutes to caramelise the sugar. You should be able to see the sugar bubbling up around the edges of the pastry – watch it carefully as it turns from golden to dark brown in colour. Transfer to the oven and cook for another 10 minutes, until the puff pastry is golden brown.

COOK AHEAD

These can be made up to 2 days in advance and kept chilled in the fridge on a plastic tray covered with clingfilm until needed. To reheat, preheat the oven to 190°C (375°F/gas mark 5), place them on a preheated baking sheet and cook for 6–8 minutes, until heated through.

Beetroot Carpaccio

Serves 4–8

2 large raw beetroot

450ml (3/4 pint) red wine

100ml (3 1/2fl oz) ruby red port

2 tbsp crème de cassis (optional)

To prepare the beets, it's best to put a pair of gloves on, otherwise you will stain your hands. Trim the tops off the beets and then peel. Using a mandolin, carefully slice each beetroot as thinly as possible. You'll need 24 even-sized slices for this recipe in total. Stamp out the slices with a 3.5cm (1 1/4in) straight-sided cutter.

Place the wine in a pan with the port and crème de cassis, if using. Bring to the boil, then add the thinly sliced beetroot and cook for 8–10 minutes, until just cooked through. Drain well and dry with kitchen paper. Use as required.

COOK AHEAD

This can be made 2–3 days in advance and kept in the liquid in a non-metallic bowl covered with clingfilm in the fridge until needed. Drain and dry with kitchen paper to use.

Pickled Cucumber

Serves 4

4 tbsp rice wine vinegar

2 tbsp caster sugar

sea salt

1/2 small cucumber, peeled, halved, seeded and thinly sliced

Place the vinegar in a bowl and stir in the sugar and a good pinch of salt until dissolved. Tip in the cucumber, stirring to combine, and set aside for 1 hour to allow the flavours to develop. Use as required.

COOK AHEAD

This can be made up to 1 week in advance and kept covered in the fridge until needed.

Garlic Confit

Serves 6

300ml (1/2 pint) duck fat

1 garlic bulb, separated into cloves (but not peeled)

2 fresh thyme sprigs

Warm the duck fat in a pan until it's no longer solidified. Add the garlic cloves and thyme sprigs and simmer very gently over a low heat for about 40 minutes, until meltingly soft. Remove from the oil and gently squeeze the cloves out of their skins. Use as required.

COOK AHEAD

This can be made up to 2 days in advance and kept covered in the fridge until needed.

Oven-dried Cherry Tomatoes

Makes 20

10 cherry tomatoes, halved

4 tbsp olive oil

good pinch chopped fresh thyme

sea salt and freshly ground black pepper

Preheat the oven to 100°C (200°F/gas mark 1/4).

Arrange the cherry tomato halves cut side up on a baking sheet lined with parchment paper. Drizzle over the olive oil, scatter the thyme on top and season to taste. Place in the middle of the oven for 4–5 hours, checking every hour to ensure the tomatoes at the edge aren't overcooking. Remove the tomatoes from the oven and leave to cool, then use as required.

COOK AHEAD

These tomatoes can be kept covered with olive oil in a sterilised jar in the fridge for up to 2 weeks. Drain and bring back to room temperature to use.

Other Sides and Accompaniments

Red Pepper Polenta

Serves 8 (makes 16 discs)

300ml (1/2 pint) vegetable stock

1 small roasted red pepper, cored, seeded and finely diced

1 tbsp sweet chilli sauce

1 tbsp basil pesto (page 256)

1 tbsp freshly grated Parmesan

100g (4oz) instant polenta (maize meal)

sea salt and freshly ground black pepper

rapeseed oil, for cooking and greasing

knob of butter

Pour the stock into a pan and bring to the boil. Add the diced pepper, chilli sauce, pesto and Parmesan. Pour in the polenta and seasoning, stirring all the time. Cook for 4–5 minutes, until the mixture starts to come away from the sides of the pan.

Pour the polenta onto 2 sheets of clingfilm and form into a 20cm (8in) sausage shape that is approximately 3.5cm (1 1/2in) wide. Chill for at least 30 minutes (or overnight is fine), until firm.

Remove the polenta from the fridge and using a sharp knife, cut straight through the clingfilm into 16 x 1cm (1/2in) slices (discarding the ends), then carefully remove the clingfilm. Heat a large frying pan over a medium heat and add the rapeseed oil and butter. Gently fry the polenta discs for 1–2 minutes on each side, until heated through and light golden. Use as required.

COOK AHEAD

The polenta can be made up to 2 days in advance, cut as needed and kept chilled in the fridge covered with clingfilm. Pan-fry to order and they can then be kept warm in a preheated oven (140°C/275°F/gas mark 1) for 5–10 minutes if necessary.

Mediterranean Couscous

Serves 6

1 tbsp rapeseed oil

1 small red onion, diced

1 small courgette, trimmed and finely diced

1 garlic clove, crushed

1 red pepper, roasted, cored and finely diced

150ml (1/4 pint) tomato juice

1 tbsp tomato purée

dash of balsamic vinegar

pinch of sugar

1 tbsp chopped fresh basil

sea salt and freshly ground black pepper

400ml (14fl oz) vegetable stock (page 252)

finely grated rind and juice of 1 lemon

175g (6oz) couscous

2 tbsp lemon oil (shop bought)

4 tbsp toasted pine nuts

4 tbsp chopped fresh mixed herbs (such as mint, coriander and flat-leaf parsley)

Heat the rapeseed oil in a pan over a medium heat. Add the red onion, courgette and garlic and cook for 2 minutes, stirring. Add in the red pepper and cook for 1 minute more, stirring. Using a wooden spoon, stir in the tomato juice, purée, vinegar and sugar and cook for 5–6 minutes, then add the basil and season to taste. Keep warm.

Meanwhile, bring the stock to the boil and add in the lemon juice, then season to taste. Keep warm.

Toast the couscous on a dry pan for 2–3 minutes, until golden brown, tossing constantly and being careful not to let it burn. Transfer to a large bowl and add in the lemon oil and rind and mix well to combine. Pour in the hot stock, then cover with clingfilm and leave to sit until all the liquid is absorbed.

Just before serving, stir in the warm vegetable mixture along with the pine nuts and herbs. Mix well to combine and season to taste – you should have about 900g (2lb) in total. Use as required.

COOK AHEAD

The couscous and vegetable mixture can be prepared and kept separately in the fridge for up to 2 days. Reheat the couscous in a pan over a gentle heat, fluffing up the grains with a fork. Place the vegetable mixture in a separate pan and allow to warm through, then stir into the couscous with the pine nuts and herbs to serve.

Quinoa

Serves 4

125g (4 1/2oz) mixed black, red and white quinoa

1 tsp salt

25g (1oz) butter

1 tbsp chopped fresh flat-leaf parsley

Rinse the quinoa through a fine sieve under cold running water. Drain well and place in a pan with 450ml (3/4 pint) water. Add the salt, bring to the boil and cover with a lid. Reduce the heat and simmer gently for 15–20 minutes, until tender.

Remove the quinoa from the heat and allow to sit for 5 minutes with the lid on to swell up – all the water should now be absorbed. Fluff the quinoa gently with a fork – you should now have about 400g (14oz) in total. Gently fold in the butter and parsley and use as required.

COOK AHEAD

The quinoa can be cooked up to 2 days in advance and kept covered in the fridge – just add the parsley at the last minute to retain the vibrant colour. Reheat in the microwave or over a gentle heat in a pan, using a fork to help separate the grains.

Creamed White Beans

Serves 6–8

175g (6oz) dried haricot beans

2 fresh thyme sprigs

2 streaky bacon rashers, cooked and finely diced

200ml (7fl oz) cream

1 tbsp chopped fresh flat-leaf parsley

1 tbsp snipped fresh chives

sea salt and freshly ground black pepper

Soak the haricot beans overnight in a large bowl of cold water. Drain and place in a very large pan and cover with fresh water and add the thyme. Bring to the boil and boil rapidly for 10 minutes, then cover and simmer for 45–50 minutes, until the beans are just cooked and tender but still holding their shape. Refresh under cold running water and store in the fridge until needed.

Preheat the grill and cook the bacon until golden and sizzling on both sides. Drain on kitchen paper, then finely chop.

Place the cream in a pan and bring to the boil, then add the cooked bacon, parsley, chives and cooked haricot beans – you should have about 450g (1lb) in total. Return to the boil, then reduce the heat to a simmer and allow to warm through. Season to taste and use as required.

COOK AHEAD

The cooked beans can be left to cool and kept chilled in a non-metallic bowl covered with clingfilm for up to 2 days in the fridge. Put into a pan and reheat gently to serve.

Bread Croûtes

Serves 4

1 slice of white bread, crusts removed

1 tbsp softened butter

Using a rolling pin, roll and flatten the slice of bread until it's about 3mm (1/8in) thick. Cut out 1cm (1/2in) rounds or cut into quarters, depending on the recipe you are using them for.

Heat the butter in a small heavy-based frying pan over a medium heat. Cook the bread shapes for 1–2 minutes on each side, until golden. Drain on kitchen paper and use as required.

Balsamic Lentils

Serves 4

100g (4oz) Puy lentils

1 tbsp rapeseed oil

1 tbsp finely chopped carrot

1 tbsp finely chopped celeriac

150ml (1/4 pint) beef stock (page 253)

1 tbsp balsamic vinegar

pinch of sugar

1 tbsp finely chopped smoked bacon

1 tsp chopped fresh flat-leaf parsley

sea salt and freshly ground black pepper

Rinse the lentils under plenty of cold running water, then place in a pan, cover with water and bring to the boil. Simmer for 15–20 minutes, until the lentils are just tender but still holding their shape. You may need to top them up with water as they are cooking. Drain well and then refresh under cold running water.

Heat the rapeseed oil in a pan over a low heat and add the cooked lentils. Add the carrot, celeriac, stock, vinegar and sugar to the lentils and cook for about 5 minutes, until heated through. Keep warm.

Meanwhile, in a separate frying pan, sauté the smoked bacon until golden brown and sizzling, then stir into the lentils with the parsley and season to taste. Use as required.

COOK AHEAD

These will keep for up to 5 days in a bowl covered with clingfilm in the fridge. Reheat gently in a pan to serve. They can also be frozen quite successfully.

Fresh Pasta Sheets

Serves 4–6

550g (1lb 4oz) strong pasta flour, plus extra for dusting

5 egg yolks

4 eggs

1 tsp olive oil

pinch of salt

Place the flour, egg yolks, eggs, oil and salt into a food processor and pulse for about 10 seconds, until the mixture binds together. Be careful not to overwork the dough. Remove from the processor and bring together with your hands to form a semi-soft dough. Work the dough hard for about 2 minutes, until smooth, silky and elastic. Wrap in clingfilm and allow it to rest in the fridge for at least 1 hour.

Remove the dough from the fridge and divide into 4 balls. Re-cover 3 balls and work with one at a time. Flatten the ball slightly with the base of the palm of your hand and run through the thickest setting on your pasta machine, which will roll it into a thick sheet. Fold the two ends into the middle and run the pasta through, on the thickest setting, 3–4 times. This will make the sides of the pasta fill out to the full width of the pasta machine.

Lightly dust both sides of the sheet with flour and run it through the machine on a thinner setting. Repeat this process through the settings until the sheets are 1–1.5mm thick. Cut each pasta sheet into rectangles that are about 10cm (4in) in length. Use as required.

COOK AHEAD

Place the pasta sheets on a plastic tray and cover them completely with a very well wrung-out damp tea towel. This will keep it fresh for 3–4 hours.

Yorkshire Puddings

Serves 6–8

100g (4oz) plain flour

pinch of salt

4 eggs, beaten

200ml (7fl oz) milk

sea salt and freshly ground black pepper

4 tbsp beef dripping or rapeseed oil

Sift the flour and a pinch of salt into a bowl. Make a well in the centre, then pour in the beaten egg and gradually draw in the flour. Add the milk and whisk until you have achieved a smooth batter the consistency of single cream. Season to taste, cover with clingfilm and leave to rest for 1 hour in the fridge, if time allows.

Preheat the oven to 220°C (425°F/gas mark 7).

Place the dripping or oil into 2 x 12-hole bun trays and heat on the top shelves of the oven for 5 minutes. The fat needs to be very hot to enable the puddings to rise quickly and to stop them from sticking to the moulds. Stir the batter, then using a small ladle, pour the batter into the hot fat so that it comes halfway up the sides. Bake the puddings for about 20 minutes, until well risen, crisp and golden brown. Use immediately.

COOK AHEAD

The batter can be made up to 1 hour in advance and kept in the fridge.

Vegetable Purées

Pea Purée

Serves 4–6

4 tbsp cream

2 tbsp milk

225g (8oz) fresh or frozen peas

1 tbsp softened butter

sea salt and freshly ground black pepper

Place the cream and milk in a pan and bring to the boil. Add the peas and butter and cook for another 2 minutes (or 4 minutes if the peas are frozen). Season to taste and place in a Thermomix (see page 273 for details) or blender. Whizz until well blended to a smooth purée, then pass through a sieve into a clean pan to reheat gently – you should end up with about 275g (10oz) in total. Keep warm and use as required.

VARIATION

Pea and Mint Purée
Add 2 tablespoons chopped fresh mint before blending the pea purée in the food processor.

COOK AHEAD

This will keep for up to 3 days in a bowl covered with clingfilm in the fridge. Reheat gently in a pan to serve. It can also be frozen quite successfully.

Aubergine Purée

Serves 4–6

225g (8oz) aubergine

1 tbsp rapeseed oil

1 garlic clove, crushed

1 tsp chopped fresh thyme

sea salt

5 tbsp cream

1/4 tsp ground cumin

knob of butter

Preheat the oven to 190°C (375°F/gas mark 5).

Cut the aubergine in half lengthways, cut off the top and lay the halves on a large piece of tin foil, cut side up. Drizzle over the oil, scatter the garlic and thyme on top and season with salt. Wrap in the tin foil and place on a baking sheet. Cook in the oven for 25–30 minutes, until the flesh has completely softened. Scrape the cooked flesh away from the skin and discard the skin.

Place the aubergine flesh in a Thermomix (see page 273 for details) or blender. Add the cream, cumin and butter, then blend for 5 minutes, until really smooth. Pass through a fine sieve into a clean pan and keep warm.

COOK AHEAD

This will keep for up to 3 days in a bowl covered with clingfilm in the fridge. Reheat gently in a pan to serve. It can also be frozen quite successfully.

Cauliflower Purée

Serves 4–6

1 small cauliflower

25g (1oz) butter

100ml (3 1/2fl oz) milk

sea salt and freshly ground black pepper

Trim the cauliflower into small florets, discarding the leaves and tough stalk. Melt the butter in a pan. Add the florets and cook for 3 minutes, until they're just beginning to soften, stirring regularly. Add the milk and cover and simmer for another 8 minutes, until the cauliflower is completely soft and the milk mixture is slightly reduced.

Place the cauliflower mixture in a Thermomix (see page 273 for details) or blender and whizz to a smooth purée. Pass through a sieve into a bowl. Season to taste and either leave to cool completely and cover with clingfilm in the fridge until needed, or if using immediately, keep warm.

COOK AHEAD

This will keep for up to 3 days in a bowl covered with clingfilm in the fridge. Reheat gently in a pan to serve. It can also be frozen quite successfully.

Red Pepper Purée

Makes 300g (11oz)

1 tbsp rapeseed oil

1/2 onion, finely chopped

1 garlic clove, finely chopped

3 large red peppers, cored and chopped

2 tsp red vine vinegar

2 tsp tomato purée

1 tsp caster sugar

sea salt and freshly ground black pepper

Heat the rapeseed oil in a pan over a medium heat and sauté the onion and garlic for a few minutes, until softened but not coloured. Tip in the red peppers with the vinegar, tomato purée and sugar. Season to taste and simmer for 20–25 minutes, until the peppers are completely tender.

Remove the red pepper mixture from the heat and leave to cool completely, then place in a Thermomix (see page 273 for details) or a blender. Blitz to a smooth purée texture, then pass through a fine sieve into a bowl.

Basil Purée

Makes 700ml (1 1/4 pints)

350g (12oz) fresh basil leaves

250g (9oz) spinach leaves, tough stalks removed

200ml (7fl oz) rapeseed oil

sea salt and freshly ground black pepper

Blanch the basil and spinach for 2–3 minutes in a pan of boiling water. Strain out the water, reserving 300ml (1/2 pint). Place the basil and spinach in a Thermomix (see page 273 for details) or blender. Take the reserved water that was used for blanching and the oil and gradually add them to the blending basil and spinach. Blend for 30 seconds, until smooth, and season to taste. Place in a squeezy bottle and use as required.

COOK AHEAD

This can be kept for up to 1 week in the fridge.

243

Celeriac Purée

Makes 650g (1lb 7oz)

550g (1lb 4oz) celeriac, peeled and cut into chunks

200ml (7fl oz) cream

200ml (7fl oz) vegetable stock (page 252)

20g (3/4oz) butter

sea salt and freshly ground black pepper

Place the celeriac in a pan with the cream and stock. Bring to the boil, then reduce the heat and simmer for 20–25 minutes, until the celeriac is completely soft.

Once the celeriac is cooked, place the mixture into a Thermomix (see page 273 for details) or blender and blitz until smooth. Add the butter and blitz again for 5–7 minutes. Season to taste and use as required.

VARIATIONS

Sweet Potato Purée
Makes 550g (1lb 4oz)
Replace the celeriac with sweet potatoes.

Carrot Purée
Makes 550g (1lb 4oz)
Replace the celeriac with 575g (1lb 5oz) of carrots.

Carrot and Ginger Purée
Makes 550g (1lb 4oz)
Add 1 teaspoon freshly grated root ginger to the carrots while they are cooking.

Mushroom Purée

Makes 350g (12oz)

1 tbsp rapeseed oil

25g (1oz) butter

1 onion, finely chopped

1 garlic clove, crushed

550g (1lb 4oz) Portobello mushrooms, diced

2 tbsp Madeira

1 tsp chopped fresh thyme

100ml (3 1/2fl oz) cream

Heat the oil and 1 teaspoon of the butter in a frying pan over a medium heat. Add the onion and garlic and sauté for a couple of minutes, until softened. Tip in the mushrooms, Madeira and thyme and simmer for 15–20 minutes, until the mushrooms are completely softened and almost mushy.

Pour the cream into the pan and stir to combine, then allow to reduce down for a couple of minutes. Place the mixture into a Thermomix (see page 273 for details) or blender with the rest of the butter and blitz for 5–7 minutes. Use as required.

Spinach or Watercress Purée

Makes 75g (3oz)

50g (2oz) spinach or watercress leaves, tough talks removed

100ml (3 1/2fl oz) rapeseed oil

sea salt and freshly ground black pepper

Blanch the spinach or watercress in a pan of boiling salted water for 30 seconds, then refresh quickly under cold running water. Drain well and pat dry with kitchen paper.

Place in a Thermomix (see page 273 for details) or blender for 5–7 minutes, adding the oil in a slow, continuous stream until the purée comes together. Season to taste and use as required.

Beetroot Purée

Serves 4–6

3 raw beetroot

3 tbsp red wine vinegar

sea salt and freshly ground black pepper

Preheat the oven to 180°C (350°F/gas mark 4).

With a scouring brush, scrub the beetroots gently but do not trim. Wrap in tin foil and place in a small baking tin. Bake for 1 1/2–2 hours, until tender.

Place the vinegar in a small non-reactive pan and boil for about 1 minute, until reduced by half. Leave to cool.

Unwrap the beets and leave until they are cool enough to handle, then peel and coarsely chop them – you can use gloves to prevent your hands from getting stained.

Transfer the chopped beets to a Thermomix (see page 273 for details) or blender with the reduced vinegar and blend to a smooth purée. Season to taste and then transfer to a squeezy bottle. Chill until needed and use as required.

COOK AHEAD

This will keep in the fridge for up to 1 week.

Foams, Gels and Powders

Basic Foam

Makes about 300ml (1/2 pint)

flavouring (see variations below for quantities)

300ml (1/2 pint) milk

1 tsp soya lecithin granules

sea salt and freshly ground white pepper

Place the flavouring variation in a pan with the milk and cook gently for 10–15 minutes, until the garlic has softened and is completely tender (if making the garlic variation). Blitz with a hand blender and pass through a fine sieve into a clean pan. Keep warm.

Add the soya lecithin granules to the pan, whisking until smooth. Season to taste and bring to the boil, then blitz with a hand blender to create a foam by bringing the head of the blender from the very bottom of the pan to the top of the liquid. Use immediately.

VARIATIONS

Mushroom

Add 100g (4oz) of the mushroom purée (page 244) to the milk.

Smoked Garlic or Garlic

Add 4 peeled smoked garlic cloves or regular garlic cloves to the milk. Add 1 tablespoon freshly grated Parmesan before blitzing with a hand blender.

Parmesan

Add 50g (2oz) freshly grated aged Parmesan to the pan before blitzing with a hand blender.

Smoked Bacon or Bacon

Add 50g (2oz) diced rindless smoked or regular bacon to the milk.

Carrot and Ginger

Use vegetable stock (page 252) instead of the milk. Add 2 tablespoons carrot purée (page 244), 1 tablespoon freshly squeezed orange juice and 1 teaspoon freshly grated ginger before blitzing with a hand blender.

Cauliflower

Use vegetable stock (page 252) instead of the milk. Add 2 tablespoons cauliflower purée (page 243) and 1 tablespoon freshly grated Parmesan before blitzing with a hand blender.

Caramel

Add 100ml (4fl oz) caramel sauce (page 262) to the pan before blitzing with the hand blender.

COOK AHEAD

All these foams can be made in advance up to the stage where they are passed through a sieve. Store in the fridge covered in clingfilm for up to 2 days, then reheat in a pan and add the soya lecithin at the last minute just before frothing.

Red Pepper Foam

Makes about 600ml (1 pint)

1 tbsp rapeseed oil

1 red pepper, roasted, cored and diced

1 small garlic clove, crushed

1 tsp tomato purée

pinch of smoked paprika

150ml (1/4 pint) vegetable stock (page 252)

150ml (1/4 pint) milk

1 tbsp chopped fresh basil

sea salt and freshly ground white pepper

1 tbsp soya lecithin

Place the rapeseed oil in a pan and add the red pepper, garlic, tomato purée, paprika, stock and milk. Bring to the boil, then add the basil and season to taste. Blend to a purée with a hand blender, then pass through a sieve into a clean pan. Add the soya lecithin and hand blend to achieve a foam by bringing the head of the blender from the very bottom of the pan to the top of the liquid. Use immediately.

COOK AHEAD

This can be made in advance up to the stage where it is passed through a sieve. Store in the fridge covered in clingfilm for up to 2 days, then reheat in a pan and add the soya lecithin at the last minute just before frothing.

Lemon Grass Foam

Makes about 300ml (1/2 pint)

1 tsp softened butter

1 shallot, finely chopped

1 lemon grass stalk, outer leaves removed and the core halved

finely grated rind and juice of 1 lemon

50ml (2fl oz) dry white wine

200ml (7fl oz) coconut milk

100ml (3 1/2fl oz) vegetable stock (page 252)

sea salt and freshly ground white pepper

1 tsp soya lecithin

Melt the butter in a pan. Add the shallot, lemon grass and lemon rind and cook for 2–3 minutes, stirring occasionally, until the shallot and lemon grass have softened but not coloured. Pour in the wine and reduce by half, stirring occasionally. Stir in the coconut milk and vegetable stock and bring to the boil, then reduce the heat and simmer for 5 minutes, until slightly reduced and thickened.

Remove from the heat and discard the lemon grass, then season to taste and stir in the lemon juice. Blitz with a hand blender and pass through a fine sieve into a clean pan. Keep warm and add the soya lecithin to the sauce. Place the hand blender in the lemon foam just before serving and blitz to lighten by bringing the head of the blender from the very bottom of the pan to the top of the liquid. Use immediately.

COOK AHEAD

This can be made in advance up to the stage where it is passed through a sieve. Store in the fridge covered in clingfilm for up to 2 days, then reheat in a pan and add the soya lecithin at the last minute just before frothing.

Mango Gel

Makes 500ml (18fl oz)

5g agar agar
500ml (18fl oz) mango coulis (shop bought)

Place the agar agar in a pan with the mango coulis and blitz until smooth with a hand blender. Bring to the boil, remove from the heat and leave to set in the fridge for 20 minutes. Transfer to a food processor and blend again until smooth. Place in a squeezy bottle and use as required.

VARIATIONS

Red Pepper Gel
Replace the mango coulis with 300g (11oz) of red pepper purée (page 243).

Apple Gel
Replace the mango coulis with freshly pressed apple juice.

Apple and Vanilla Gel
Replace the mango coulis with freshly pressed apple juice. Whisk in the scraped out seeds from one vanilla pod while bringing to the boil with the agar agar.

Raspberry Gel
Replace the mango coulis with raspberry coulis (shop bought).

Cherry Gel
Replace the mango coulis with cherry coulis (shop bought).

Balsamic Gel
Replace the mango coulis with 400ml (14fl oz) balsamic vinegar, 100g (4oz) caster sugar and use 7g (1/4oz) agar agar.

COOK AHEAD

These will keep for up to 1 week in the fridge.

Lemon Olive Oil Powder

Makes about 150g (5oz)

80g (3oz) N-Zorbit M powder (tapioca maltodextrin)

40g (1 1/2oz) icing sugar

50ml (2fl oz) lemon extra virgin olive oil

2g fine salt

Place the N-Zorbit M powder in a bowl and whisk in the icing sugar. Slowly whisk in the lemon extra virgin olive oil and salt until evenly combined. Press through a fine sieve to remove any lumps. Store in an airtight container in a cool, dry place. Use as required.

COOK AHEAD

This keeps well for up to 1 month as long as it is stored in a cool, dry place.

Jams and Chutneys

Chilli Jam

Makes about 450ml (3/4 pint)

2 tbsp olive oil

2 onions, roughly diced

2 red peppers, cored, seeded and roughly diced

1 garlic clove, crushed

1 red chilli, finely chopped

1 tbsp tomato purée

50g (2oz) light brown sugar

4 ripe tomatoes, diced

1 tbsp balsamic vinegar

1 tbsp dark soy sauce

sea salt and freshly ground black pepper

Heat the olive oil in a heavy-based pan on a medium heat. Add the onions, red peppers and garlic and sauté for 2 minutes, until just beginning to soften. Stir in the chilli and tomato purée and cook for 3 minutes, stirring occasionally. Stir in the sugar, tomatoes, balsamic vinegar and soy sauce and pour in 300ml (1/2 pint) of water to just cover. Simmer for 45–50 minutes, until well reduced and thickened, stirring occasionally.

Remove the chilli jam from the heat and leave to cool completely, then tip into a food processor or liquidiser and blend to a purée. Pass through a sieve set over a bowl and season to taste. Transfer to a rigid plastic container and store in the fridge. Use as required.

Date Jam

Apple Chutney

Makes about 450g (1lb)

50g (2oz) granulated sugar

450g (1lb) Medjool dates

2 tbsp brown sugar

2 tbsp crème de cassis

2 tsp balsamic vinegar

Place 300ml (1/2 pint) of water and the sugar in a heavy-based pan. Bring to the boil, then reduce the heat and simmer for 10 minutes, until the dates are completely soft. Stir in the brown sugar, crème de cassis and vinegar, then blend in a food processor for 5 minutes, until smooth. Transfer to a squeezy bottle and use as required.

COOK AHEAD

This keeps very well in the fridge for up to 3 weeks in the squeezy bottle.

Makes about 1.5kg (3lb)

900g (2lb) cooking apples

450g (1lb) dessert apples

225g (8oz) onions, diced

225g (8oz) sultanas

225g (8oz) light brown sugar

225ml (8fl oz) cider vinegar

1 tsp sea salt

1 tsp ground mixed spice

1 tsp ground cloves

1 tsp freshly grated root ginger

Peel, core and chop the apples and place into a large preserving pan. Add the onions, sultanas, brown sugar, cider vinegar, salt, mixed spice, cloves and ginger. Bring to the boil, then reduce the heat and simmer gently for 1 hour, stirring occasionally, until the chutney has nicely reduced and all of the fruit is completely tender.

Remove the chutney from the heat and leave to cool a little, then pack into warm, sterilised jars. Cover with a wax disc and seal when hot. Once opened, keep it in the fridge and use as required within a couple of weeks.

COOK AHEAD

This chutney can be kept in a cool dark place for up to 1 year as long as the jars have been correctly sterilised.

COOK AHEAD

This keeps very well in the fridge for up to 3 weeks and can be put into a squeezy plastic bottle if you would like to use it to garnish plates. This can also be frozen.

Oils, Dressings and Mayonnaise

Parsley Oil

Makes about 100ml (3 1/2fl oz)
100g (4oz) fresh flat-leaf parsley
100ml (3 1/2fl oz) rapeseed oil
sea salt

Pick the leaves from the parsley and place in a mini blender, discarding the stalks. Add the rapeseed oil and a pinch of salt and blend for 5 minutes, until completely smooth. Pass the parsley mixture through a fine sieve into a jug and then transfer to a squeezy bottle. Use as required.

COOK AHEAD

This keeps very well in the fridge for up to 3 weeks in the squeezy bottle.

Chilli Oil

Makes about 600ml (1 pint)
600ml (1 pint) rapeseed oil
1 large red chilli, split in half
1 lemon grass stalk
1 garlic clove
20g (3/4oz) root ginger, sliced but not peeled

Gently warm the oil through in a heavy-based pan but do not allow it to boil. Bring to a gentle simmer, then add the chilli, lemon grass, garlic and ginger. Continue to simmer very gently for 20–30 minutes, until the flavours are well infused. It's important not to allow it to boil at any stage. Pour into a squeezy bottle, leaving the bits in, as the flavours will continue to infuse. Use as required.

COOK AHEAD

This keeps very well in the fridge for up to 3 weeks in the squeezy bottle.

Lentil Vinaigrette

Makes about 200ml (7fl oz)
25g (1oz) Puy lentils
100ml (3 1/2fl oz) rapeseed oil
1 tbsp white truffle oil
2 tbsp white wine vinegar
sea salt and freshly ground black
pepper
1 tsp snipped fresh chives

Rinse the lentils under plenty of cold running water and place in a pan. Cover with water and bring to the boil. Simmer for 15–20 minutes, until the lentils are just tender but still holding their shape. You may need to top them up with water as they are cooking. Drain well and refresh under cold running water.

Mix together the rapeseed and truffle oils in a bowl. Stir in the vinegar and season to taste. Add the cooked Puy lentils and the chives and mix well to combine. Cover with clingfilm and store in the fridge until needed. Use as required.

COOK AHEAD

This will keep happily for up to 1 week in the fridge.

Mayonnaise

Makes about 250ml (9fl oz)
1 egg, at room temperature
2 tsp white wine vinegar
1 tsp Dijon mustard
pinch of caster sugar
100ml (3 1/2fl oz) olive oil
100ml (3 1/2fl oz) rapeseed oil
sea salt and freshly ground white
pepper

Break the egg into a food processor and add 1/2 teaspoon salt and the vinegar, mustard, sugar and half of the olive oil. Secure the lid and whizz for 10 seconds.

Leave to stand for a couple of seconds, then turn on again and pour the remaining olive oil and rapeseed oil through the feeder tube in a thin, steady stream. This should take 25–30 seconds.

Switch off the machine, take off the lid, scrape down the sides and whizz again for 2–3 seconds, then season to taste. Transfer to a squeezy bottle and chill until needed. Use as required.

VARIATIONS

Truffle Mayonnaise
Add 1/2 teaspoon black or white truffle paste into the food processor.

Aioli
Add 2 chopped garlic cloves with the egg into the food processor.

Lemon Mayonnaise
Add the juice and rind of 1 small lemon and 2 tablespoons snipped fresh chives.

Curried Mayonnaise
Beat in 2 teaspoons mild curry paste with a good squeeze of lemon juice. Season to taste, then cover with clingfilm and chill until needed.

COOK AHEAD

This mayonnaise or any of the variations keeps very well in the fridge for up to 1 week in the squeezy bottle.

Ginger Sesame Dressing

Stocks

Vegetable Stock

Makes about 100ml (3 1/2fl oz)

2 tbsp white wine vinegar

1 tbsp dark soy sauce

1 tsp finely grated root ginger

2 tbsp vegetable oil

2 tbsp toasted sesame oil

sea salt and freshly ground black pepper

Place the vinegar, soy sauce and ginger in a small bowl. Stir until well combined, then slowly whisk in the vegetable and sesame oils to emulsify and thicken. Season to taste and store covered with clingfilm in the fridge until needed. Use as required.

COOK AHEAD

This will keep happily for up to 1 week in the fridge.

Makes about 1.2 litres (2 pints)

2 leeks, trimmed and finely chopped

2 onions, peeled and finely chopped

2 carrots, peeled and cut into 1cm (1/2in) dice

2 celery sticks, finely chopped

1 fennel bulb, cut into 1cm (1/2in) dice

1 garlic bulb, sliced in half crossways

100ml (3 1/2fl oz) dry white wine

1 fresh thyme sprig

1 bay leaf

1 star anise

1 tsp pink peppercorns

1 tsp coriander seeds

pinch of salt

Place all the ingredients in a large pan and cover with 1.75 litres (3 pints) cold water. Cover with a lid and bring to a simmer, then remove the lid and cook for another 30 minutes, until the vegetables are tender.

Either set aside to marinate for 2 days in a cool place, or if you're short of time, strain through a sieve. Taste – if you find the flavour isn't full enough, return to the pan and reduce until you are happy with it. Leave to cool completely and transfer to a plastic jug with a lid and store in the fridge until needed. Use as required.

COOK AHEAD

This will keep in the fridge for up to 3 days or freeze in 600ml (1 pint) cartons and defrost when you need it.

Chicken Stock

Makes about 1.2 litres (2 pints)

1 large raw or cooked chicken carcass, skin and fat removed and bones chopped

2 leeks, trimmed and chopped

2 onions, peeled and chopped

2 carrots, peeled and chopped

2 celery sticks, chopped

1 fresh thyme sprig

1 bay leaf

handful of fresh parsley stalks

1 tsp white peppercorns

If using a raw chicken carcass, preheat the oven to 220°C (450°F/gas mark 7) and roast the chicken carcass in a tin for about 40 minutes, until golden. Drain through a colander to get rid of excess fat, then chop it up.

Place the chopped up chicken carcass in a large pan and cover with 1.8 litres (3 1/4 pints) cold water. Bring to the boil, then skim off any fat and scum from the surface. Reduce the heat to a simmer and tip in all the remaining ingredients.

Simmer gently for another 1–1/2 hours, skimming occasionally and topping up with water as necessary. Taste regularly to check the flavour. When you're happy with it, remove from the heat and pass through a sieve. Leave to cool and remove any fat that settles on the top, then store in the fridge in a plastic jug with a lid and use as required.

COOK AHEAD

This can be stored in the fridge for up to 3 days or freeze in 600ml (1 pint) cartons and defrost when you need it.

Beef Stock

Makes about 1.75ml (3 pints)

675g (1 1/2lb) shin of beef, cut into pieces

675g (1 1/2lb) marrow bones or knuckle of veal, chopped

1 tbsp olive oil

1 onion, peeled and sliced

1 carrot, peeled and sliced

1 celery stick, sliced

1 tbsp tomato purée

150ml (1/4 pint) red wine

1 small garlic bulb, halved

1 bouquet garni (parsley stalks, sprigs of thyme and bay leaf tied together)

Preheat the oven to 220°C (425°F/gas mark 7). Place the shin of beef and marrow bones or knuckle of veal in a roasting tin and cook in the oven for 30–40 minutes, until well browned. Drain off all the excess oil and discard.

Meanwhile, heat the oil in a large pan over a medium heat. Add the onion, carrot and celery and sauté for 6–7 minutes, until just beginning to colour. Stir in the tomato purée, then pour in the red wine and allow it to bubble down for 1 minute.

Add the roasted meat bones to the vegetable and wine mixture along with the garlic and bouquet garni. Pour in 1.75 litres (3 pints) water and bring to the boil. Skim off any scum, then partially cover and reduce the heat to simmer for 4–5 hours, until you have achieved a well-flavoured stock, topping up occasionally with a little water – you'll need to add another 1.2 litres (2 pints) in total over the whole cooking time.

Strain the stock and leave to cool completely before chilling down. Once it's cold, remove any trace of solidified fat from the surface using a large spoon, then cover with a lid and return to the fridge until needed. Use as required.

COOK AHEAD

This stores very well in the fridge for 3 days or freeze in 600ml (1 pint) cartons and defrost when you need it.

Fish Stock

Makes about 1.2 litres (2 pints)

250g (9oz) white fish trimmings and/or bones (such as lemon sole, brill or plaice bones)

3 leeks, trimmed and chopped

3 carrots, chopped

1 fennel bulb, chopped

large handful of fresh parsley, roughly chopped

175ml (6fl oz) dry white wine

Rinse the fish bones and trimmings of any blood, which would make the stock look cloudy and taste bitter. Place into a large heavy-bottomed stockpot with the leeks, carrots, fennel and parsley. Pour in the white wine, then add 2.4 litres (4 pints) cold water to cover the fish and vegetables. Place on a high heat and bring to a simmer. After 5 minutes, remove the scum that forms on the surface with a spoon and discard. Reduce the heat and simmer, covered, for about 25 minutes, skimming as necessary.

At the end of the cooking time, remove the stock from the heat and strain, discarding the fish trimmings and the vegetables. Cool and store in a plastic covered jug in the fridge and use as required.

COOK AHEAD

Store in the fridge for up to 3 days. Alternatively, once the stock is made you can reduce it further and then freeze it in ice cube trays (freezing it this way means you can defrost as little or as much as you need at a time).

Sauces, Syrups and Jus

Tomato Sauce

Makes 350ml (12fl oz)

1 tbsp olive oil

1 onion, finely chopped

1 garlic clove, crushed

6 large ripe tomatoes, peeled, seeded and cut into chunks, or 400g canned chopped tomatoes

2 tsp red wine vinegar

2 tsp tomato purée

1 tsp caster sugar

sea salt and freshly ground black pepper

1 tbsp chopped fresh basil

Heat the olive oil in a pan over a medium heat. Add in the onion and garlic and sauté for a few minutes, until softened but not coloured. Tip in the tomatoes with the vinegar, tomato purée and sugar. Cook on a low heat for a few minutes while stirring to help break down the tomatoes. Season to taste.

Simmer gently for 25–30 minutes, until the sauce has reduced and dried out a little. Stir in the basil and use immediately or leave to cool, then transfer to a bowl and cover with clingfilm and chill until needed. Use as required.

COOK AHEAD

This will keep happily in the fridge for up to 1 week covered with clingfilm.

Hollandaise Sauce

Makes about 250ml (9fl oz)

2 tbsp white wine vinegar

225g (8oz) unsalted butter, diced and chilled

3 egg yolks

sea salt and freshly ground black pepper

Place the white wine vinegar in a small pan with 1 tablespoon water and reduce to 1 tablespoon. Leave to cool.

Melt the butter in a small pan or in a dish in the microwave. Set aside and keep warm.

Beat 2 tablespoons water into the egg yolks, then beat into the reduced vinegar mixture. Stir with a whisk over a low heat until smooth and velvety, beating continuously.

Add the melted butter to the egg yolk mixture, little by little, until you have achieved a thick, smooth sauce. If it becomes too thick, add 1 tablespoon warm water. Season to taste and keep warm but not hot or the sauce will split.

Sauce Vierge

Makes about 175ml (6fl oz)

1 tbsp extra virgin lemon olive oil (shop bought)

1 small red onion, finely diced

1 small roasted red pepper, finely diced (from a jar is fine)

5 tbsp extra virgin olive oil

1 tbsp white wine vinegar

finely grated rind of 1/2 lemon

2 tsp caster sugar

sea salt and freshly ground black pepper

2 tsp snipped fresh chives

1 tsp chopped fresh basil

Warm the lemon oil in a small pan. Gently fry the onion and roasted pepper for 5 minutes, stirring occasionally. Pour in the olive oil and vinegar, then add the lemon rind and sugar. Cook for another 2–3 minutes, until bubbling and warmed through. Season to taste and stir in the herbs. Keep warm and use as required.

COOK AHEAD

This will keep up to 1 week in the fridge in a rigid plastic container.

Chinese Black Bean Sauce

Makes about 300ml (1/2 pint)

1 1/2 tbsp fermented Chinese black beans

2 tbsp clear honey

1 tbsp balsamic vinegar

1 tbsp dark soy sauce or kecap manis

1 tsp tomato ketchup

300ml (1/2 pint) beef stock (page 253)

sea salt and freshly ground black pepper

Place the black beans in a bowl and cover with hot water, then leave to soak for 5 minutes. Meanwhile, place the honey, balsamic vinegar, soy sauce or kecap manis and tomato ketchup in a pan. Cook for 1 minute, stirring, then add in the beef stock. Simmer for 10–15 minutes, until nicely reduced to a sauce-like consistency. Drain the soaked black beans and add to the sauce. Return to a simmer and season to taste. Remove from the heat and leave to cool completely. Cover with clingfilm and set aside until needed. Use as required.

COOK AHEAD

This will keep up to 1 week in the fridge in a rigid plastic container.

Basil Pesto

Makes about 250ml (9fl oz)

1 large bunch of fresh basil leaves (at least 50g/2oz)

2 garlic cloves, peeled

25g (1oz) toasted pine nuts

175ml (6fl oz) olive or rapeseed oil

50g (2oz) freshly grated Parmesan

sea salt and freshly ground black pepper

Place the basil in a food processor with the garlic, pine nuts and a quarter of the oil. Blend to a paste, then slowly add the remaining oil through the feeder tube. Transfer to a bowl and fold in the Parmesan, then season to taste. Cover with clingfilm and chill until needed.

COOK AHEAD

This will keep happily in the fridge for up to 1 week – just top it up with a little extra olive oil to keep it tasting lovely and fresh. It can also be frozen.

Sun-dried Tomato Pesto

Makes about 400ml (14fl oz)

175g (6oz) semi sun-dried tomatoes, roughly chopped

8 large fresh basil leaves

2 garlic cloves, peeled

200ml (7fl oz) olive or rapeseed oil

sea salt and freshly ground black pepper

Place the semi sun-dried tomatoes in a food processor or blender with the basil leaves and garlic and pulse to finely chop. Switch the machine back on and slowly pour in the oil through the feeder tube until the pesto has emulsified. Transfer to a bowl with a spatula and season to taste.

COOK AHEAD

This can be made up to 3–4 days in advance and kept covered with clingfilm in the fridge.

Horseradish Cream

Makes about 225ml (8fl oz)

200ml (7fl oz) crème fraîche

4 tbsp creamed horseradish (from a jar)

1 tbsp snipped fresh chives

1 tsp prepared English mustard

sea salt and freshly ground black pepper

Mix the crème fraîche, horseradish, chives and mustard together in a bowl. Season to taste and spoon into a serving dish. Cover with clingfilm and chill until needed. Use as required.

COOK AHEAD

This can be kept in the fridge for up to 24 hours before serving.

Pineapple Salsa

Serves 4–6

1 small ripe pineapple, peeled, cored and finely diced

1 small roasted red pepper, finely diced (from a jar is fine)

2 tbsp sweet chilli sauce

1 tbsp rapeseed oil

1 tbsp chopped fresh coriander

1 tbsp shredded fresh basil

sea salt and freshly ground black pepper

Place the pineapple in a bowl and stir in the roasted red pepper, sweet chilli sauce, rapeseed oil, coriander and basil. Season to taste. Cover with clingfilm and set aside at room temperature until needed. Use as required.

VARIATION

Mango Salsa
Replace the pineapple with 2 firm ripe mangoes that have been peeled and finely diced, with their stones discarded.

COOK AHEAD

This salsa is much better made fresh, but it can be left at room temperature for up to 2 hours until needed.

Prawn Velouté

Makes about 300ml (1/2 pint)

1 tbsp rapeseed oil

100g (4oz) Dublin Bay prawn shells

1 small carrot, chopped

1 onion, chopped

1 celery stick, chopped

1 fresh vine tomato

1/4 fennel bulb, chopped

1 garlic clove

1 1/2 tbsp tomato purée

150ml (1/4 pint) dry white wine

2 tbsp Cognac

300ml (1/2 pint) fish stock (page 254)

2 star anise

1 fresh thyme sprig

1 fresh tarragon sprig

1 fresh basil sprig

100ml (3 1/2fl oz) cream

50ml (2fl oz) milk

sea salt and freshly ground black pepper

1 tsp soya lecithin

Heat a large heavy-based pan over a medium heat. Add the oil and sauté the prawn shells for 2–3 minutes, until just beginning to colour. Add the carrot, onion, celery, tomato, fennel and garlic and sauté for another 5 minutes.

Stir the tomato purée into the vegetable and prawn shell mixture. Deglaze with the wine and Cognac, then reduce down until almost all of the liquid has evaporated. Pour in the fish stock, then add the star anise and herbs. Bring to the boil, then simmer for 25 minutes, until well reduced. Finally, stir in the cream and milk and reduce for another 10 minutes. Pass the sauce through a fine sieve into a clean pan. Season to taste and keep warm.

Add the soya lecithin to the sauce. Place the hand blender in the sauce just before serving and blitz to lighten by bringing the head of the blender from the very bottom of the pan to the top of the liquid. Use immediately.

COOK AHEAD

This can be made in advance up to the stage where it is passed through a sieve. Store in the fridge covered in clingfilm for up to 2 days, then reheat in a pan and add the soya lecithin at the last minute just before frothing.

Sun-dried Tomato and Saffron Velouté

Makes about 500ml (18fl oz)

1 tsp softened butter

1 small onion, finely chopped

150ml (1/4 pint) white wine

2 tsp tomato purée

large pinch of saffron, soaked in 1 tbsp warm water

50g (2oz) sun-dried tomatoes, chopped

300ml (1/2 pint) vegetable (page 252) or fish stock (page 254)

150ml (1/4 pint) cream

150ml (1/4 pint) milk

sea salt and freshly ground black pepper

Melt the butter in a pan over a medium heat. Add the onion and cook for 2 minutes, stirring, until softened but not coloured. Stir in the wine, tomato purée and saffron mixture. Simmer on a medium heat for about 5 minutes to reduce by half, then add the sun-dried tomatoes and stock. Bring to the boil, then simmer for 10 minutes.

Stir in the cream and milk and simmer for another 8–10 minutes, until reduced by half and thickened. Blitz with a hand blender or food processor, then pass through a fine sieve into a clean pan, squeezing the pulp dry with the back of a spoon and discarding. Season to taste, then return to a pan, cover and set aside until needed. Keep warm and use as required.

COOK AHEAD

This will keep for up to 1 week in the fridge in a rigid plastic container. It can also be frozen.

Marmalade Sauce

Makes about 200ml (7fl oz)

225ml (8fl oz) beef stock (page 000)

4 tbsp marmalade

2 tbsp light brown sugar

2 tbsp dark soy sauce

2 tbsp balsamic vinegar

2 tbsp tomato ketchup

1 tbsp Cointreau liqueur

1 tsp chopped fresh thyme

sea salt and freshly ground black pepper

Place the stock, marmalade, sugar, soy sauce, vinegar, ketchup, Cointreau and thyme in a small pan. Bring to the boil, then reduce the heat and simmer vigorously for 5 minutes, until the mixture has thickened to a sauce consistency that coats the back of a spoon. Season to taste, then pass through a sieve into a clean pan, discarding the thyme. Reheat gently and use as required.

COOK AHEAD

This sauce keeps for up to 1 week in a rigid plastic container in the fridge.

Honey and Clove Sauce

Makes about 200ml (7fl oz)

225ml (8fl oz) beef stock (page 000)

4 tbsp clear honey

2 tbsp dark soy sauce

2 tbsp balsamic vinegar

2 tbsp light brown sugar

2 tbsp tomato ketchup

2 tsp whole cloves

sea salt and freshly ground black pepper

Place the stock, honey, soy sauce, vinegar, sugar, ketchup and cloves in a small pan. Bring to the boil, then reduce the heat and simmer vigorously for 5 minutes, until the mixture has thickened to a sauce consistency that coats the back of a spoon. Season to taste, then pass through a sieve into a clean pan, discarding the cloves. Reheat gently and use as required.

COOK AHEAD

This will keep for up to 1 week in the fridge in a rigid plastic container. It can also be frozen.

Balsamic and Port Syrup

Makes about 120ml (4fl oz)
100g (4oz) caster sugar
100ml (3 1/2fl oz) ruby red port
100ml (3 1/2fl oz) balsamic vinegar

Place the sugar, port and balsamic vinegar in a heavy-based pan. Bring to the boil, then reduce the heat and simmer for 15–20 minutes, until the mixture has reduced by one-third and has become thick and syrupy, like a honey consistency. Serve at once or allow to cool completely and store in a bowl covered with clingfilm in the fridge for up to 1 month. Use as required.

COOK AHEAD

This will keep in the fridge for 1 month. When you're ready to use it, if you find that it has solidified too much, either warm it in a small pan or in the microwave. Or if you want to use it cold, add a few drops of boiling water to it, stirring to loosen.

Sherry Vinegar Caramel

Makes about 100ml (3 1/2fl oz)
100g (4oz) caster sugar
2 tbsp sherry vinegar
2 fresh thyme sprigs

Place the sugar and 100ml (3 1/2fl oz) water in a heavy-based pan. Bring to the boil and cook for about 15 minutes without stirring, until golden brown.

Quickly stir the sherry vinegar into the golden caramel, then add another 100ml (3 1/2fl oz) cold water and the thyme, stirring well to combine. Reduce the heat and simmer for 2 minutes, until you have achieved a honey-like consistency. Set aside to cool. Transfer to a squeezy bottle and store in the fridge. Use as required.

COOK AHEAD

This will keep happily for up to 2 months in the fridge.

Rosemary Jus

Makes about 100ml (3 1/2fl oz)
50ml (2fl oz) balsamic vinegar
200ml (7fl oz) red wine jus (page 261)
1 tsp light brown sugar
1 tsp chopped rosemary
1 tsp tomato purée
sea salt and freshly ground black pepper

Heat a medium-sized pan until quite hot. Add the balsamic vinegar, and as soon as the bubbling subsides, add the red wine jus, sugar, rosemary and tomato purée. Boil for about 5 minutes, until reduced by three-quarters and well flavoured. Season to taste and use as required.

COOK AHEAD

This will keep for up to 1 week in the fridge in a rigid plastic container.

Red Wine Jus

Makes 200ml (7fl oz)
300ml (1/2 pint) red wine
2 tbsp balsamic vinegar
200ml (7fl oz) beef stock (page 253)
2 tbsp chopped fresh thyme
2 heaped tsp light brown sugar
sea salt and freshly ground black
pepper

Heat a small pan and pour in the
red wine and vinegar. Boil for about
5 minutes, until reduced by half.
Add the stock, sugar and thyme
and reduce again for another 10–12
minutes, stirring occasionally, until
you have achieved a good sauce
consistency. Season to taste and use
as required.

VARIATION

Madeira Jus
Replace the red wine with Madeira.

COOK AHEAD

This will keep for up to 1 week in the
fridge in a rigid plastic container. It can
also be frozen.

Honey Jus

Makes about 200ml (7fl oz)
100ml (3 1/2fl oz) crème de cassis
1 tbsp clear honey
1 tbsp sherry vinegar
300ml (1/2 pint) beef stock (page 253)
2 fresh thyme sprigs, chopped
sea salt and freshly ground black
pepper

Heat a heavy-based pan. Add the
crème de cassis, honey and vinegar,
stirring to combine. Simmer until
the mixture has reduced to a syrup
consistency, stirring occasionally so
that it doesn't catch on the bottom
of the pan. Add the beef stock and
thyme and simmer until reduced by
half. Pass the honey jus through a
sieve into a clean pan and season to
taste. Keep warm and use as required.

COOK AHEAD

This will keep for up to 1 week in the
fridge in a rigid plastic container.

Dessert Sauces

Caramel Sauce

Makes about 450ml (3/4 pint)

275g (10oz) caster sugar

75g (3oz) butter

250ml (9fl oz) cream

1/2 vanilla pod, split in half and seeds scraped out

Place the sugar and 150ml (1/4 pint) water in a pan. Bring to the boil and cook for approximately 15 minutes, until golden brown. Stir in the butter, cream and vanilla seeds and mix well over a low heat until it's a thick consistency. Serve hot or transfer to a large bowl and leave to cool. Cover with clingfilm and chill until needed. Use warm or cold as required.

VARIATIONS

Salted Caramel Sauce

Add 1 teaspoon sea salt flakes with the vanilla seeds and cook as described above.

Caramel Whiskey Sauce

Add 1 tablespoon Irish whiskey to the sauce after the vanilla seeds and cook as described above.

COOK AHEAD

This sauce will keep in the fridge covered with clingfilm for 2 weeks.

Butterscotch Sauce

Makes about 120ml (4fl oz)

100g (4oz) caster sugar

25g (1oz) butter, diced

100ml (3 1/2fl oz) cream

1 vanilla pod, split in half and seeds scraped out

2 tbsp dark rum

Bring the sugar and 200ml (7fl oz) water to the boil, stirring until the sugar has dissolved. Reduce the heat and simmer for 15–20 minutes, until reduced by a quarter and syrupy.

Add the butter, cream, vanilla seeds and rum to the caramel, stirring until combined, then simmer gently for another 5 minutes, until thickened. Leave to cool for 10–15 minutes, until thickened a little further.

This is ready to serve warm or transfer to a bowl and leave to cool completely, then cover with clingfilm and keep in the fridge until needed. This can also be put in a squeezy bottle. Use warm or cold as required.

VARIATION

Salted Butterscotch Sauce

Add 1 teaspoon sea salt flakes with the vanilla seeds and cook as described above.

COOK AHEAD

This will keep happily for up to 1 week covered with clingfilm in the fridge.

Chocolate Fudge Sauce

Makes about 400ml (14fl oz)

25g (1oz) caster sugar

25g (1oz) butter

150ml (1/4 pint) cream

175g (6oz) plain chocolate, finely chopped (at least 70% cocoa solids)

Place the sugar, butter and cream in a pan and bring to the boil, stirring. Reduce the heat and simmer gently for 4–5 minutes, until thickened and beginning to become syrupy, stirring occasionally to prevent the mixture from catching. Remove from the heat and leave to cool a little.

Meanwhile, place the chocolate in a heatproof bowl set over a pan of simmering water until melted. Whisk the chocolate into the sauce until smooth and well combined. This is ready to serve warm or transfer to a bowl and leave to cool completely, then cover with clingfilm and keep in the fridge until needed. Use warm or cold as required.

COOK AHEAD

This will keep happily for up to 1 week covered with clingfilm in the fridge.

Crème Anglaise

Makes about 400ml (14fl oz)

5 egg yolks

3 tbsp caster sugar

1/2 vanilla pod, split in half and seeds scraped out

300ml (1/2 pint) milk

100ml (3 1/2fl oz) cream

Place the egg yolks in a large bowl with the sugar and vanilla seeds. Whisk with an electric mixer for a few minutes, until pale and thickened.

Place the milk and cream in a medium pan and bring to the boil, then immediately remove from the heat.

Gradually whisk the heated milk and cream into the egg yolk mixture until smooth, then pour back into the pan and place over a gentle heat. Cook gently for 6–8 minutes on a medium heat, stirring constantly, until the custard coats the back of a wooden spoon. Serve hot or transfer to a large bowl. Press a sheet of clingfilm directly onto the surface of the custard to help prevent a skin from forming and leave to cool, then chill until needed. It can also be put into a squeezy bottle depending on how you want to use it. Use warm or cold as required.

VARIATIONS

Coole Swan Crème Anglaise
Add 2 tablespoons Coole Swan Dairy Cream Liqueur to the crème anglaise before it gets cooked to thicken.

COOK AHEAD

This will keep in the fridge for 2–3 days.

Apple Coulis

Makes 300ml (1/2 pint)

2 eating apples, cored and diced (skin still on)

1 vanilla pod

300ml (1/2 pint) freshly pressed apple juice

squeeze of lemon juice

Place all the ingredients in a pan and cook for 5–10 minutes, until softened. Leave to cool slightly, then place in a food processor. Blend to make a smooth purée, then pass through a sieve and place in an airtight container. Store in the fridge until needed and use as required.

COOK AHEAD

This can be made up to 1 week in advance.

Citrus Mascarpone Cream

Makes about 275g (10oz)

250g mascarpone cheese

finely grated rind of 1 orange

finely grated rind of 1 lemon

finely grated rind of 1 lime

1/2 vanilla pod, split in half and seeds scraped out

1–2 tbsp sifted icing sugar

Place the mascarpone in a bowl and beat in the orange, lemon and lime rinds. Fold in the vanilla seeds and enough of the icing sugar to just sweeten, making sure it isn't too sweet. Be careful not to overmix. Cover with clingfilm and chill in the fridge until needed. Use as required.

COOK AHEAD

This will keep for up to 3 days in the fridge.

Ice Creams, Sorbets and Parfaits

Vanilla Ice Cream

Serves 6–8

5 egg yolks

125g (4 1/2oz) caster sugar

1/2 vanilla pod, split in half and seeds scraped out

300ml (1/2 pint) milk

100ml (3 1/2fl oz) cream

Place the egg yolks in a large bowl with the sugar and vanilla seeds. Whisk with an electric mixer for a few minutes, until pale and thickened.

Place the milk and cream in a medium pan and bring to the boil, then immediately remove from the heat.

Gradually whisk the heated milk and cream into the egg yolk mixture until smooth, then pour back into the pan and place over a gentle heat. Cook gently for 6–8 minutes on a medium heat, stirring constantly, until the custard coats the back of a wooden spoon.

Plunge the base of the pan into a sink of cold water and beat occasionally until cold. Freeze in an ice cream maker according to the manufacturer's instructions. You should end up with about 400ml (14fl oz) of ice cream. Use as required.

VARIATIONS

Malteser Ice Cream
Roughly crush a 37g bag of Maltesers with a rolling pin and fold into the ice cream, following the ice cream maker's manufacturer's instructions on when to add the flavourings (normally when it's half-frozen).

Caramel Ice Cream
Reduce the sugar in the basic custard mixture to 3 tablespoons and fold in 200ml (7fl oz) caramel sauce (page 262), following the ice cream maker's manufacturer's instructions on when to add the flavourings (normally when it's half-frozen).

COOK AHEAD

This can be made up to 1 month in advance and kept in an airtight container in the freezer until needed.

Raspberry Sorbet

Serves 6–8

100g (4oz) caster sugar

100ml (3 1/2fl oz) raspberry coulis (shop bought)

Place the sugar in a heavy-based pan with 200ml (7fl oz) water and put over a gentle heat, stirring until dissolved. Stir in the raspberry coulis and then remove from the heat. Leave to cool completely. Freeze in an ice cream maker according to the manufacturer's instructions. You should end up with about 400ml (14fl oz) of sorbet. Use as required.

VARIATIONS

Coconut Sorbet
Replace the raspberry coulis with coconut coulis (shop bought) or even coconut milk. Proceed as described above.

COOK AHEAD

This can be made up to 1 month in advance and kept in an airtight container in the freezer until needed.

Apple Parfait

Serves 10–12

rapeseed oil, for greasing

100g (4oz) caster sugar

5 egg yolks

1/4 tsp ground cinnamon

600ml (1 pint) cream

200ml (7fl oz) apple coulis (page 264)

Line a 1kg (2 1/4lb) loaf tin with oiled clingfilm. Place the sugar and 100ml (3 1/2fl oz) water in a heavy-based pan and simmer gently until the sugar has dissolved. Bring to the boil, then continue to boil without stirring until the mixture has reached 116°C (240°F), or the soft ball stage. That means that when you drop a bit of it into cold water to cool it down, it will form a soft ball.

Meanwhile, whisk the egg yolks and cinnamon in a separate bowl until they look pale yellow in colour and have become thick and creamy in consistency. When the sugar has reached the correct temperature, quickly whisk it into the egg yolks and continue to whisk until the mixture is cold.

Pour the cream into another bowl and whisk until it forms soft peaks. Mix the apple coulis into the cooled egg yolk mixture and gently fold in the cream. Pour into the lined loaf tin, then cover with clingfilm and freeze for at least 4 hours, or preferably overnight, until solid.

To serve, carefully remove the parfait from the tin and peel away the clingfilm. Using a sharp knife dipped in boiling water, cut into slices and arrange on plates.

COOK AHEAD

This can be made up to 1 month in advance and kept in an airtight container in the freezer until needed.

Rapberry and White Chocolate Parfait

Serves 6

50g (2oz) white couverture chocolate

50g (4oz) caster sugar

3 egg yolks

150ml (1/4 pint) cream

25ml (1fl oz) raspberry coulis (shop bought)

Line a 18cm (7in) square tin with parchment paper.

Place the white chocolate in a heatproof bowl set over a pan of simmering water. Leave to melt, stirring until smooth.

Place the sugar and 100ml (3 1/2fl oz) water in a heavy-based pan and simmer gently until the sugar has dissolved. Bring to the boil, then continue to boil without stirring until the mixture has reached 116°C (240°F), or the soft ball stage. That means that when you drop a bit of it into cold water to cool it down, it will form a soft ball.

Meanwhile, whisk the egg yolks in a separate bowl until they look pale yellow in colour and have become thick and creamy in consistency. When the sugar has reached the correct temperature, quickly whisk it into the egg yolks and continue to whisk until the mixture is cold, then fold in the melted white chocolate.

Pour the cream into another bowl and whisk until it forms soft peaks. Mix the raspberry coulis into the cooled egg yolk mixture and gently fold in the cream. Pour into the lined tin, then cover with clingfilm and freeze for at least 4 hours, or preferably overnight, until solid.

To serve, carefully remove the parfait from the tin and peel away the parchment paper. Cut out 6 x 5cm (2in) rounds using a straight-sided cutter. Use as required.

COOK AHEAD

This can be made up to 1 month in advance and kept in an airtight container in the freezer until needed.

Dessert Decorations

Spun Sugar

100g (4oz) caster sugar

1 tsp powdered glucose

Place the sugar, powdered glucose and 120ml (4fl oz) water into a heavy-based pan. Bring to the boil, then reduce the heat and simmer for 15–20 minutes, until the mixture turns a golden caramel colour. Use a pure bristle pastry brush dipped in cold water to brush the inner sides of the pan to prevent sugar crystals from forming while simmering. Do not stir the sugar, as this will cause the syrup to crystallise and become hard.

Using a sugar/jam thermometer, cook the syrup until it reaches 140°C (280°F). The sugar syrup should be a thick honey consistency and should not be too runny. It will thicken a little as it cools, but if it gets too thick, simply heat again and it will quickly loosen. Immediately remove from the heat and plunge the base of the pan into cold water to halt the cooking.

To spin the sugar, dip a teaspoon into the syrup, then flick the teaspoon back and forth over a broom handle or rolling pin to create long hair-like strands. Gather up the strands of spun sugar and create shapes by simply moulding the strands in your hands. Arrange on a piece of parchment paper and do not touch until needed.

VARIATIONS

Spun Sugar Curls

Once you have the caramel, you can make sugar curls. Using a teaspoon and a knife-sharpening steel, dip the spoon into the caramel and lift it out again, then twist it around the steel to create sugar curls, working very carefully as the caramel is extremely hot. Remove the curls from the steel once they are cool and hardened. Repeat until you have enough spun sugar curls for your purpose. Arrange on a piece of parchment paper and do not touch until needed.

Spun Sugar Baskets

Place a liberal amount of groundnut oil over the back of a ladle. When the sugar has become a state of liquid thread, use a spoon to scoop some of the sugar up and weave it backwards and forwards over and around your ladle to form a fine and intricate sugar basket. Gently remove the basket from the ladle and repeat until you have enough sugar baskets for your purpose. Arrange on a piece of parchment paper and do not touch until needed.

COOK AHEAD

These should be made about 30 minutes before you want to serve them, otherwise they will start to disintegrate. However, if you store them in an airtight container with a silica gel pack, they will keep for up to 3–4 hours in airtight conditions.

Plain Chocolate Curls

Makes 20–30

200g (7oz) plain chocolate, broken into squares (at least 70% cocoa solids)

I find that this works best in a plastic container in a microwave, as it's quicker and saves washing up and time. However, the same process can be done in a heatproof bowl set over a pan of hot water – just remember to take the bowl off the heat when there is a small amount of chocolate that is still unmelted, then stir the melted chocolate to melt the final little pieces.

Break up the chocolate and put it in a plastic container such as a large measuring jug. Start by giving the chocolate bursts of 30 seconds in the microwave, stirring between each burst. When the chocolate starts to melt, reduce the bursts to 20 or 10 seconds and finally 5 seconds. The aim is to stop heating the chocolate when there is still a small amount of unmelted chocolate. The final melting should be done by stirring the chocolate.

Spread the tempered chocolate in a thin, even layer on a sheet of acetate paper. When the chocolate turns matte and is just beginning to set, cut it into 0.5cm (1/4in) strips with a trellis wheel. Carefully roll up the acetate of chocolate and secure it with sellotape until the chocolate is set.

When the chocolate is set, carefully open out the acetate over a piece of parchment paper and the chocolate curls will drop out. Use as required.

COOK AHEAD

These can be made up to 24 hours in advance and carefully layered up in pieces of parchment paper in a large airtight container. Just be careful that none of the curls are touching each other or they may get damaged. Keep in a cool place, but not the fridge, as the chocolate may lose some of its wonderful sheen.

White Chocolate Curls

Makes 10–15

100g good-quality bar of white chocolate

Using a large-bladed knife held with both hands or a cheese slice, pull the blade across the chocolate, pressing down slightly. As the blade comes towards you, the chocolate will form curls (if the chocolate is too hard, it will be brittle and will break rather than forming curls, in which case leave at room temperature for 5 minutes before trying again). You will find that as the chocolate bar gets thinner it will be harder to form nice curls. Use as required.

COOK AHEAD

These can be made up to 24 hours in advance and carefully layered up in pieces of parchment paper in a large airtight container. Keep in the fridge and just be careful that none of the curls are touching each other or they may get damaged.

Food Suppliers

ALBATROSS SEAFOODS
WWW.ALBATROSSSEAFOODS.IE
Lobsters, prawns, crabmeat, scallops, oysters, monkfish, cod and kippers

THE APPLE FARM
WWW.THEAPPLEFARM.COM
Premium apple juice

B.D. FOODS
WWW.BDFOODS.IE
Kataifi pastry, mushrooms, fresh yeast, couverture chocolate, puff pastry, paillette feulletine, mini Maltesers (chocolate pearls) and quail

BURREN SMOKEHOUSE
WWW.BURRENSMOKEHOUSE.IE
Smoked salmon

CARRAIG NA BREAC SMOKEHOUSE
UNIT 6/7, THE FOOD HUB,
DRUMSHANBO, CO. LEITRIM
Smoked pigeon, smoked bacon, smoked butter and smoked duck

CLONARN CLOVER
WWW.CLONARNCLOVER.IE
Eggs

CONNACHT GOLD
WWW.CONNACHTGOLD.IE
Milk, cream and butter

COOLE SWAN DAIRY CREAM LIQUEUR
WWW.COOLESWAN.COM
Coole Swan liqueur

CORLEGGY CHEESE
WWW.CORLEGGYCHEESES.COM
Corleggy cheese

DONEGAL RAPESEED OIL COMPANY
WWW.DONEGALRAPESEEDOILCO.COM
Rapeseed oil

EDEN PLANT, EDEN, ROSSINVER
CO. LEITRIM
Micro herbs, herbs and salad leaves

FINNEABROGUE
WWW.FINNEBROGUE.COM
Venison saddle

FIVEMILETOWN CREAMERY
WWW.FIVEMILETOWN.COM
Boilie cheese

HANNAN MEATS
WWW.HANNANMEATS.COM
Dry cure bacon, breakfast and regular sausages and pork fillet

NOEL HOEY BAKERS
TULLYHORKY, DONEGAL ROAD,
BALLYSHANNON, CO. DONEGAL
Bread and cakes

HOLLAND & BARRETT
WWW.HOLLANDANDBARRETT.IE
Rice bran and quinoa

KELLY'S BUTCHERS
WWW.KELLYSBUTCHERS.COM
Black and white puddings

KILBEG DAIRY DELIGHTS
WWW.KILBEGDAIRYDELIGHTS.IE
Natural plain yoghurt, crème fraîche and Greek yoghurt

HUGH MAGUIRE FAMILY BUTCHER
3-4 ASHBOURNE TOWN CENTRE,
ASHBOURNE, CO. MEATH
Craft butcher

MCDAID FRUIT & VEGETABLES
DERRYMACAUSEY, DERRYLIN,
ENNISKILLEN, CO. FERMANAGH,
BT92 9NU
Fruit and vegetables and micro herbs

MCGETTIGANS BUTCHERS
MAIN STREET, DONEGAL
Craft butchers

JAMES MCGOUGH BUTCHER
WWW.CONNEMARAFINEFOODS.IE
Air-dried beef

MCGOVERN MEATS
37 MAIN ST, BELLEEK, ENNISKILLEN,
CO. FERMANAGH, BT93 3FY
Lamb loin, beef fillets, smoked pork belly, rolled pork belly and minced beef

MILEEVEN HONEY
WWW.MILEEVEN.COM
Honey

MOURNE SEAFOOD
WWW.MOURNESEAFOOD.COM
Turbot, skate, halibut, sea trout, organic salmon, crab meat, plaice and sole

MSK
WWW.MSK-INGREDIENTS.COM
N-Zorbit M powder, Ultra-Tex, dried raspberries, xanthan gum, tomato powder and beetroot powder

ODAIOS FOODS
WWW.ODAIOS-FOODS.COM
Kettyle 28 days dry-aged beef sirloin, rib eye of beef, pork cheek, lamb rump, veal sweetbreads and Fermanagh chicken

THE ORGANIC CENTRE
WWW.THEORGANICCENTRE.IE
Seedlings, salad leaves, herbs and herb flowers

PALLAS FOODS
WWW.PALLASFOODS.EU
General catering suppliers

PRIOR BROTHERS
WWW.PRIORBROTHERS.COM
Fruit and vegetables, micro herbs and samphire

REDMOND FINE FOODS
WWW.REDMONDFINEFOODS.IE
Agar agar and dried egg whites

RING OF KERRY LAMB
WWW.RINGOFKERRYQUALITYLAMB.IE
All lamb cuts

SHERIDANS CHEESEMONGERS
WWW.SHERIDANSCHEESEMONGERS.
COM
Tomato relish, cheese crackers and cheese

STRATHROY DIARY LTD
WWW.STRATHROYDAIRY.COM
Irish milk and dairy produce

THAI FOOD COMPANY LIMITED
WWW.THAI.IE
Thai Gold coconut milk, rice, sweet chilli sauce, lime leaves and soy sauce

THORNHILL DUCK
WWW.THORNHILLDUCK.COM
Whole ducks (or breasts and legs) and geese

VANILLA BAZAAR
WWW.VANILLABAZAAR.COM
Vanilla pods and vanilla essence

Specialist Kitchen Equipment

If you're a keen cook, you've probably got most of the basic kit. Some of the techniques I use depend on modern technology, but I've tried to keep specialist gadgets to a minimum. Most of them are not completely necessary but will take your cooking to a different level and make a big difference to what you achieve in the kitchen. In the restaurant, I love the technical challenge of some of our dishes and the thrill of taking an idea and turning it into something wonderful to eat. Most things can be purchased at a good kitchen shop; otherwise, try online Irish catering websites such as www.gduke.com or www.nisbets.ie.

I've also included some information on a sous-vide machine and water bath, which restaurants are increasingly depending on to cook all sorts of dishes. If you're lucky enough to have one you'll probably have some understanding of the process and technology. As far as I'm concerned, sous-vide is a wonderful addition to any domestic kitchen.

BALLOON WHISK: This is used to blend ingredients smooth or to incorporate air into a mixture in a process known as whisking or whipping. Most whisks consist of a long, narrow handle with a series of wire loops joined at the end. Just make sure the whisk you have has enough wires to really get some air into a mixture. You may find that you need a couple of different sizes depending on the tasks you want to use them for.

BAMBOO STEAMER SET: These are the traditional round steamers made from bamboo like those used in Chinese cuisine. They can be stacked on top of each other so that the steam can cook many different servings simultaneously. They are available in numerous sizes, so choose whatever suits your purposes. Just make sure you have a pan that's the correct size to fit them comfortably on top.

BLOWTORCH: Essential in my book for caramelising the sugar and getting rid of the bubbles on top of a crème brûlée or parfait. We also use them to flame alcohol, melt cheese and, occasionally, brown meat or fish. I think that the ones from a DIY store are best, as they are much more robust than the little ones available in most kitchen shops.

DISPOSABLE PIPING BAGS: Cotton piping bags are notorious for harbouring bacteria if not boil washed and dried after every use, which is one of the reasons professional chefs choose disposable piping bags. Simply cut the end of the bag to fit the nozzle of your choice. They are great for speedy microwave melting and are very reasonable to buy.

ESPUMA GUN: Otherwise known as a cream whipper or whipped cream dispenser. It's very useful for aerating cream, but it has also proved to be an invaluable tool for creating foams. It works by injecting air into the ingredients by means of an N_2 cartridge (or cream charger) or a CO_2 cartridge (or soda charger). There are other ways of getting bubbles into a liquid, such as a hand blender or balloon whisk, but the cream whipper is less labour intensive and produces a light, delicate structure. The dispenser and its cartridges are available to purchase separately.

FOOD DEHYDRATOR: I like to occasionally serve dried fruit and vegetables as a garnish to some of my more complicated dishes, as they offer a different texture and shape to the finished plate. A food dehydrator uses a constant heat source and airflow to reduce the water content of foods. The water content of food is usually very high – typically 80% to 95% for various fruits and vegetables. Removing moisture from food restrains various bacteria from growing and spoiling food.

FOOD MIXER: The KitchenAid is an iconic piece of equipment that has changed little in appearance since its original design from the 1930s. They are built to last and in my opinion are the most powerful and best-performing stand mixers out there. My pastry chef uses it on a daily basis for making cakes, biscuits and breads. It's also excellent for whipping large quantities of cream. Check out www.kitchenaid. co.uk for local stockists.

HAND BLENDER: I find the Bamix hand blender the best by far and use it almost as an extension to my hand in the kitchen. I use the multi-purpose blade to froth up sauces and blend small amounts of ingredients to a purée. It also comes with whisk and beater attachments.
See www.bamix.com.

ICE CREAM MAKER: If you like ice cream and make it a lot, a Pacojet makes life so much easier. It produces exquisite mousses, ice creams and sorbets at the press of a button. However, if that's too expensive an option, you can also use a machine that has a canister that can be pre-frozen in the freezer. These are reasonably priced and freeze quickly, which is important, because the faster it freezes, the smoother the final ice cream will be. See www. pacojet.com.

JUICER: All the juice recipes in the book can be made using a juice extractor alone. Unfortunately, high-powered juicers can be expensive. We have a fantastic one we use in the restaurant – check out www.santos.fr. Like most things in life, you tend to get what you pay for – the more expensive juicers are likely to have a hardier motor and extract more juice per piece of fruit. They also tend to be easier to clean and I would always suggest doing this immediately, when it won't take you more than a couple of minutes. Juicers are what are called centrifugal extractors, which means they grate the fruit and vegetables and quickly spin it toward a mesh, which catches the pulp and sends the juice down into a jug. In

separating the pulp, juicers concentrate the nutrition naturally present in fruits and vegetables and allow the body to more easily absorb the nutrition than digesting the solid produce. The use of juicers also makes it easier to consume more raw produce.

MANDOLIN: This is a plane-slice tool, which originated in the Far East and is used to cut potatoes or other vegetables. Most offer various cuts and thicknesses but typically they have three blades – one each for fine, medium and large ribbons. If you haven't used a mandolin before, try to purchase one that has a tripod and a guard for your fingers. I also have a Benriner mandolin slicer, which creates long spiral strings of raw potatoes, which I like to use for making crispy potato rosti.

MELON BALLER: Otherwise known as a Parisienne scoop, this is a small spoon-like tool used to cut round or oval-shaped sections of melon, known as melon balls, by pressing into the melon's flesh and rotating. It can also be used to cut other soft fruit. The diameter of a melon baller's bowl varies from around 1cm to 3cm (3/8in to 1in). Some brands have the handle in the middle and a different-sized bowl on each end, and the bowl typically has a small hole in the middle to allow air and juice through.

MICROPLANE GRATERS: This is one of those fortunate culinary accidents – what originated as an excellent smoothing tool for woodworkers proved to be an indispensable grating tool for cooks. With a soft-grip handle for a firm, comfortable hold, they have razor-sharp stainless steel teeth that allow grating in both directions, saving time and en-

ergy. The paddle-shaped grater is available in three versions: fine, for zesting citrus fruits and puréeing onions, garlic, peppers and ginger; medium ribbon, for grating soft cheeses and chocolate as well as shredding coconut; and coarse, for grating hard cheeses and chocolate as well as shredding cabbage and potatoes.

MSK STARTER KIT: This is molecular gastronomy made easy and will enable you to create everything from caviar pearls to a flaming sorbet! Packed full of specialist ingredients such as N-Zorbit M powder. This kit is a great way to experiment with this novel way of cooking and contains a micro scale necessary for precise measuring with a capacity of 500g. It enables you to make rapid-setting and heat-resistant jellies and hot and cold foams that will last for hours without losing body or texture. See www.msk-ingredients. com.

OYSTER OPENER: Otherwise known as an oyster shucker or oyster knife, this has a short, thick blade that is used to pry open oysters and separate their meat from the shell. Some models have a shield built into the handle that prevents the knife (and hand) from slipping and going too far into the shell. It's almost impossible to deal with oysters without one.

PASTA MACHINE: For me, this is the simple and easy way to make homemade pasta sheets and even the most basic model comes with a detachable duo cutter for knocking up tagliatelle and fettuccine. Choose a robust machine with a good roller and detachable handle functions to make it even easier to use. Even standard models have fully adjustable rollers for kneading and rolling pasta in up to nine different thicknesses and a table/worktop clamp to hold the machine securely in place when in use.

POTATO RICER: This might sound a bit unnecessary, but believe me, they make the very best mashed potato. If you overwork the starch in the potatoes it becomes gluey, whereas what you're looking for is fluffy. Pressing the potatoes through a ricer keeps the starch granules separate. One of the best on the market is from a company called Metalex and is made from white plastic, has interchangeable metal plates with different-sized holes, depending on what you want to mash, and is dishwasher safe too. They are relatively inexpensive and perfect for use in a domestic kitchen.

SIEVE: I find that the sieves we use in the kitchen are in constant demand for straining sauces and soups, purées and custards. Picking up this habit can have a real impact on the food you serve at home. Straining is actually a very simple thing to do and any fine sieve will cover your needs for the recipes in this book. However, in my opinion it's worth investing in a conical sieve (chinois) because it holds a decent amount and its shape makes it much easier to filter large quantities.

SOUS-VIDE: This is a revolutionary cooking method that has the ability to transform any amateur chef. It heats food to exactly the temperature you want so that it's perfectly cooked with no risk of overcooking. It is clean, efficient, versatile and user friendly. I love it because it enables whatever you cook in it to hold onto all its juices, keeping

the food succulent and full of flavour. The best part about it is that sous-vide is so precise that it gives exactly the same result every time. It is certainly an indispensible part of my restaurant kitchen. The technology itself is simple: a vacuum-packing machine and a water bath. Vacuum packing the food makes it easy to handle and helps to protect it during the cooking process. It ensures that it heats through evenly and prevents the juices from leaking out. The water bath cooks the food efficiently (because water is a better medium for heat transfer than the air in the oven) and at a far more precise temperature than what can be achieved with a pan on the hob. Together, the vacuum packer and the water bath give the cook fantastic control. You can heat at the sort of low temperatures that really bring out the best in many ingredients. The system is exceptionally well suited to cooking food in advance and reheating it. This makes it an excellent option if you want to plan ahead or try out complex multi-stage dishes. We use Grant sous-vide baths in the restaurant and they have a distributer in Ireland: www.eurolec-instruments.com.

STOCKPOT: A vital part of any kitchen, the one we use in the restaurant is built-in and so big that you could almost climb into it! Obviously this isn't necessary for a domestic kitchen, but a good large, sturdy stockpot is worth investing in.

SUGAR THERMOMETER: This is a thermometer used to measure the temperature and therefore the stage of a cooking sugar solution. I also use them to measure hot oil for deep-frying. The digital ones are the best, as they read the temperature more quickly

and accurately and some models have an alarm when the thermometer hits a certain temperature. Many models have markers for the various stages of sugar cooking. It's similar to a meat thermometer except that it can read higher temperatures (usually 200°C (400°F) or more).

THERMOMIX: This German-designed machine weighs, chops, grates, whisks, blends, kneads, cooks and steams. Despite its extensive uses, it's actually quite neat and will sit comfortably on any countertop without demanding too much space. I use it to make silky soups and sauces without any stirring or straining. It's the one piece of equipment I'd miss most and it's in heavy use all day in the restaurant's kitchen. See www.ukthermomix.com.

TWEEZERS: The Western answer to kitchen chopsticks, which have been used to assemble intricate plates in Asia for centuries. The ones we use at the restaurant are actually medical tweezers normally used by surgeons. They are much more gentle than tweezers designed for plucking eyebrows or extracting pin bones from a halibut. There are three main types: offset, curved tip and needle and they're about 15cm (6in) long. They allow me to assemble meticulous compositions on plates quickly and with such consistency that they look the same every time. In some recipes there might be ten things on a plate, but tweezers keep your hands clean and you keep the plate clean. As a rule of thumb, the more intricate and immaculate the plate, the more likely it is that tweezers played a role in the final presentation.

Index

A

agar agar
  crispy goat's cheese with beetroot panna cotta, 60, 61
  mango gel, 247
almonds
  bircher muesli with granola, 4
  warm prunes marinated in tea and vanilla with yoghurt, 6, 7
apples
  apple chutney, 249
  apple coulis, 264
  apple parfait, 266
  apple and potato purée, 229
  bircher muesli with granola, 4
  celeriac, smoked bacon and apple soup, 76
  confit prawn spring rolls with mango and apple, 30, 31
  the orchard (apple panna cotta with apple jelly, glazed apple tart, apple crumble and apple parfait), 150–1, 152–3
  roast goose with cranberry and apple sausage stuffing, 109
  vanilla crème brûlée with poached Irish apple compote, 174, 175
apricots: poached apricots with star anise and yoghurt, 5
asparagus
  bruschetta of wild mushrooms and asparagus, 58, 59
  sea trout with aubergine purée and crispy courgette flowers stuffed with crab, 92, 93
aubergine
  aubergine and potato dhansak, 144, 145
  aubergine purée, 242
    sea trout with aubergine purée and crispy courgette flowers stuffed with crab, 92, 93
  Mediterranean vegetable and Boilíe pizza tart, 146, 147
  open lasagne with roasted vegetables, 136, 137
  pappardelle pasta with vegetables and parmesan foam, 140, 141
avocado
  avocado spring roll with red pepper polenta, 138, 139
  deconstructed prawn cocktail, 32, 33

B

bacon
  assiette of rare-breed pork (caramelised belly, smoked bacon-wrapped fillet and pork and leek sausage), 120, 121

bacon rashers: roast woodcock with creamed spinach and offal croûte, 104, 105
    trio of MacNean chicken with baby carrots, 98–9, 100
  celeriac, smoked bacon and apple soup, 76
  smoked belly of pork with creamed white beans and date jam, 52, 53
baked Alaska, 164, 165
balsamic and port syrup, 260
banana and pineapple smoothie, 16
barley: vegetable soup with barley, 73
basil pesto, 256
  gratin of cod with prawns, spinach and pesto, 82, 83
basil purée, 243
beans
  creamed white beans, 239
  hake with cassoulet of beans and chorizo, 86, 87
  rump of local lamb with pea purée and rosemary jus, 118, 119
  satay vegetable noodles: 143
  smoked belly of pork with creamed white beans and date jam, 52, 53
beef
  air-dried beef carpaccio with roasted beetroot and mustard cream, 54, 55
  beef satay with pickled cucumber, 50, 51
  beef stock, 253
  fillet of dry-aged beef with braised blade and celeriac purée, 122–2, 124–5
  roast rib of beef on the bone with Yorkshire pudding and horseradish cream, 128
beetroot
  air-dried beef carpaccio with roasted beetroot and mustard cream, 54, 55
  beetroot carpaccio, 236
  beetroot purée, 245
  crispy goat's cheese with beetroot panna cotta, 60, 61
  salad of wood pigeon with trio of beetroot, 36, 37
bircher muesli with granola, 4
biscuits
  jammie dodgers, 221
  oatmeal cookies, 218, 219
  oaty chocolate chip cookies, 217
  Sophie's chocolate biscuit cake, 224, 225

see also shortbread biscuits

black beans: Chinese black bean sauce, 256

black pudding

    baked eggs with black pudding hash browns, 14

    saddle of rabbit stuffed with black pudding, 47

    and white pudding: MacNean special breakfast, 8, 9

Boilíe cheese: Mediterranean vegetable and Boilíe pizza tart, 146, 147

boxty: MacNean special breakfast, 8, 9

brandy snaps with chilli and passion fruit cream, 197

bread

    bread croûtes, 240

    brioche, 214

    goat's cheese and red onion and rosemary focaccia, 210, 211

    Irish tea bread, 207

    MacNean wheaten bread, 200, 201

    pizza bread, 204, 205

    rosemary and cranberry soda bread, 202, 203

    sun-dried tomato gluten-free bread, 212, 213

breakfast berry zinger, 15

breakfast: MacNean special breakfast, 8, 9

buttermilk mousse: raspberry plate, the (baked raspberry shortcake, buttermilk mousse, raspberry and white chocolate parfait and raspberry sorbet), 172, 173

butterscotch sauce, 262

C

cabbage

    creamed Savoy cabbage, 233

    red cabbage: braised red cabbage, 234

        roast goose with cranberry and apple sausage stuffing, 109

    Savoy cabbage: curried chicken spring rolls with pineapple salsa, 42, 43

cakes: the MacNean celebration cake, 222, 223

cannelloni: roast turbot with crab cannelloni and prawn velouté, 84, 85

caramel sauce, 262

carrots

    celeriac and baby carrot risotto with sherry vinegar caramel and crispy potato rosti, 134, 135

    fillet of dry-aged beef with braised blade and celeriac purée, 122-2, 124-5

    Mum's special roast chicken with lemon, garlic and thyme, 101, 102-3

    tasting of Irish lamb (herb-crusted loin, confit of neck and sweetbreads), 112-13, 114

    trio of MacNean chicken with baby carrots, 98-9, 100

    veal sweetbreads with carrot and star anise, 48, 49

caul fat: saddle of rabbit stuffed with black pudding, 47

cauliflower

    aubergine and potato dhansak, 144, 145

    cauliflower purée, 243

    dried cauliflower, 234

celeriac

    celeriac and baby carrot risotto with sherry vinegar caramel and crispy potato rosti, 134, 135

    celeriac purée, 244

        fillet of dry-aged beef with braised blade and celeriac purée, 122-2, 124-5

    celeriac, smoked bacon and apple soup, 76

chard

    Frisée and baby Ruby chards: salad of wood pigeon with trio of beetroot, 36, 37

    ravioli of Swiss chard and ricotta with smoked garlic foam, 62, 63

cheese

    Ballyoak cheese in kataifi pastry and sauce vierge: 64

    Cheddar cheese: MacNean fish pie, 91

        pizza bread, 204, 205

    crispy goat's cheese with beetroot panna cotta, 60, 61

cheesecake: MacNean cheesecake with raspberries and white chocolate, 156, 157

chestnut and wild mushroom soup with smoked duck, 68, 69

chicken

    chicken liver parfait with cherry gel, 38

    chicken stock, 252

    curried chicken spring rolls with pineapple salsa, 42, 43

    Mum's special roast chicken with lemon, garlic and thyme, 101, 102-3

    saddle of rabbit stuffed with black pudding, 47

    sautéed breast of guinea fowl and stuffed leg with leeks and girolle mushrooms, 106-7, 108

    trio of MacNean chicken with baby carrots, 98-9, 100

chilli jam, 248

chilli oil, 250

Chinese black bean sauce, 256

chocolate

    chocolate delice, 182

    chocolate fudge sauce, 263

    chocolate ganache: the MacNean celebration cake, 222, 223

        trio of chocolate (warm fondant, delice and opera cake), 178-9, 180-1

        vanilla macaroons with chocolate and peanut butter cream, 194, 195

    chocolate roulade: trio of chocolate (warm fondant, delice and opera cake), 178-9, 180-1

    chocolate truffles: MacNean chocolate orange truffles, 188, 189

MacNean cheesecake with raspberries and white chocolate, 156, 157

oaty chocolate chip cookies, 217

plain or white chocolate curls, 269

raspberry plate, the (baked raspberry shortcake, buttermilk mousse, raspberry and white chocolate parfait and raspberry sorbet), 172, 173

raspberry and white chocolate parfait, 267

Sophie's chocolate biscuit cake, 224, 225

sticky toffee pudding and salted whiskey butterscotch sauce, 176, 177

trio of chocolate (warm fondant, delice and opera cake), 178–9, 180–1

warm chocolate and pecan brownie with boozy fudge sauce, 154, 155

white chocolate and pistachio fudge, 192, 193

chorizo: hake with cassoulet of beans and chorizo, 86, 87

cinnamon

cinnamon roasted quail with pea and truffle risotto, 34, 35

cinnamon sticks: duck confit with crispy fried vegetables, 39, 40–1

poached apricots with star anise and yoghurt, 5

citrus mascarpone cream, 264

coconut

coconut cream, aubergine and potato dhansak, 144, 145

coconut floating islands with Coole Swan crème anglaise, raspberries and spun sugar basket, 162, 163

coconut and Malibu marshmallows, 186, 187

coconut milk: sweet potato and coconut soup, 66, 67

toasted coconut and Malibu parfait with pineapple carpaccio and coconut sorbet, 158, 159

cod: gratin of cod with prawns, spinach and pesto, 82, 83

courgette

courgette flowers, sea trout with aubergine purée and crispy courgette flowers stuffed with crab, 92, 93

Mediterranean vegetable and Boilíe pizza tart , 146, 147

open lasagne with roasted vegetables, 136, 137

pappardelle pasta with vegetables and Parmesan foam, 140, 141

couscous

braised shoulder of lamb with Mediterranean couscous, 116, 117

Mediterranean couscous, 238

crab

crab ravioli, 20

crab wontons with enoki mushrooms and Thai broth, 28, 29

roast turbot with crab cannelloni and prawn velouté, 84, 85

sea trout with aubergine purée and crispy courgette flowers stuffed with crab, 92, 93

cranberries: rosemary and cranberry soda bread, 202, 203

crème anglaise, 263

coconut floating islands with Coole Swan crème anglaise, raspberries and spun sugar basket, 162, 163

warm chocolate and pecan brownie with boozy fudge sauce, 154, 155

crème brûlée: vanilla crème brûlée with poached Irish apple compote, 174, 175

cucumber

cucumber, beef satay with pickled cucumber, 50, 51

pickled cucumber, 236

D

date jam, 249

smoked belly of pork with creamed white beans and date jam, 52, 53

dates: sticky toffee pudding and salted whiskey butterscotch sauce, 176, 177

delice: trio of chocolate (warm fondant, delice and opera cake), 178–9, 180–1

duck

breast of Thornhill duck with sweet potato fondants, 96, 97

chestnut and wild mushroom soup with smoked duck, 68, 69

duck confit with crispy fried vegetables, 39, 40–1

E

eggs

baked eggs with black pudding hash browns, 14

chicken liver parfait with cherry gel, 38

MacNean eggs Benedict, 12, 13

MacNean special breakfast, 8, 9

scrambled eggs with Burren smoked salmon, 10, 11

F

feuilletine: the MacNean celebration cake, 222, 223

fish

fish pie: MacNean fish pie, 91

fish stock, 254

see also entries for each species

foam: basic, 245

focaccia: goat's cheese and red onion and rosemary focaccia, 210, 211

frangipane filling: prune and Armagnac tart, 215

G

garlic: confit garlic, 236

ginger
    aubergine and potato dhansak, 144, 145
    brandy snaps with chilli and passion fruit cream, 197
    ginger sesame dressing, 252
    rhubarb and strawberry pudding, 167
goat's cheese and red onion and rosemary focaccia, 210, 211
goose: roast goose with cranberry and apple sausage stuffing,
    109
granola
    bircher muesli with granola, 4
    warm prunes marinated in tea and vanilla with yoghurt, 6, 7
guinea fowl: sautéed breast of guinea fowl and stuffed leg
    with leeks and girolle mushrooms, 106-7, 108

H

hake with cassoulet of beans and chorizo, 86, 87
haricot bean and white truffle oil velouté, 78, 79
hash browns: baked eggs with black pudding hash browns,
    14
hollandaise sauce, 255
honey and clove sauce, 259
honey jus, 261
horseradish cream, 257

I

ice cream
    baked Alaska, 164, 165
    sticky toffee pudding and salted whiskey butterscotch
        sauce, 176, 177
    vanilla ice cream, 265
    warm chocolate and pecan brownie with boozy fudge
        sauce, 154, 155
Irish tea bread, 207

J

jammie dodgers, 221
    MacNean cheesecake with raspberries and white
        chocolate, 156, 157
juices, fruit, vegetables and herbs, 15

K

kataifi pastry
    Ballyoak cheese in kataifi pastry and sauce vierge: 64
    kataifi pastry, with prawns, 20
    rabbit confit with wild mushrooms in kataifi pastry, 44-5,
        46
kiwi fruit: lime meringues with fresh fruit and cream, 160

L

lamb
    braised shoulder of lamb with Mediterranean couscous,
        116, 117
    rump of local lamb with pea purée and rosemary jus, 118,
        119
    tasting of Irish lamb (herb-crusted loin, confit of neck and
        sweetbreads), 112-13, 114
lasagne: open lasagne with roasted vegetables, 136, 137
leeks
    creamed leeks, 234
    sautéed breast of guinea fowl and stuffed leg with leeks
        and girolle mushrooms, 106-7, 108
    turkey and leek stroganoff with wild and basmati rice, 110
    warm potato pancakes with leeks and wild mushrooms,
        142
lemon grass foam, 246
lemon and sultana scones, 216
lentil vinaigrette, 251
lentils: balsamic lentils, 240
lettuce: wilted cos lettuce, 232
lime meringues
    lime meringues with fresh fruit and cream, 160
    toasted coconut and Malibu parfait with pineapple
        carpaccio and coconut sorbet, 158, 159

M

macaroons: vanilla macaroons with chocolate and peanut
    butter cream, 194, 195
madelines, 190, 191
Malibu rum
    coconut and Malibu marshmallows, 186, 187
    toasted coconut and Malibu parfait with pineapple
        carpaccio and coconut sorbet, 158, 159
mango
    confit prawn spring rolls with mango and apple, 30, 31
    lime meringues with fresh fruit and cream, 160
    mango gel, 247
marmalade sauce, 259
mascarpone cheese: classic tiramisu, 166
mascarpone cream
    citrus mascarpone cream, 264
    summer fruit crumble, 171
mayonnaise, 251
Mediterranean vegetable and Boilíe pizza tart , 146, 147
meringues
    lime meringues with fresh fruit and cream, 160
    toasted coconut and Malibu parfait with pineapple
        carpaccio and coconut sorbet, 158, 159

monkfish with gnocchi, wild mushrooms, sun-dried tomato
and saffron velouté, 88, 89
morning reviver juice, 15
muesli: bircher muesli with granola, 4
mushrooms
    beech mushrooms: cinnamon roasted quail with pea and
        truffle risotto, 34, 35
    bruschetta of wild mushrooms and asparagus, 58, 59
    chestnut and wild mushroom soup with smoked duck, 68,
        69
    enoki mushrooms: crab wontons with enoki mushrooms
        and Thai broth, 28, 29
    MacNean special breakfast, 8, 9
    monkfish with gnocchi, wild mushrooms, sun-dried
        tomato and saffron velouté, 88, 89
    mushroom purée, 244
    peppered steak with gratin potatoes and whiskey sauce,
        126, 127
    pork and wild mushroom wontons with Chinese black
        bean sauce, 56, 57
    rabbit confit with wild mushrooms in kataifi pastry, 44–5,
        46
    sautéed breast of guinea fowl and stuffed leg with leeks
        and girolle mushrooms, 106–7, 108
    scrambled eggs with Burren smoked salmon, 10, 11
    trio of MacNean chicken with baby carrots, 98–9, 100
    turkey and leek stroganoff with wild and basmati rice,
        110
    warm potato pancakes with leeks and wild mushrooms,
        142
mustard cream: air-dried beef carpaccio with roasted
    beetroot and mustard cream, 54, 55

N

noodles: satay vegetable noodles, 143

O

oatmeal cookies, 218, 219
oaty chocolate chip cookies, 217
onions
    caramelised baby onions, 235
    onion tart tatin, 235
    open lasagne with roasted vegetables, 136, 137
oranges: passion fruit and orange jelly with vanilla yoghurt
    and granita, 168, 169
oysters, 21

P

pak choi: pork and wild mushroom wontons with Chinese
    black bean sauce, 56, 57
pancakes: warm potato pancakes with leeks and wild
    mushrooms, 142
pappardelle pasta with vegetables and Parmesan foam, 140,
    141
Parma ham: smoked belly of pork with creamed white beans
    and date jam, 52, 53
Parmesan
    salad of grilled vegetables and aged Parmesan, 65
    tomato and Parmesan twister bread rolls, 206
parsley oil, 250
passion fruit
    brandy snaps with chilli and passion fruit cream, 197
    passion fruit and orange jelly with vanilla yoghurt and
        granita, 168, 169
    toasted coconut and Malibu parfait with pineapple
        carpaccio and coconut sorbet, 158, 159
pasta: fresh pasta sheets, 241
pastry
    pastry cream: raspberry plate, the (baked raspberry
        shortcake, buttermilk mousse, raspberry and white
        chocolate parfait and raspberry sorbet), 172, 173
    Mediterranean vegetable and Boilíe pizza tart , 146, 147
    the orchard (apple panna cotta with apple jelly, glazed
        apple tart, apple crumble and apple parfait), 150–1,
        152–3
pea purée, 242
peanut butter: vanilla macaroons with chocolate and peanut
    butter cream, 194, 195
peanut frosting: the MacNean celebration cake, 222, 223
pecan nuts: warm chocolate and pecan brownie with boozy
    fudge sauce, 154, 155
peppered steak with gratin potatoes and whiskey sauce, 126,
    127
peppers
    Mediterranean vegetable and Boilíe pizza tart, 146, 147
    open lasagne with roasted vegetables, 136, 137
    pappardelle pasta with vegetables and Parmesan foam, 140,
        141
    red pepper foam, 246
    red pepper polenta, 237
        avocado spring roll with red pepper polenta, 138, 139
        rump of local lamb with pea purée and rosemary jus, 118,
            119
    red pepper purée, 243
    roast pepper and tomato soup, 74, 75
    satay vegetable noodles: 143
pigeon, see wood pigeon

pineapple
  pineapple salsa, 257
  curried chicken spring rolls with pineapple salsa, 42, 43
  roasted pineapple and coconut rice pudding, 161
  toasted coconut and Malibu parfait with pineapple
    carpaccio and coconut sorbet, 158, 159
pistachio nuts: white chocolate and pistachio fudge, 192, 193
pizza bread, 204, 205
polenta: red pepper polenta, 237
pork
  assiette of rare-breed pork (caramelised belly, smoked
    bacon-wrapped fillet and pork and leek sausage), 120, 121
  pork cheeks: seared scallops with confit of pork cheek and
    cauliflower textures: 26, 27
  pork and wild mushroom wontons with Chinese black
    bean sauce, 56, 57
  stout-braised shoulder of pork with potato and apple
    purée, 130
  see also bacon
porridge: MacNean special porridge with honey and cream,
  2, 3
potato
  aubergine and potato dhansak, 144, 145
  celeriac and baby carrot risotto with sherry vinegar caramel
    and crispy potato rosti, 134, 135
  monkfish with gnocchi, wild mushrooms, sun-dried
    tomato and saffron velouté, 88, 89
  peppered steak with gratin potatoes and whiskey sauce,
    126, 127
  potato sides
    apple and potato purée, 229
    crispy potato rosti, 228
    potato gnocchi, 231
    potato gratin, 230
    potato purée, 228
    roast potatoes, 229
    sweet potato fondants, 231
  warm potato pancakes with leeks and wild mushrooms,
    142
  Vera's seafood chowder, 70, 71
prawns, 20
  confit prawn spring rolls with mango and apple, 30, 31
  deconstructed prawn cocktail, 32, 33
  gratin of cod with prawns, spinach and pesto, 82, 83
  prawn velouté, 258
    roast turbot with crab cannelloni and prawn velouté, 84,
      85
    sea trout with aubergine purée and crispy courgette
      flowers stuffed with crab, 92, 93
  salmon sausages with creamed leeks and lemon butter
    sauce, 94

prunes
  prune and Armagnac tart, 215
  warm prunes marinated in tea and vanilla with yoghurt, 6, 7

Q

quail
  cinnamon roasted quail with pea and truffle risotto, 34, 35
  quail eggs: salad of wood pigeon with trio of beetroot, 36,
    37
quinoa, 239
  loin of venison with quinoa and spinach, 132, 133

R

rabbit
  rabbit confit with wild mushrooms in kataifi pastry, 44–5,
    46
  saddle of rabbit stuffed with black pudding, 47
raspberries
  coconut floating islands with Coole Swan crème anglaise,
    raspberries and spun sugar basket, 162, 163
  MacNean cheesecake with raspberries and white
    chocolate, 156, 157
  raspberry plate, the (baked raspberry shortcake, buttermilk
    mousse, raspberry and white chocolate parfait and
    raspberry sorbet), 172, 173
  raspberry sorbet, 266
  raspberry and white chocolate parfait, 267
ravioli of Swiss chard and ricotta with smoked garlic foam,
  62, 63
red berry smoothie, 16
red cabbage, see under cabbage
red wine jus, 261
rhubarb and strawberry pudding, 167
rice
  aubergine and potato dhansak, 144, 145
  roasted pineapple and coconut rice pudding, 161
    turkey and leek stroganoff with wild and basmati rice,
      110
ricotta: ravioli of Swiss chard and ricotta with smoked garlic
  foam, 62, 63
risotto
  celeriac and baby carrot risotto with sherry vinegar caramel
    and crispy potato rosti, 134, 135
  cinnamon roasted quail with pea and truffle risotto, 34
rosemary
  rosemary and cranberry soda bread, 202, 203
  rosemary jus, 260

S

saffron orzo: smoked salmon and saffron orzo, 90
salad of grilled vegetables and aged Parmesan, 65
salmon
    roast turbot with crab cannelloni and prawn velouté,
        84, 85
    salmon sausages with creamed leeks and lemon butter
        sauce, 94
    scrambled eggs with Burren smoked salmon, 10, 11
    smoked salmon: gratin of cod with prawns,
        spinach and pesto, 82, 83
    smoked salmon and saffron orzo, 90
satay sauce: beef satay with pickled cucumber, 50, 51
satay vegetable noodles, 143
sauce vierge, 256
    Ballyoak cheese in kataifi pastry and sauce vierge, 64
sausage
    assiette of rare-breed pork (caramelised belly, smoked
        bacon-wrapped fillet and pork and leek sausage), 120,
        121
    roast goose with cranberry and apple sausage stuffing,
        109
scallops, 20–1
    seared scallops with confit of pork cheek and
        cauliflower textures, 26, 27
scones: lemon and sultana scones, 216
sea trout, *see* trout
sesame and poppy seed white bread, 208, 209
shellfish, a study of, 20–1, 22, 23
sherry vinegar caramel, 260
shortbread biscuits, 220
    MacNean cheesecake with raspberries and white
        chocolate, 156, 157
    raspberry plate, the (baked raspberry shortcake,
        buttermilk mousse, raspberry and white chocolate
        parfait and raspberry sorbet), 172, 173
smoothies, 16, 17
sole: tempura of sole with curried mayonnaise and chilli
    jam, 25
Sophie's chocolate biscuit cake, 224, 225
soup
    celeriac, smoked bacon and apple soup, 76, 77
    chestnut and wild mushroom soup with smoked duck,
        68, 69
    haricot bean and white truffle oil velouté, 78, 79
    roast pepper and tomato soup, 74, 75
    sweet potato and coconut soup, 66, 67
    vegetable soup with barley, 73
    Vera's seafood chowder, 70, 71
speckled canary juice, 15

spinach
    aubergine and potato dhansak, 144, 145
    creamed spinach, 233
    fillet of dry-aged beef with braised blade and celeriac
        purée, 122–2, 124–5
    gratin of cod with prawns, spinach and pesto, 82, 83
    loin of venison with quinoa and spinach, 132, 133
    MacNean eggs Benedict, 12, 13
    roast woodcock with creamed spinach and offal croûte,
        104, 105
    spinach purée, 244
    wilted spinach, 233
spring onions: warm potato pancakes with leeks and wild
    mushrooms, 142
spun sugar, 267
star anise
    duck confit with crispy fried vegetables, 39, 40–1
    poached apricots with star anise and yoghurt, 5
    summer fruit crumble, 171
    toasted coconut and Malibu parfait with pineapple
        carpaccio and coconut sorbet, 158, 159
    vanilla crème brûlée with poached Irish apple compote,
        174, 175
    veal sweetbreads with carrot and star anise, 48, 49
sticky toffee pudding and salted whiskey butterscotch
    sauce, 176, 177
strawberries
    lime meringues with fresh fruit and cream, 160
    rhubarb and strawberry pudding, 167
    strawberry booster smoothie, 16
sugar snap peas: satay vegetable noodles, 143
sultanas: lemon and sultana scones, 216
summer fruit crumble, 171
sun-dried tomato
    avocado spring roll with red pepper polenta, 138, 139
    braised shoulder of lamb with Mediterranean couscous,
        116, 117
    monkfish with gnocchi, wild mushrooms, sun-dried
        tomato and saffron velouté, 88, 89
    sea trout with aubergine purée and crispy courgette
        flowers stuffed with crab, 92, 93
    sun-dried tomato gluten-free bread, 212, 213
    sun-dried tomato pesto, 257
    sun-dried tomato and saffron velouté, 258
sunrise juice, 15
sweet potato
    breast of Thornhill duck with sweet potato fondants,
        96, 97
    loin of venison with quinoa and spinach, 132, 133
    sweet potato and coconut soup, 66, 67
    sweet potato fondants, 231
sweetcorn: satay vegetable noodles, 143

T

Tia Maria liqueur: classic tiramisu, 166
tiramisu: classic tiramisu, 166
toasted coconut and Malibu parfait with pineapple
  carpaccio and coconut sorbet, 158, 159
tomatoes
  cherry vine tomatoes: deconstructed prawn cocktail, 32,
    33
  MacNean special breakfast, 8, 9
  open lasagne with roasted vegetables, 136, 137
  oven-dried cherry tomatoes, 237
  roast pepper and tomato soup, 74, 75
  scrambled eggs with Burren smoked salmon, 10, 11
  tomato and Parmesan twister bread rolls, 206
  tomato sauce, 255
trout: sea trout with aubergine purée and crispy courgette
  flowers stuffed with crab, 92, 93
truffle oil: haricot bean and white truffle oil velouté, 78,
  79
turbot: roast turbot with crab cannelloni and prawn
  velouté, 84, 85
turkey and leek stroganoff with wild and basmati rice, 110

V

veal sweetbreads with carrot and star anise, 48, 49
vegetable soup with barley, 73
vegetable stock, 252
venison: loin of venison with quinoa and spinach, 132,
  133

W

walnuts: air-dried beef carpaccio with roasted beetroot
  and mustard cream, 54, 55
watercress purée, 244
white chocolate and pistachio fudge, 192, 193
wood pigeon: salad of wood pigeon with trio of beetroot,
  36, 37
woodcock: roast woodcock with creamed spinach and
  offal croûte, 104, 105

Y

yoghurt
  Bircher muesli with granola, 4
  passion fruit and orange jelly with vanilla yoghurt and
    granita, 168, 169
  poached apricots with star anise and yoghurt, 5
  warm prunes marinated in tea and vanilla with yoghurt,
    6, 7
Yorkshire puddings, 241